THE AFGHAN HOUND

POPULAR DOGS' BREED SERIES

ON THE WAY

THE AFGHAN HOUND

CHARLES HARRISSON

POPULAR DOGS

London

POPULAR DOGS PUBLISHING CO LTD
178–202 Great Portland Street, London W1

AN IMPRINT OF THE HUTCHINSON GROUP

London Melbourne Sydney
Auckland Johannesburg Cape Town
and agencies throughout the world

First published 1971

© Charles Harrisson 1971

*This book has been set in Garamond type, printed in Great Britain
on antique wove paper by Anchor Press, and
bound by Wm. Brendon, both of Tiptree, Essex*

ISBN 0 09 106930 0

To my wife, and to all our dogs
which have given us both so much devotion
and pleasure

ACKNOWLEDGMENTS

I wish to acknowledge with sincere gratitude the generous help of the following in the production of *The Afghan Hound*.

To Mrs. Kay Finch for her kind cooperation in sending me photographs and magazines from the U.S.A.; to Mrs. Angela Mulliner for her drawings of the Afghan Hound skeleton and anatomical notes, produced especially for this book; to Miss Patricia Keane for kindly placing her notes on hip displasia at my disposal; to Dr. and Mrs. Wascow of the U.S.A., for their help in sending me documents from the Jackson Sanford papers; to Mr. Bo. Bengtson of Sweden for his notes on Scandinavian Afghan Hounds; to Miss Stephanie Hunt-Crowley for her notes on the Afghan Hound in Australia; to Mr. C. A. Binney and the staff of the Kennel Club for their help, and for permission to use the K.C. library; to Mrs. Wendy Graham for lending me many documents, photographs, and items of historical interest concerning the breed; to Mrs. Rene John for the loan of books and magazines on the breed; to Mr. Richard Gie for his help with contacts in the U.S.A.; to Mr. Ronald Adams for allowing me to use his article in the *Afghan Hound Association Newsletter* of 1966; to Mrs. Ann Adams for the list of pedigrees of champions; to the Afghan Hound Association for the loan of the 'Amps' file; to the Southern Afghan Hound Club for back numbers of their magazine; to the British Museum (Natural History) for their general help and cooperation and permission to photograph the dog Shahzada; to Mrs. Joan Ludwig of the U.S.A. for her help with photographs; and to thank all those who have sent me photographs. Unfortunately, space will not permit me to name them all.

Finally, my thanks to Mrs. Daphne Gie and Mr. Alan Brooks for checking some of my manuscript; and to my wife for the constant use of her memory, and her general help throughout the production of this book.

C.H.H.

CONTENTS

ILLUSTRATIONS

IN THE TEXT

Figs 1, 2, 3, 4, 8, 10 and 12 are by Angela Mulliner and those numbered 5, 6, 7, 9, 11, 13, 14 and 15 are by the author.

AUTHOR'S INTRODUCTION

It is the primary aim of this book to cater for the new Afghan Hound owner and novice breeder, although it is hoped that the more experienced will also find something of interest.

My greatest difficulty has been to decide the comparative importance of the various aspects covered, and to apportion the available space accordingly. Of necessity only a part of the data collected can be used. For obvious reasons I have not discussed dogs which are currently being exhibited, but a list of champions is included as Appendix C.

Owing to its sudden popularity, the Afghan Hound is at a critical stage in its history. Increased classifications at shows have caused a shortage of experienced judges, which in turn has resulted in much pursuing of the false gods of coat, colour, and glamour, to the detriment of conformation, type, and soundness. The most serious outcome of popularity is wanton and indiscriminate breeding for financial gain. Much of this is carried out by inexperienced people, but some established kennels cannot be absolved from the charge.

It is therefore imperative that Breed Clubs should be diligent in facing their responsibilities, and that newcomers should acquire a knowledge of and, I hope, a love for this ancient breed, so that they can play their part in safeguarding its future. If this book can help to achieve this end I shall be more than satisfied.

C.H.H.

I

History of the Breed

WRITING the history of a breed such as the Afghan Hound, with its origins buried in such distant and inaccessible regions of the world is a formidable undertaking fraught with difficulties that are often insurmountable.

Unlike many of our native breeds, which appear with frequency in old paintings and drawings, and concerning which references and descriptions in literature abound, there is very little reliable documentation about the Afghan Hound prior to its appearance in this country in the late nineteenth century. It is also a disappointing fact that there is no known illustration of an Afghan Hound, as we know it today, before the early nineteenth century.

At the risk of the inevitable unpopularity that is the lot of those who destroy cherished illusions, I confess I have reached the conclusion that many of the generally accepted beliefs concerning the origins and ancient history of this fascinating breed are a mixture of legend, wishful thinking, romantic sentimentality, and very little fact. It is, furthermore, true that people tend to believe what they want to believe, ignoring or minimising facts that do not support their preconceived ideas, while overemphasising or distorting information that would seem to lend credence to what they earnestly wish to establish. This tendency is particularly relevant in the Afghan Hound, where the lack of early information in either art or the written word leaves the field wide open to speculation and imagination, so that people have tended to fill in the gaps in authenticated knowledge with attractive, but apocryphal facts, much as nature, which abhors a vacuum, will fill one whenever it occurs.

Furthermore, the generally accepted requisites of anyone carrying out research, i.e. an unbiased and analytical mind, free from emotion and sentiment, are seldom part of the equipment of dog enthusiasts, whatever other worthy qualities they may possess. It

B

is not surprising, therefore, that vague rumour and speculation, and unconfirmed reports, have been instantly accepted as fact, and frequently passed on with embellishment, while descriptions of dogs in ancient literature that could well be any number of breeds have been quoted as proof that the breed was known in this or that part of the world at any given time.

It is generally accepted that dogs were the first animals to be domesticated by man. Wall paintings show Stone Age man in hunting scenes accompanied by animals of a distinctly doglike appearance, although how far these primitive canidae can be identified with the present day domestic dog is debatable.

There is no doubt that the parent stock of the domestic dog is the wolf, but there is evidence that jackal and other wild canine blood has been introduced at some stages. The Greek historian Xenophon (430–355 B.C.), who, among other things, became an enthusiastic dog breeder, mentions Fox Dogs, which were the results of the union of dog and fox. Aristotle also mentions the crossing of dogs with foxes, although some authorities claim that there is no authenticated record of such a cross. The practice, indulged in in many parts of the world, of tethering bitches in season where they could be mated by wolves and possibly other wild canidae would lend further weight to the possibility of the dog not being derived from a single stock. Some authorities have sought to exlude the jackal from the stock because of the cingulum (ridge) on the upper molars, which is not present or is less well developed in the dog and wolf. Richard and Alice Fiennes in *The Natural History of the Dog,* published by Weidenfeld and Nicolson, state: 'The possession of a cingulum could not be used to exclude the jackal from the ancestry of the domestic dog unless it were known that this feature was a genetically dominant characteristic which would be inherited in hybrids', and 'There is therefore no reasonable doubt that the ancestors of domestic dogs were wolves; but at some stage there may well have been some admixture of jackal blood.'

Dr. Konrad Lorenz, the eminent authority on animal behaviour, also claims the jackal as an important ancestor of the domestic dog, although I believe he has to some extent modified his theories.

Richard and Alice Fiennes propose that the domestic dog can be classified into four main groups, each group having its origins in a different wolf type. They are: the northern group (including the Spitz), derived from the northern grey wolf (canis lupus); the dingo group (including pariahs), derived from the pale-footed Asian wolf (canis lupus pallipes); the Greyhound group, derived from a cursorial form of C.l. pallipes, possibly the small desert wolf of Arabia (canis lupus arabs), and, lastly, the Mastiff group, derived from the woolly-coated mountain wolf of India and Tibet (canis lupus chanco or laniger).

The Greyhound group, the origins of which are lost in antiquity, are not, of course, true hounds, and are incorrectly grouped with them for show purposes. They are the most clearly defined of all the groups, and for thousands of years have retained their basic characteristics, tending to vary only in size and coat, variations in coat being resultant on different climatic conditions. This lack of basic variation could well indicate the derivation of this group from a single wolf type. This group hunt by sight.

Known also as gaze hounds, the Greyhound family comprise the following breeds; Afghan Hound, Borzoi; Deerhound; Greyhound; Irish Wolf Hound; Italian Greyhound; Saluki; and Whippet.

Various types of Greyhound have been depicted in Egyptian art as far back as 4000 B.C., the type being much bred and used by the ancient Egyptians, and further developed by the Greeks. The Greyhound probably reached India by way of the Greek invaders under Alexander the Great, and during the Seleucid Empire which followed. It is interesting to note that this empire stretched to the borders of India, and included part of Afghanistan.

Richard and Alice Fiennes suggest that, 'pride of ancestry in this group can possibly be claimed by the Saluki breed, said by some to be the oldest pure-bred dog in the world, though the Pekingese might dispute this'. They do not, unfortunately, give any opinions as to the Afghan Hounds' claim to this distinction. Certainly there is ample proof that dogs of the Saluki type have been carefully bred from ancient times, in contrast to the astonishing lack of reliable evidence to support a similar claim on behalf of the Afghan Hound.

In the many instances where representations of the basic Greyhound type have appeared in art throughout the ages, some have been portrayed with long hair on ears or tails, or other characteristics that might vaguely suggest the Afghan Hound. None of these, however, could, without quite unwarranted demands on the imagination, be called Afghan Hounds as we know them to-day. They can, none the less, be claimed as Saluki types.

This almost complete absence of documentary or pictorial evidence that the more heavily coated Afghan Hound existed in antiquity, compared to the comparatively plentiful evidence as to the existence of the Saluki in ancient times, may well be taken as an indication that the Afghan Hound was, historically speaking, a recent development.

It must be stated at this point, that the actual lines of demarcation between the Saluki and the Afghan Hound are somewhat blurred. Exactly where the sparsely coated Afghan Hound ends, and the heavily coated Saluki begins, is not entirely clear. It is true that breeders have made a definitely recognisable difference between the two, with or without coats, but in dealing with periods dating back hundreds, even thousands of years, these differences, brought about largely, if not wholely, by man in his selective breeding, are not present. In fact the whole concept of what we mean by a breed presumes the consciously planned breeding by man.

In history and antiquity there were no controls as we know them, and no rigid lines of demarcation. Countries with land borders made it possible for various types of dog to mingle and mate either by chance, or by the deliberate intent of their owners, who would naturally introduce any new blood to their dogs for the quite praiseworthy purpose of improving their working or hunting qualities. It is, therefore, in my opinion, wrong to attempt to label or pigeonhole breeds of dogs in antiquity. Types are the most that we can attempt to isolate, but even then a wide variation within these types must be accepted. The practice of giving dogs as gifts, in addition to the nomadic character of many tribes, would all contribute to the intermingling of different types of dogs from widely separated areas.

The scarcity of historical data on the Afghan Hound is highlighted by Edward Ash, who claims to have searched the British Museum high and low when collecting material for his book *Dogs Their History and Development* published in 1927, but to have found no material on the Afghan Hound. I can confirm this, as I have combed museums, libraries, and other likely sources of possible information on the breed, including the examination of wall hangings, tapestries, paintings and illuminations from India in the Victoria and Albert Museum, many of which depict hunting or hawking scenes with dogs, but always clearly, and disappointingly, Saluki types.

Before jumping to any too hasty conclusions as the result of this frustrating lack of information on the breed, it would be well to consider some possible explanations.

In the first place the remote geographical position of their native habitat could be a contributory factor and, added to this, the nomadic character of many of the tribes would further reduce the possibility of recorded information on the breed, since wandering peoples are not prone to leave much art or literature. Another possible reason is the Moslem law forbidding the drawing of animals, on the grounds that it might constitute idolatry.

Some twenty-five years ago, Jackson Sanford of the U.S.A., carried out some exhaustive research to substantiate his theories concerning the ancient history of the Afghan Hound, and produced some interesting descriptions of early dogs. Among these was an exciting account of the central Asiatic Yeuchi peoples who conquered northern Afghanistan in the year 125 B.C. The account, contained in a Chinese manuscript runs as follows:

'They are of the race that inhabits the Land of the Frozen Earth. They are keepers of herds, breeders of horses, and drinkers of mares' milk . . . At night . . . their dogs stand watch by the common herd. . . . These dogs are as large as the foals in the herd, black and exceedingly fierce; the hair on them is long, and on the ear is of such texture that the women shear them as sheep, and make from the ear wool a felt, which is the material of their finest headgear. . . . When they hunt no animal stands before the ferocity of the dogs, and the mounted huntsman are hard-pressed to keep in view of the pack.'

Thrilling as the above account undoubtedly is, great caution must be exercised, and more details obtained before identifying the dogs as Afghan Hounds.

I understand from Dr. and Mrs. Waskow of the U.S.A., to whom I am indebted for the above extract, that they have much material on the origins of possible Afghan Hounds, which they intend to make available to those interested in the breed.

Other documents of varying ages have been discovered that contain descriptions of dogs that could possibly be Afghan Hounds, but not with sufficient detail to enable a positive identification to be made.

One of the most famous, certainly the most quoted, sources of the Afghan Hounds' claim to ancient origins, is the now well-known story of the rock carvings on the walls of the caves at Balkh. This information was contained in correspondence from a Major McKenzie to W. D. Drury, the author of *British Dogs*, published in 1903. The Major had become fascinated with the native dogs while serving on the North-West Frontier of India at the close of the nineteenth century, and had subsequently taken some specimens back to Europe with him. He described the carvings as of colossal size, and depicting dogs 'exactly like the Barukzie hounds of today'. He further stated that on these carvings were inscriptions of a much later date, written by invaders under Alexander the Great.

This fact, if true, would certainly establish the carvings as prior to the fourth century B.C. Unfortunately, subsequent and diligent enquiries among a wide circle of individuals and organisations who would be expected to have knowledge of these carvings has so far not produced anyone who has seen them, nor has any scientific evidence been unearthed to substantiate their existence. Even more perlexing, it now appears increasingly clear that there are no caves at all in the Balkh area.

Quite apart from the disappointment that is naturally felt at the apparent discrediting of this interesting story, it unfortunately creates a certain reserve in accepting other information from the same source. It is the more disturbing because Major McKenzie was the most fruitful source of information on the breed when it first arrived in this country.

Another popular and widely accepted story, purporting to prove not only the antiquity of the breed but also its exact place of origin, is contained in the history of the breed in the American Kennel Club's *Complete Dog Book*. It begins as follows: 'It was near Jebel Musa on the Mountain of Moses, on that small peninsular called Sinai, between the Gulf of Suez and the Gulf of Aqaba, that the breed now known as the afghan hound became a recognisable type of dog.' The authority given for this sweeping statement is described as a papyrus, attributed to a period between 3000 to 4000 B.C., which is alleged to have mentioned the dog so many times 'that there can be little doubt'.

The foundation on which this whole thesis rests is the translation of the word 'cynocephalus'. According to a Major Blackstone, who made the translation, this word can be freely translated as 'monkey-faced hound', and this is the meaning that he ascribes to it, claiming support for this in the illustrations on nearby tombs that, it is stated, 'offer convincing proof that even then the afghan hound's head was suggestive of the baboon'.

I have consulted the Department of Egyptian Antiquities at the British Museum concerning the translation of the word cynocephalus, and they inform me that the correct translation is dog-faced monkey or baboon, and not monkey-faced dog. A small, but vital rearrangement of three words.

Moreover, they were not very encouraging as to possible illustrations of Afghan Hounds, pointing out that in their experience the dogs usually represented were of the smooth-coated Greyhound or Saluki type.

On the other hand, the baboon was held sacred to the Gods Thoth and Khonsu by the Egyptians, and representations of it in wood, stone, and on papyrus are plentiful.

I have examined many of these, and in fairness it must be stated that to anyone not really familiar with Afghan Hounds, there could, in some instances, be a strong resemblance to these dogs more particularly if the representations were indistinct; and it must be borne in mind that those in question were thousands of years old.

I have also inspected the skulls and mummified remains of cynocephali, and found them to be unquestionably baboons.

Apart from the important points discussed above, this whole account has an air of the Arabian Nights, and at times borders on the flippant, as when it states 'there is no doubt that an Egyptian Princess claimed him [Afghan Hound] as her pet and applied to him the nickname "Monkeyface"'.

Finally, if the account is to be accepted, one must ask how the breed became established in the mountains of Afghanistan, and why there are no traces of it in Arabia or Persia, across which it must have passed.

An Englishman, the Hon. Mountstewart Elphinstone, wrote a book, published in the year of Waterloo, entitled *An Account of the Kingdom of Caubul and its Dependencies*. I, like other enthusiasts before me, have searched hopefully in this book for some reference to the Afghan Hound, but although the author goes into great detail in describing people, animals, and customs of the country, as far as dogs are concerned he mentions only the Greyhounds, with no hint of long coats or other characteristics that would enable them to be identified as Afghan Hounds. This is surprising, considering the detailed nature of some of his descriptions and observations, and might reasonably be taken as indicating that he saw only smooth-coated dogs, reminiscent of the English Greyhound, a breed that would be familiar to an Englishman of his background.

It was about this time (1813) that the earliest known illustration depicting an actual, recognisable Afghan Hound appeared. I refer to the picture of the Meena of Jajurh with his Afghan Hound, which appeared in a book by Thomas D. Broughton entitled *Letters written in a Mahrotta Camp, during the year 1809*. It shows a fairly well-coated Afghan Hound with a ring tail, but considerably smaller than the dogs of today, even if it is assumed to be a bitch. As this is a drawing, not a photograph, it is possible that the dog is not strictly to scale. If the scale was correct, much would depend on whether the man represented was short or tall. Clifford Hubbard says that the man was of a race known to be tall, so the dog may not be as small as it appears.

It is of interest that the dog is a better specimen, by today's standards, than many of the first imported dogs to arrive in this country nearly a century later. This may well have been due to frequently mentioned difficulty experienced by the early importers in obtaining good specimens from their native owners.

During the nineteenth century several writers on dogs made tentative and sometimes obscure references to the breed, referring to Afghan Hounds, Barukzie Hounds, Kabul Hounds, Persian Greyhounds, or Baluchi Hounds.

Barukzie was the name of the ruling Sirdars, much associated with the breed, and the plains of Baluchistan were the home of the plains or desert type. The association with the town of Kabul is obvious.

Early writers on dogs, in many instances, used the term 'Persian Greyhound' to cover various Saluki types as well as Afghan Hounds. Compt. Henri de Bylandt, in his book *Les Races de Chiens,* published in 1894, seems undecided which was which, and illustrations of both Afghan Hounds and Persian Greyhounds appear with the same joint title of 'Afghan Hound Persian Greyhound'.

Another colourful account of dogs, claimed to be Afghan Hounds in their native environment, comes from a visitor to the North-West Frontier writing under the name of Mali. This is printed in Hutchinson's *Dog Encyclopedia,* describes the mud forts at Chaman, and tells us that the complement of these forts were troops and dogs. The writer states:

'What strikes the newcomer . . . are the large extraordinary-looking creatures sprawling all over the place, fast asleep. In size and shape they somewhat resemble a large greyhound, but such slight resemblance is dispelled by the tufts with which all are adorned; some having tufted ears, others tufted feet, and others again possessing tufted tails.

They are known as Baluchi hounds, and. . . . They will have no truck with any stranger, white or black.

When retreat sounds, the pack awakes, yawns, pulls itself together, and solemnly marches out to take up positions close to the newly arrived night guard. They appear to be under no leadership, yet, as the patrols are told off, a couple of dogs attach themselves to each patrol, and they remain with their respective patrols till "Reveille" next morning. . . . Immediately one couple has completed the circuit of the walls and arrived back at the main gate, another couple starts out.

When it is remembered that these extraordinary hounds have never had any training whatsoever, that their duties are absolutely self imposed—for no human being has the slightest control over them—the perfection of their organisation and the smoothness with which they carry out their tasks, make mere man gasp.'

While making reasonable allowances for some licence in the interests of a good story (the idea of dogs with an inborn ability to carry out sentry duties with an efficiency that would rival her Majesty's Brigade of Guards is a little far-fetched), I feel that these dogs could well be Afghan Hounds.

It is unlikely that the old controversy over which came first, the Saluki or the Afghan Hound, will ever be satisfactorily resolved. The arguments put forward by both sides are frequently logical and plausible. It is worth quoting the contradictory views of two authorities.

H. D. Richardson in *Dogs their Origins and Varieties,* published in 1847, claims that the original Greyhound was unquestionably a long-haired dog, and that the modern thin and smooth-coated animal now known by that name is of comparatively recent date. Conversely, Croxton Smith, writing in *About Our Dogs,* published in 1931, claims that the Afghan Hound is an offshoot of the Saluki. He states that if the Saluki moved north from its native habitat into the mountains of Afghanistan, it would then have been quite natural for the higher altitude, with its attendant climate, to produce a heavier coat.

An important scientific fact, frequently overlooked by breed historians, is mentioned by Richard and Alice Fiennes in *The Natural History of the Dog.* They state, 'The adults [Afghan Hounds] have thick fleecy coats, which no doubt are very necessary in their cold, adopted habitat. The puppies, however, do not have fleecy coats and so reveal their origins in warmer climates.' And further, 'These dogs tend to segregate when developed in isolation and vary in size and conformation according to the district where they are kept.'

When seeking evidence for the Afghan Hounds' claim to antiquity, we must not entirely ignore the belief of the Afghan people that these dogs were the ones chosen by Noah to go with him into the Ark, an attractive legend, unfortunately not substantiated by historical record. Nevertheless, the Afghan people, as Mohammedans, would be familiar with the biblical story of the flood, and it is therefore fair to say that they at least consider the breed to be of ancient origin.

It will be apparent by now that there is very little dependable information available concerning the origins and early history of the breed. It is also difficult to ignore the strong probability that the Afghan Hound did, in fact, spring from an early Saluki type.

Among the many documents and scraps of information that helpers have sent to assist me in writing this book, I found an old page torn from a magazine which, from the contents and illustrations, I would date as from the 1920s. It contains an article entitled 'The Afghan Hound', but there is no indication of who wrote it, or from which publication it was taken. The author, however, puts forward some sound, commonsense views concerning the possible origins of the Afghan Hound, and for that reason I reproduce an extract here. It is also interesting in that it reveals, even at that early date, a certain scepticism concerning the story of the caves at Balkh.

The writer states:

'Assuredly the Afghan Hound is a primitive breed of conservative type quite distinct from any of our acclimatised foreign dogs. Yet it is hard to believe that it can have had an independent origin centuries ago in so wild and isolated a country as Afghanistan. . . .

Certain rock carvings and inscriptions discovered in the caves of Balkh are supposed to give proof of the use of this hunting dog in the chase long before the greyhound was known in Europe, and even before the lion-hunting mastiff was known in Assyria. But it is a dog of racy greyhound shape and make, and it is difficult to believe that breeds so similar in type were evolved independently from separate sources of origin. A sporting dog of such definite character as the barukhzy hound could hardly have sprung into perfect being on its own initiative thousands of years ago on the steppes of Bokhara and Hindu-Kush. The resemblance between it and the Russian borzoi, the English greyhound, and the Arabian saluki is too close to admit of a doubt that these breeds were all derived from a kindred ancestral stock, and superficially modified by a changed environment.

When one remembers that Afghanistan is crossed by the several trade routes and pilgrim ways connecting India with the Mediterranean, the question of the origin of the afghan dog is simplified. No explanation is more likely than that many centuries ago the nomadic Arabs, who took their horses and camels to the east, took also their gazelle hounds. So useful a hunting dog would not be omitted from the caravans passing from Syria into Persia, and thence across Afghanistan into India.'

In the many accounts that we have of the Afghan Hound in its native land, many and varied are the roles that it is claimed to have fulfilled; hunter, herd dog, guard dog, shepherd dog, sentry, and even trained thief on behalf of its master. Clifford Hubbard suggests that they may also have been used as fighting dogs, in the manner of cock fighting in early days in this country.

Some of these claims may be hard to credit, but there is no doubt about the true role of these dogs. They are sight hunters of game of varying types, especially over mountainous and uneven country. The Afghan Hound is not designed for pure speed on the flat. We are told that when hunting the larger types of game they are used in couples, one being trained to take the hind-quarters and the other the throat. These are the tactics of the ancestral wolves.

That the breed is highly valued in its native land there can be no doubt. The term 'Tazi' applied to the breed throughout Afghanistan clearly separates them from the ordinary dogs.

It has been stated earlier that the Afghan Hound varies in size and conformation according to the district from which it comes. The early imports into this country can be broadly grouped into two main types; the desert, or plains type, and the mountain type.

The desert dogs were large, long, with fairly light bone, and were more reminiscent of the Greyhound and Saluki, being very elegant and fast, with rather long loins. Shoulders were well laid back with long necks, carried slightly forward, and little front angulation. Feet, especially hind feet, were long. The heads were long and fine, with little stop, and slanting oriental eyes. The coats were sparse, but of silky texture; temperaments were said to be aloof and inclined to be unfriendly.

The mountain dogs, on the other hand, were smaller and altogether more sturdy and compact, with heavier bone, more spring of rib, shorter loin, and more pronounced front angulation. The necks were shorter than the desert dogs, but carried upright, with heads that were heavier and deeper, with a more definite stop. The eyes were less slanting, and set facing the front. The coats, although much more profuse, were woolly rather than silky in texture; temperaments were said to be perhaps more friendly. (Ch. Buckmal, illustrated facing page 48, is an example of the desert type; and Ch. Sirdar of Ghazni, facing page 49, shows the mountain type. For further notes on these two types see extract from *A.H.A. Newsletter* in Chapter 2.)

It will be apparent from the contents of this chapter that any attempt to be dogmatic concerning the place of origin, or the exact degree of antiquity of the Afghan Hound, on the evidence so far available, would be rash indeed. It is clear that for a very long time these dogs have been established in the areas known as Afghanistan and Baluchistan, but beyond this I would hesitate to go.

Perhaps the aura of mystery that surrounds the origins of these intriguing dogs is part of their charm and fascination. If we, like the poet, choose to imagine them running with Genghis Khan, then why not? It is true that it cannot be proved that they actually did, but neither has anyone so far proved that they did not.

We are left with the old Afghan saying: 'No man knoweth whence they came, but there they are and there they stay'.

2

The Afghan Hound up to the Second World War

THE closing years of the nineteenth century saw the first appearance of the Afghan Hound in this country. These early arrivals were mostly introduced by Army officers who had acquired them while serving on the North-West Frontier of India, and in many cases were very poor specimens of the breed, bearing little resemblance to the Afghan Hound we now know. As there were naturally no classes scheduled for them at the shows of the time, they were exhibited in the foreign dog class and initially seem to have made little impact on either the show enthusiasts or the general public. The tendency was to look upon them as curiosities, rather than serious examples of a hitherto unknown breed. Among the names that come down to us from those early days was Mustapha, owned by the Shah of Persia, but about whom little is known. Khelat, another dog which was exhibited successfully in the 1880s, although sometimes referred to as an Afghan Hound was in fact a black and white Afghan sheepdog, and closely resembled a Bobtail. He was, apparently, seriously considered by breeders of Bobtail Sheepdogs as a stud, and actually had a docked tail. Another early import at the turn of the century was Shahzada, illustrated in Charles Henry Lane's *All about Dogs*. This dog together with his kennel companion, the bitch Mooroo, after death were presented to the British Museum of Natural History, where they remain today. Shahzada, sometimes called Gazelle and exhibited under both names, is claimed to have had a moderately successful show career. I have, by the courtesy of the Museum authorities, examined the documents connected with the presentation of these two specimens to the Museum in 1901 and 1903, but no details of show activities or progeny are given.

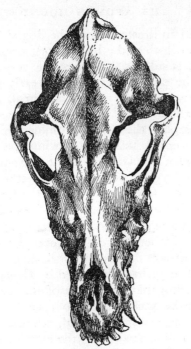

FIG 1 Afghan skull: bitch Mooroo

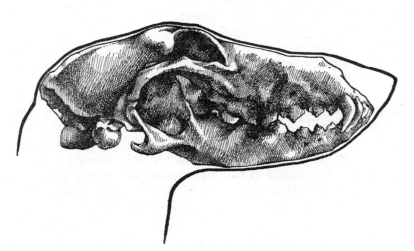

FIG 2 Profile of skull (Mooroo)

I have included an illustration of the dog since he appears to be a better specimen than the bitch; both would be considered small by today's standards, and they are very sparsely coated. This might be the ravages of time, but early drawings of this dog certainly show a virtually coatless animal. It must be borne in mind that this is a stuffed skin, without the skeleton, which would probably explain the lack of prominent hip bones. Assuming, however, a certain skill in following the original conformation on the part of the taxidermist, the dog appears to have had a short coupled body, good depth of brisket, sturdy legs, and good neck: but the most interesting of all are the feet, well down, of great size and in contrast to the rest of the dog very heavily coated, giving a bizarre appearance even to eyes accustomed to the Afghan foot. (Alas, where have these feet gone today?) Another name from those distant days is Dilkoosh described as an Afghan Barakhzy Hound. Afghan Bob owned by Captain Cary Barnard was exhibited during the early years of the century with some success, although he was reputed to resemble an Irish Setter. Other early specimens were Mukmul, Khulm, and Moroo, the property of Major Mackenzie, and the pair Roostam and Motee owned by Mr. T. R. Tufnell which mated produced Rajah II, considered at the time to be typical. It is fairly clear from the foregoing that these early imports were a somewhat motley collection, which is not surprising, since there was no standard to which to refer, and no recognised authority to give guidance. They were, moreover, probably different types from widely separated areas.

It was not until 1907 that the Afghan Hound made a definite impact on the British scene. In that year, the now legendary Zardin, owned by Captain John Barff, was exhibited at the Kennel Club Championship Show at Crystal Palace, and won the foreign dog class, a class in which he was subsequently never to be beaten. In contrast to the comparative indifference shown to the earlier arrivals in this country, Zardin made an immediate and considerable impression, so much so that Queen Alexandra expressed a wish to see him, which, we are told, resulted in Zardin visiting Buckingham Palace. He was described in the phraseology of the time as 'the finest oriental greyhound ever

(British Museum)

South Italian (Lucanian) figured pottery, 400–280 B.C., depicting the death of Actaeon. The dogs are greyhound types carrying their tails, which are feathered, high

(Gerald Massey)

A Meenah of Jajurh with his Afghan Hound, 1813

Zardin

(Peter Ward)
Shahzada—presented to the British Museum, 1901

seen in England', and from his photographs he would appear to have merited his success. Imported by his owner, Captain John Barff, from Seistan Province, he was exhibited successfully in India on his way to this country. Zardin came out of quarantine in time to compete at the aforementioned Kennel Club Show, and it is interesting to note that Mr. R. Temple, the judge who started him on his great career, placed Afghan Bob second to him.

An article in the *Indian Kennel Gazette* of 1906 gives a description of this famous dog, and as it must be one of the earliest, detailed descriptions of an undoubted Afghan Hound, it is worth printing in full.

'Zardin is a light coloured hound, almost white, with a black muzzle. He has a very long, punishing jaw of peculiar power and level mouth. His head resembles that of a deerhound, but with skull oval and prominent occiput, surmounted by a topknot; ears fairly large, well feathered and hanging to the side of the head rather than carried to front. He has a keen, dark eye, and little or no stop. A long, strong, clean neck, fairly well arched, running in a nice curve to shoulder, which is long and sloping and well laid back; his back is strong, loin powerful and slightly arched. He, as well as all this class of hound, falls away towards the stern (tail), which is set on low, almost destitute of hair, and usually carried low. He is well ribbed, tucked up under loin; forelegs straight and strong and covered with hair; great length between elbow (which is straight) and ankle. The forefeet are long, fairly broad and covered with long hair. Not too narrow in brisket, which is deep, with good girth of chest. Hindquarters very powerful, furnished with plenty of muscle; great length between hip and hock, which is low and strong, a fair bend of stifle, hind feet not so long as forefeet, but fairly wide and well protected with hair. The hindquarters, flanks, ribs and forequarters are well clothed with protective hair, thick and fine in texture, showing some undercoat. The coat on the back is shorter.'

This careful and observant description used in conjunction with the illustrations that we possess provide a very good represen-

C

tation of the dog as he was. Zardin was considered by the Barffs to be about five years old.

Captain Barff exhibited other dogs besides Zardin in the years subsequent to 1907, but none of them appears to have enjoyed the same success.

Although this great and much publicised dog is known to have been used at stud, it is almost certain that his strain has completely died out. I cannot find any evidence or trace of him in any Afghan pedigrees. The final chapter in the chronicle of his life is vague, very depressing, and something of an anticlimax. He was sold by his owner to an animal dealer called Shackleton, situated in the Leadenhall Market, who bought several other dogs from Captain Barff and bred from them. Just prior to the First World War, all these Afghan Hounds died in rather mysterious circumstances. Thus passed from the scene probably the best known Afghan Hound of all time, leaving nothing tangible behind him in the form of progeny but gaining immortality by providing the basis upon which our breed standard was built.

Many articles and books on the Afghan Hound state that Zardin's embalmed body is to be seen in the British Museum (Natural History). This probably arose from a statement in Hutchinson's *Dog Encyclopedia*. Regrettably I must contradict this story. Never during my lifelong visit to this Museum has Zardin been on exhibition, and I am assured by the Museum authorities that he has never been in their possession. They did, however, possess a photograph of him.

It was natural that in 1912, when a standard was required, Zardin should be the model upon which it was based. This, and subsequent standards, are more fully discussed in Chapter 4.

Mention should be made of one more Afghan Hound of this period, who achieved fame in a rather unusual way. Baz, a red dog, was bought from a caravan in Baluchistan by an Indian Army officer, who sold him to Mr. N. Dunn, the racing Greyhound breeder. Mr. Dunn mated Baz to a Greyhound bitch Explosion, in order to give stamina. The progeny were all smooth-coated, but with ringed tails and, I understand, were reasonably fast. Logically enough, it seems these puppies were not permitted to be entered in the Greyhound Stud Book. Baz however, the father, and as far as we know a thoroughbred Afghan Hound, was, due to the efforts of his owner, entered in the Greyhound Stud Book of 1911, an achievement that is unlikely to be equalled by any other Afghan Hound.

During the four years of the First World War, of necessity there were no further importations, and little or no breeding of Afghan Hounds. But after the Armistice a new and vigorous phase in the history of the breed began.

In 1921, Miss Jean Manson, who, like other early enthusiasts had been captivated by the breed while living in India, arrived in this country accompanied by Major and Mrs. Bell Murray and a team of twelve Afghan Hounds. These new arrivals, which were established at Cove Kennels in Scotland, were the foundation of the well-known Bell Murray Kennel, and were to play an important part in the development of the breed in the 1920s. They were predominantly of the plains or desert type, described in the last chapter, being Greyhound-like with sparse and tufted coats, but of considerable size, some reaching a height of 32 inches at the shoulder. In short, they were very different from the much publicised Zardin, who had so impressed the British scene some years earlier. This kennel was firmly established by 1925, when the next important influx of hounds occurred.

In 1925, Major and Mrs. Amps arrived in England from the North-West Frontier, where they had established their Ghazni Kennels in the hills of Afghanistan. Among the dogs they brought with them was the great Sirdar of Ghazni, described as a rich red dog bred in the Royal Kennels of King Amanullah of Afghanistan, and considered by the Amps to be approximately five years old. Sirdar was destined to become a great stud force in this country, siring three champion sons, three champion daughters and many champion grandchildren, thereby making his mark on the breed and establishing himself in the strains of many present-day hounds. Also with the Amps was Khan of Ghazni, another stud force who was reputed to have killed three leopards. The Ghazni hounds, as opposed to those owned by the Bell Murrays, were of the mountain type (also described in the last chapter), being much smaller and more compact but carrying more profuse coats.

Mrs. Amps was a great enthusiast and champion of the Afghan

Hound in this country. A tireless writer on the subject of her favourite breed, her ample correspondence has provided much material for works on the Afghan Hound. Although I corresponded with Mrs. Amps in my early days in the breed, I never actually met her: I am particularly indebted, therefore, to Mrs. Wendy Graham and the Afghan Hound Association for placing at my disposal many documents, press cuttings, and photographs given to Mrs. Graham by Major and Mrs. Amps, from which I have been able to draw much useful information and material for this book. Among these documents I was interested to find Sirdar's challenge certificates, a very tangible link with this famous dog of the past. While Mrs. Amps was responsible for supplying so much first-hand and authentic information concerning the Afghan Hound in its native country, she also took pains and, I suspect, some pleasure in shooting down many of the myths and misconceptions that surrounded them in Great Britain at that time. It was Mrs. Amps who provided the information printed in an early copy of *Our Dogs,* concerning possible Afghan and Saluki crosses. She states in a letter to the Editor, 'The Afghans who live in the heat of the plains near the Indian frontier sometimes cross a Saluki bitch with an Afghan hound dog, in order to get a less profuse coat. These crosses are often seen with the Powindah caravans on the various Afghan frontiers, but around Kabul and in the hill country which forms the greater part of Afghanistan, the best strains always have an abundant coat to enable them to stand the bitter cold of the winter.'

A further reference to the possibility of Afghan Saluki crosses appears in a letter written by Major Amps to the Maharajah of Patiala dated August 31st 1926. Major Amps, who was still resident in Afghanistan writes, '. . . My wife is having a most successful time with the dogs in England. She found that the type which has been shown there in the past is not the pure-bred Afghan hound but shows unmistakable signs of a cross with the Saluki. The result is that they are too light in build and short of coat.' This paragraph also contains, for the perceptive, a hint of the coming press battle between Mrs. Amps and Major Bell Murray.

While the Amps and the Bell Murrays are generally considered to be the main importers of hounds from Afghanistan in the

immediate post-war years, others were also playing a part in the
introduction and establishment of the breed in this country at
that time. Miss Clara Bowring, was one of these. A notice in the
Dog World of 1925 reads, 'Miss Bowring's brother is sending her
two more bitches from India. He had a job to get them and only
managed it through a Rajah friend', yet another reference to the
difficulty experienced in getting dogs out of Afghanistan.

Miss Evelyn Denyer, another breeder and exhibitor of the
early 1920s was the first Afghan Kennel owner to have an affix—
'of Kaf'—and was the owner of Taj Mahip of Kaf. Miss Denyer—
who on marriage became Mrs. J. Barton—was a prime mover
behind the formation of the Afghan Hound Club, formed in 1925,
with herself as Secretary, Captain T. S. Waterlow Fox as President,
and Miss Clara Bowring as Treasurer. When Mrs. Barton went
overseas with her husband, most of her dogs were acquired by
Captain Waterlow Fox, whose affix 'of Wyke' was well known
in the breed.

By the middle of the 1920s we have a situation where two
pioneer kennels of the breed are established in this country, each
producing and extolling a different type of hound. Major Bell
Murray with his desert or plains type, and Mrs. Amps with her
mountain type, and as would be expected other kennels based on
stock obtained from one or the other.

Purists will hasten to inform me that this is something of an
oversimplification, and I am well aware that some of the Bell
Murray hounds did have some pretension to a fair coat, while it
is equally true that not all the Ghazni hounds were heavily
coated, nonetheless the generalisation is broadly correct and the
image is one with which I am sure neither of these two breeders
would have quarrelled.

A situation like this in dog breeding and showing circles was
bound to erupt into open confrontation, and the controversy that
raged in the press between these two early enthusiasts makes
interesting, informative, and sometimes amusing reading today.
Mrs. Amps, on her arrival in this country, seems to have been
quick to seize upon the natural advantage of the obvious simi-
larity between her own hounds and the famous Zardin, who as
another mountain type, clearly resembled the Ghazni hounds,

rather than the desert hounds of the rival kennel. Both sides referred to the dogs of the other as imposters. Major Bell Murray, on the one hand, appears to have made the most of the superior size of his hounds, while Mrs. Amps, as would be expected, relied on the more profuse coat of hers. Evidence of this is contained in the following paragraph from the previously mentioned letter from Major Amps to the Maharajah of Patiala. Referring to showing in England in 1925, he states, 'My wife was very amused to find that at all the shows the owners of Afghan hounds were careful to explain that their dogs were "temporarily out of coat" . . . my wife has been bombarded by visits from most of the leading judges who were anxious to see her dogs, and she has had no difficulty in convincing them that most of the dogs bred in England were not quite true to type.' One cannot help feeling that the last sentence has a rather ominous ring for Major Bell Murray and his hounds. Mrs. Amps seems to have been a formidable opponent, and from my own experiences of crossing swords with forceful doggy ladies I cannot suppress a certain sympathy springing up for the Major in his battle of nearly fifty years ago.

It is interesting to note, on the question of size, that Mrs. Amps admitted that Sirdar was a 'bit on the small side' but offers the explanation that this was due to his legs having been broken and badly set in his youth, otherwise she claimed, he would undoubtedly have grown a further two inches. An ingenious theory, which, if it proves nothing else shows that Afghan Hound owners of the past were as adept as their present-day counterparts in offering plausible excuses for the shortcomings of their dogs.

It would appear, looking back on this old battle between these early breeders, that in the main Mrs. Amps did succeed in persuading many people to her views. The natural appeal of her more glamorously coated hounds must have been an advantage, apart from their other attributes. The breed today, however, has much to thank the Bell Murray hounds for, more particularly their fine heads and excellent shoulders.

I am indebted to Mr. Ronald Adams for placing at my disposal for this book his record of a discussion on this subject between

Dr. Betsy Porter and Mrs. Eileen Drinkwater, which appeared in the *Afghan Hound Association Newsletter* of 1966. As both these ladies had direct personal experience of these two early strains this discussion is of great interest to all Afghan Hound enthusiasts, and I therefore include it in full.

EXTRACT FROM AFGHAN HOUND ASSOCIATION NEWSLETTER

Neither Mrs. Drinkwater nor Dr. Porter was much impressed with the Ghazni heads and Ch. Sirdar, it appears, had a somewhat heavier head than we are accustomed to seeing nowadays. (By 'nowadays' I think both ladies had in mind the current state of the breed at the time of the discussion. Undoubtedly this is what I intended to convey at the time I originally wrote it. In the mid-fifties some very coarse and heavy heads were still to be seen—and seem to be reappearing here and there at the present time—1966.) He was, incidentally, rather a small dog—at least by modern standards—a fact which is certainly not apparent in his photographs which, almost without exception, provide no idea of scale.

Bell Murray hounds, on the other hand, had beautifully modelled skulls, being finer in the head altogether although by no means lacking in power. They had long cleanly chiselled forefaces, rather Roman-nosed, and possessed strong, powerful underjaws. As to eyes, the Bell Murrays excelled in this department—not only in colour, shape and placement, but also in expression. Both ladies assured me that the hounds of this strain had a most beautiful expression in the eye, and that this particular characteristic has now completely disappeared from the breed. Generally speaking, the typical Bell Murray head combined elegance with power and was very oriental both in type and expression.

Both strains were said to have had rather straighter stifles than are preferred today although, of the two, the Ghaznis had probably the better angulation. Nevertheless, although the Bell Murrays were straighter in the stifle, they had very well sloped pasterns and Mrs. Drinkwater was convinced that nothing could touch these hounds for speed and turning power.

They also had long and beautifully sloped quarters, and very long tails set on low and ending in good strong rings. No comments were made on Ghazni tails—unless my notes are at fault—but most of the photographs in my possession indicate that these were probably not very good.

Apparently the Bell Murray hounds also scored in neck and shoulder, the former being long and arched while the latter were generally fine and well laid. Mostly, they had excellent head carriage and good fronts. Ghazni necks, it was said, were quite definitely shorter in comparison, and the fronts of this strain were inclined to be narrow and straight.

Feet? The Bell Murrays had very long arched toes and stood with their pads absolutely flat on the ground. They were notable for their tremendously long hind feet. Not that Ghazni feet were by any means bad, although they did, in general, tend to be a little smaller. Terrier feet were virtually unknown in either strain and throughout the early days of the breed; this undesirable feature seems first to have made its appearance during the thirties.

Both ladies were of the opinion that the Ghaznis had the better temperaments—the Bell Murrays being aloof, dignified and quite distinctly unfriendly. Not, on the whole, that the Ghaznis could really be said to be overfond of strangers either. (It is, perhaps, only fair to note here that Ch. Sirdar was frequently described as being a very friendly character by various writers of his time.)

For sheer quantity, the Ghaznis had by far the better coats and the profuse hair we are accustomed to seeing nowadays is a part of their legacy to the breed. However, although in comparison the Bell Murray coats tended to be on the sparse side, they were very much silkier. Both strains had well defined saddles and were far superior in this respect to the general run of modern hounds.

Viewed as a whole, the typical Bell Murray hound could be said to have been a tallish, very racy dog, having something of the 'houndiness' of the English Greyhound. It had a fair length of back, a good deep brisket and was rather long in the loin. On the move, it could give the impression that it was just

floating over the ground and its action was exceptionally clean
and springy. The typical Ghazni hound was inclined to be
smaller and built on altogether squarer lines. It was well
coated, short backed and was much shorter coupled than its
Bell Murray opposite number.

In conclusion, both Mrs. Drinkwater and Dr. Porter expressed a decided preference for the Bell Murray hounds, although
Dr. Porter felt that the breed had definitely been improved
through the inter-breeding of the two strains. As far as I can
remember, Mrs. Drinkwater did not express an opinion on this
point, although she did say that most of our present day hounds
were rather more along Ghazni lines than Bell Murray. The
two ladies were agreed, though, that not all the changes in the
breed were the result of interbreeding; some being undoubtedly
due to climate and environment. Mrs. Drinkwater was firmly
of the opinion that environment was of very great importance
to Afghans and that freedom was an essential requirement of
their nature.

Careful perusal of the canine and lay press of the 1920s throws
interesting light on many of the problems of the early exhibitors
and breeders. They show how facilities that we take for granted
today were obtained only after much effort and trouble. The
Dog World breed columns of November 1929 contain the obviously welcome news that 'mixed sex classes for Afghan Hounds are
now a thing of the past', and the breed contributor looked forward
enthusiastically to an improved situation where bitches would no
longer be compelled to compete with dogs in the ring (presumably at the large shows). A. Croxton Smith writing in the *Dog
World* and the *Daily Telegraph* in 1926 about the Kennel Club
show of that year at the Crystal Palace, is obviously impressed by
the Afghan Hound entries, which he states were '41 strong' and
continues 'a year ago it would not have been possible to foresee
such a number'.

Again, the *Dog World* of 1929 gives the following information
from Mrs. I. Bradshaw re Sirdar's offspring, which were prominent in the show-ring at that time: 'The red or rather red golds
do seem to carry a heavier coat than the paler colours, although

these get it in time.' She then goes on to say in a mood of great optimism, 'No need for anyone going in for our breed to go wrong if they have seen the beautiful dogs winning at the large shows this year (1929). The type is fixed and coat predominates, and I am thankful to say most of the dogs are sound. The splayed footed brigade has disappeared.' This chance mention of the Afghan Hound feet brings to mind another frustration of the early years. Mrs. Gibson draws attention to this in her book when describing her early days as an exhibitor. She states that only 'advanced' judges of the day were knowledgeable about the breed but states that: 'Other judges were not so well versed in the points of the breed, and considered . . . that the Afghan hound's long feet, which are an essential characteristic of the breed, were wrong and did not hesitate to voice their incorrect opinions, even in the ring.'

This ignorance of the special breed points must have been a constant source of frustration and annoyance to the early pioneers.

Apart from interesting historical facts and valuable information, these early breed columns in the canine press throw much interesting light on the human side of dog breeding and showing at the time. Afghan Hound people have always had the reputation of being volatile, and quick to join issue on any topics that touch their breed. This is in no way to be deplored, for the opposite, which is apathy and stagnation, can only lead to deterioration. One particular piece of unconscious humour, also from a breed column of 1929 is, I think, well worth reproducing, if only to show how feelings could run away with people then, as now. The columnist writes, 'It is the good fellowship spirit of the members of the Afghan Hound Association which makes us all work together so harmoniously for the good of the breed' and in the very next paragraph goes on to say, 'No one was more welcome at the show than Mrs. Amps, who made her appearance accompanied by Champion Sirdar of Ghazni which she had sportingly entered not for competition *to prove he was still alive.*' (The italics are mine.) This somewhat baffling statement is immediately explained when she continues, 'Champion Sirdar never looked better and was the admiration of all. He was guarded by a plain clothes policeman all day, a wise precaution in view of the threats of the anonymous letter-writer we have in our midst!' A letter writer whom, we must fervently hope, was not a member of the Afghan Hound Association, or if he (or she) was, then that the dire threats were made in a spirit of good fellowship for the good of the breed!

Inevitably, with the passing of the years, breeders began to experiment with mixtures of Ghazni and Bell Murray types in order to gain size, coat or some other desired attribute that could be obtained from one or the other. So the merging of the two, in many ways different, types began, the merging that has produced the Afghan Hound of today.

I make no apologies for dealing at some length in this book with the two original types of Afghan Hound, because it is only by understanding the roots from which our hounds have sprung that a knowledgeable and correct appraisal of one's own and other people's dogs can be made, and the fact that these two types will manifest themselves in litters from time to time will be the more readily understood. I have referred elsewhere to the surprise shown by many newcomers, when they first see one of the now rare Afghan Hounds with short hair on the saddle, and bare pasterns. A similar surprise was expressed by many onlookers at a recent championship show at which I judged, when a complete throwback to the original Ghazni type entered the ring. He showed not a trace of the plains type. His sturdy, heavily boned body and upright neck carried a head with well-defined stop, level set eyes, but heavy and broad by today's standards, although perfectly correct for him. He stood out among the other exhibits in the class who were all of the accepted blends to one degree or another. Those spectators who understood the origins of our current types readily recognised him for what he was. This situation, although interesting, presents problems for a judge.

In May 1925, the Kennel Club granted the breed championship status, and the first set of challenge certificates was on offer at Cruft's Dog Show in 1926. The dog challenge certificate was won by Mrs. J. Barton's Taj Mahip of Kaf, and the bitch challenge certificate was won by Miss Jean Manson's Ranee. Taj Mahip and Ranee were bred by Major Bell Murray. The Afghan Hound was, at last, firmly on the canine map. It was a year later, in 1927, that the first champion was made up. It was the dog Buckmal, bred by Major Bell Murray and owned by Miss Jean Manson. By Ooty out of Pushum (a brindle), Ch. Buckmal was 32 inches and, therefore, over the limits of our present-day standard (just as Ch. Sirdar of Ghazni at 24 inches was below it). He was described as faintly brindle, a fact that is borne out by his picture, and very intelligent, with a good coat, presumably by the standards of his day. A bitch from this breeding, Daghai was the dam of Ch. Taj Mahip of Kaf (made up to champion in 1928), and the great grand-dam of the famous International Champion Badshah of Ainsdart. The first bitch champion also gained her title in 1927 and was the aforementioned Ranee which was by Rajah out of Begum and was a black-masked cream. Thus, it will be seen that the first two British champions, dog and bitch, were bred by Major Bell Murray. The Bell Murrays can in fact lay claim to have bred four out of the first six British champions. The other two being Mrs. Amps's Ch. Sirdar of Ghazni and Ch. Azri Havid of Ghazni which gained their titles in 1927 and 1929 respectively.

Ch. Azri Havid of Ghazni, a son of Ch. Sirdar of Ghazni and Roshni of Ghazni gained distinction as the first Afghan Hound to win a Best-in-Show award. He was a black and tan known to everyone as Rif, and was the sole Afghan owned by Mrs. Phyllis Robson, the well-known canine journalist, and President of the Afghan Hound Association for many years. Rif can be seen illustrated, with his owner, in Hubbard's *Afghan Handbook,* and it is noticeable that he is very sparsely coated on the legs.

In the 1930s, the intermingling of the two strains referred to earlier in this chapter was well advanced. Inevitably, different breeders started to form their own ideas of what the ideal mixture should be, and as a result some began to develop and produce a recognisable strain, identifiable with their own kennels.

Many and varied were the results obtained from these early experiments, and it must be admitted that some of them were far from happy. Breeders will agree that merging different types to obtain certain desirable points from each is a worthy aim, but frequently nature slaps one down by producing progeny with the undesirable attributes of each. This is beautifully and shrewdly pointed out by Bernard Shaw in a letter to Lily Langtry, who had written to him suggesting marriage between them and pointing out the wonderful prospect of children with her beauty and his brains. He is reputed to have asked her if she had considered the possibility of children with his beauty and her brains.

The task of the judges must have been unenviable in sorting out some of the strange and varied types that were paraded before them. About this time, some of the breeders with long-range breeding plans began to look further afield for their blood lines, and some overseas stock was imported. Mrs. Olive Couper of the Garrymhor prefix mated her bitch Champion Garrymhor Souria (who gained her title in 1932) to Ardmore Anthony a dog imported from India. This mating produced the Champion Garrymhor Faiz-Bu-Hassid, a golden dog owned by Mrs. Sharpe, who gained his championship status in 1937.

Another important early breeder of this pioneer era was the aforementioned Mrs. Eileen Drinkwater, whose Geufron affix appears with great frequency in the challenge certificate lists and pedigrees of the 1930s. Her stud dog, Omar of Geufron, although not a champion himself, sired many champions. An early one was Ch. Yakub Khan of Geufron out of Zabana of Kaf. A later litter out of Zabana produced four champions, namely Ch. Aga Lala of Geufron, Ch. Firdausi of Geufron, Ch. Shah Shuja of Geufron, and Ch. Manaprajapati of Geufron.

Ch. Wanawallari of Geufron, a bitch out of Sheba of Wyke, was sold to Mrs. Gibson of the Acklam Kennels. A later litter out of Sheba of Wyke produced Ch. Malati of Geufron; Ch. Kinsuka was out of Ch. Sirfreda. Surely an inspiring record for any stud dog.

Ch. Fudausi sired Ch. Chankidar of Geufron and International Ch. Chota Sahib who, in his turn, sired a champion bitch Azura Goldstar.

Mrs. Drinkwater was also one of those early breeders who used an imported sire by mating Lakki Marwat to Sita of Geufron to produce the bitch Ch. Kisagotami and the American Champion Lakshum of Geufron.

The Westmill Kennels owned by Mrs. Wood contributed much to the development of the Afghan breed and produced many champions: outstanding among these in my mind was Ch.

Westmill Tamasar a dark brindle dog that captivated me when I first saw a picture of him some twenty years ago. He was by International Ch. Badshah of Ainsdart out of Ranee of Geufron and was, therefore, a grandson of Ch. Sirdar of Ghazni and a mixture of the Bell Murray and Ghazni strains. I have included his picture in this book because I have always kept an image of him in my mind as a worthy pattern to be aimed at in breeding or selecting a dog.

The Acklam Kennels owned by Mr. and Mrs. Howard Gibson were established in Yorkshire in the twenties, but later moved to the Channel Islands, where they started in Afghan Hounds. After acquiring a dog, Hassan of Acklam, they purchased the young bitch Wanarwallari of Geufron from Mrs. Drinkwater, which was the foundation of their kennel. Wanarwallari became a champion in 1937. Their most famous champion was the bitch Mitzon of Acklam (by Ch. Westmill Ben Havid out of Wanarwallari) whose story and that of her kennelmates is told in a booklet written by Mrs. Gibson and circulated privately, entitled *The Story of Mitzon of Acklam.*

While visiting England at the outset of the Second World War, the Gibsons found that communications with the Channel Islands had ceased, thus cutting them off from their animals. The story, however, has a happy ending, for by the efforts of friends and animal lovers on the Islands, Mitzon and two of her kennelmates survived the war to welcome the Gibsons back to their home at the cessation of hostilities. Mitzon, at six and a half years, was then mated to Ch. Westmill Ben Havid.

The story of this incredible bitch did not, however, end here. After the litter, Mr. and Mrs. Gibson decided to campaign Mitzon in an attempt to gain her championship title, an undertaking that meant travelling to England to exhibit at championship shows, which, bearing in mind that Mitzon was then seven and a half years old might well have daunted the most zealous exhibitor. The final achievement of Mitzon was the gaining of her qualifying challenge certificate under Mrs. Rothwell Fielding at the great age of nine years; certainly the oldest Afghan Hound bitch to gain a championship title. This feat also proves that Afghan Hounds, although undeniably late developers, are truly great lasters.

The Acklam Kennels sold only one dog. Madame Mariette Deckars of Belgium saw Ch. Mitzon at a London show, and after much perseverance and a visit to Jersey succeeded in persuading the Gibsons to make an exception to their 'no sales' rule and part with a black-and-tan son of Mitzon, Amanullah Khan of Acklam, who accompanied her back to Belgium and soon became a French and Belgian champion, before finally settling in Sweden where he sired litters (*see* Chapter 10).

Some of the early breeders were very jealous of their strains, and would not readily allow their stud dogs to be used. Mrs. Gibson gives evidence of this in describing the reluctance of Mrs. Wood to allow her Ch. Westmill Ben Havid to be used. After much persuading, Mrs. Wood finally permitted the mating on the understanding that 'no offspring was disposed of to the breeders of the day'.

Mrs. Molly Sharpe's Chaman Kennels, established in Scotland, owned the well-known champion Garrymhor Faiz-Bu-Hassid, who sired champions including three in overseas countries: Canadian Champion Pic of Chaman, Italian Champion Sabrie of Chaman, and American Champion Juan of Chaman. This kennel also bred Ch. Taj Akbar of Chaman by Kulli Khan of Kuranda out of Safiya. Taj Akbar holds the record of winning nine challenge certificates at three years of age as well as being the first Afghan Hound to be televised, appearing before the cameras at Alexandra Palace in 1938. Mrs. Sharpe was one of those British breeders who sent stock to America during the war in order to perpetuate bloodlines. Constance O. Miller and Edward M. Gilbert in the *Complete Afghan Hound* pay tribute to this and acknowledge American indebtedness to British breeders for such dogs as Ch. Rana of Chaman of Royal Irish and Tajana Glamour Girl of Chaman which, but for the Second World War, might never have left their home kennels.

After the war the Chaman Kennels were in the van in producing winning stock, taking both challenge certificates at the first postwar championship show, and producing many champions including Ch. Taj of Chaman by Taj Akbar of Chaman out of Thopar. Taj of Chaman holds the record jointly with Sirdar of Ghazni of never having been beaten in the show-ring by another Afghan Hound.

Mrs. Sharpe was also one of the first Afghan Hound owners to experiment with racing, during the 1930s.

In 1927 the Afghan Hound Association was formed with Mrs. I. Bradshaw as secretary.

The el Kabul Kennels owned by Dr. Betsy Porter were originally situated in Kirby, as were the Geufron Kennels of Mrs. Eileen Drinkwater. Dr. Porter owned the champion dog Shah Shuja of Geufron, which, as a son of the bitch Zabana of Kaf by Omar of Geufron, was a direct link with the pioneer kennels of Miss Denyer. Dr. Porter was another of those farsighted breeders who sent some of her selected stock to America during the period of hostilities of the Second World War, and was in the lead when the Afghan Hound was being re-established in Great Britain in the early days of peace. The home-bred bitch Ch. Kyronisha El Kabul was by Kuranda Turkuman Opium Poppy out of Zara El Kabul.

The Baberbagh Kennels of Mrs. L. Prude owned Ch. Marika of Baberbagh, bred by Mrs. Cannan by Sirdar of Ghazni out of Sada of Ghazni.

The Ainsdart hounds were the property of Mrs. Morris Jones, who bred the International Ch. Badshah of Ainsdart, who was by Ch. Sirdar of Ghazni out of Ku-Mari of Kaf, a link with both the Amps and the Denyer Kennels.

Miss Marjorie Matthews of the Westover prefix was a devoted worker on behalf of the breed, and her kennels provided foundation stock for some well-known post-war breeders. She was also well known for weaving Afghan Hound hair into wool, which in many ways resembled cashmere, for garments.

Mrs. S. Rhodes's Tuclo Kennels owned pre-war champions; one, Westmill Karabagh, bred by Mrs. Woods, was by Kym out of Ranee of Geufron. Mrs. Rhodes was a prominent winner at the early post-war shows with her two bitches, Ch. Ajawaan Chita Mia, by Nosnikta's Nissim Tango out of Silvercaul Sa-De-Miranda, and Ch. Ajawaan Ranee Tamba, also out of Sa-De-Miranda by Azad of Chaman.

The first International Champion was produced by the Enriallic Kennels owned by Mr. Daniel Cronin in Ireland. International Ch. Zardi of Enriallic was by Rupee out of Souria of Enriallic.

Ch. Buckmal, the first Afghan Hound Champion, 1927

Ch. Marika of Baberbagh

Ch. Sirdar of Ghazni

Ch. Westmill Tamasar

Miss Juliette de Bairacli Levi was the owner of the Turkuman Kennels mentioned frequently in the next chapter. She was a great advocate of natural rearing methods.

Mrs. Rothwell-Fielding of the Kuranda prefix was another who helped to re-establish the breed on the cessation of hostilities.

It is fair that credit should also be given to the many smaller kennels who played their part in the interwar years. Among these were the Washdarb Kennels of Mrs. I. Bradshaw, the Jalalabad Kennels of Miss Ide, the Valdoren Kennels of Mrs. Clarke, and the Pusktikuh Kennels of Mrs. Semple.

In 1939, at the outbreak of the Second World War, showing was drastically curtailed and dog breeding very severely restricted. Breeders took heed of the Kennel Club edict that 'No bitch should be mated unless it is for the express purpose of keeping in existence a line of blood of great use to the future of the breed'. Some breeders sent stock to countries free from attack in order to ensure the continuity of important bloodlines. The Canine Defence League came into being and organised a system whereby dog owners made their homes available as shelters to other dog owners (dogs not being allowed in air raid shelters). They also produced luminous leads to combat the blackout, and even canine gas masks were manufactured, but I would shrink from persuading any of my dogs to wear one.

Feeding difficulties due to rationing and general shortages, combined with the problems of animals in air raids, made the keeping of dogs and pets generally very difficult. I recall, on one short leave from my Regiment, taking my Dachshund to be put down after an air raid had slightly wounded him, and had caused severe terror.

I have mentioned that showing continued on a restricted scale. This took the form of shows limited to exhibitors residing within a prescribed distance from the venue. While I am told that this system worked well in the main, keeping the show world alive, it also led to some conniving and cunning use of accommodation addresses. No champions during this time were, of course, made, but the whole business of showing and breeding 'ticked over' for the duration, so that breeders and other interested people were ready to go forward again on the return of peace.

D

3

The Post-war Era

IN 1945, with Great Britain again at peace, people were able once more to turn their minds and energies to the pursuit of hobbies and pleasures. Dog breeders everywhere looked forward to a return to breeding and showing their chosen breeds.

The established pre-war Afghan Hound breeders were soon active again in promoting the interests of the breed. The Afghan Hound Association set up a sub-committee to revise the breed standard, and some new kennels that had been established during the war years joined in the general reinstatement of the breed. The available breeding stock was, of necessity, limited to very young or very old dogs. Feeding was at first difficult, but eased as the time passed.

Showing was soon resumed on a normal basis (as opposed to the radius shows of the war period). In 1946 there were still no general championship shows, benching being a particular difficulty. The Afghan Hound Association held its first post-war championship show on 15th June 1946 at the London Scottish Drill Hall, Buckingham Gate. Brigadier-General Lance officiated and awarded the dog challenge certificate to Taj of Chaman and the bitch certificate to Tajavia of Chaman both owned by Mrs. Molly Sharpe. The following year, 1947, saw a limited number of general championship shows. Some new ones appeared at this time but not all stayed the course: most of the old established pre-war championship shows, however, continued with gradually increasing entries.

The first post-war Cruft's was held in October 1948. The Kennel Club had bought this famous show from the widow of Charles Cruft, and after the war it took the place of the pre-war Kennel Club Show. Apart from the year 1949, when no Cruft's was held, and the year 1954, when an electricians' strike caused a cancellation, it ran on regularly to the present time, growing in size with the years, and gaining an undisputed position as the greatest dog show in the world, the transition to the Olympia from the old Agricultural Hall at Islington having been more than justified.

The year 1947 brought the second championship show of the Afghan Hound Association, held at the Corn Exchange, Leeds, on 15th February, with Mrs. Eileen Drinkwater judging. After this date, the Association was not granted championship status again until 1952, so annual open shows were held during this period.

On 14th October 1946 the Southern Afghan Club, the first of the regional breed clubs, was formed. The first Secretary was Mrs. L. J. Southgate, who after a short time handed over to Mr. A. D. A. Munro, one of the founder members, who still holds the office. Exactly one month later, on 14th November 1946 the Northern Afghan Hound Association was launched under the Secretaryship of Mrs. R. Y. Harrison, and these two regional clubs, with the Afghan Hound Association, looked after the interests of the breed for many years.

Some names of the winning dogs of those early post-war days will be of interest.

The first post-war challenge certificates were awarded, as already stated, at the first Afghan Hound Association Show, mentioned on page 50.

The first post-war dog champion was Ch. Ravelly Patrols Ali Bey owned by Mr. Reg Floyd. The first post-war bitch champion was Ch. Ajawaan Chita Mia owned by Mrs. S. Rhodes. In 1948, the nine-year-old Vendas Tash Down, owned by Mrs. O'Toole of the Kohistan prefix gained his qualifying challenge certificate at Cruft's, becoming an International Champion and going on to win the Hound Group. And in the same year Mitzon of Acklam crowned her romantic career, as previously stated, by obtaining her qualifying certificate also at the age of nine years.

Of those breeders who started during the Second World War, the Bletchingley Kennels of Mrs. F. C. Riley were among the first to make their mark in the show-rings of the late 1940s. Mrs. Riley, who was well known in cockers, started her kennel with the bitch Ravelly Badrea which was acquired from Mr. Reg

Floyd in 1939, and the bitch Shiba of Chaman. The first champion
was Ch. Bletchingley Tajomeer. Born on 24th June 1945, he was
by Taj Ameer of Chaman, out of Shiba of Chaman. This success
was quickly followed by the beautiful bitch Ch. Bletchingley Zara,
who, after gaining her championship title in 1948, was a consistent
winner. She was a daughter of Ch. Bletchingley Tajomeer out of
Ravelly Badrea. A repeat of this mating produced the next
champion, a singleton Ch. Bletchingley Tribesman, who gained
his title in 1951. These initial successes were followed by a long
run of Bletchingley champions.

Another dog from this kennel, Ch. Bletchingley Houndsman,
was exported to Sweden where he was a great success and exercised a powerful influence on the breed in that country (*see*
Chapter 10).

Contemporary with the Bletchingley Kennels were Mr. and
Mrs. Abson's Netheroyd Kennels based in Huddersfield. Mrs.
Abson (now Mrs. Morton) owned the first black champion
bitch Ch. Netheroyd Turkuman Camelthorne, which was given
to Juliette de Bairacli Levi by Mrs. Clarke, who had her as pick
from Mrs. Polson's litter out of Golden Ranee, in lieu of a stud
service by Turkuman Pomegranite. Another bitch, Netheroyd
Camelthorne, mated to Netheroyd Ansari, produced the Absons'
famous black-and-tan Netheroyd Alibaba. Born November
1947, Alibaba gained many challenge certificates, (holding the
record until it was taken by the late Mrs. Race's bitch in 1969),
but he made history by winning Best in Show, first day, at Cruft's
in 1953.

Another litter out of Ch. Netheroyd Turkuman Camelthorne
by Chota Nissim of Ringbank produced Turkuman Nissims
Laurel who was exported to the U.S.A., where he was owned by
Mrs. Sunny Shay and Mr. Sol Malkin, and was a top winner in
the breed in the U.S.A. in the 1950s.

Mr. and Mrs. Abson used Mrs. Riley's Ch. Bletchingley Tajomeer which sired their champion Netheroyd Red Eagle, also out of
the bitch Ch. Netheroyd Turkuman Camelthorne.

Another famous sire, influencing many pedigrees, was Turkuman Damar Pine Tree, bred by Miss Venn of the Conygar prefix.
Miss Venn's kennels were to produce many top quality dogs.

Damar Pine Tree was a black and tan and was owned by Miss Matthews of the Westover prefix, who had bought him from Miss de Bairacli Levi whose prefix Turkuman he bore. A repeat of the mating produced Ch. Patrols Ali Khan, owned by Mrs. R. Y. Harrison.

The Patrols Kennels of Mrs. R. Y. Harrison were also influential in the breed at this time. The bitch Patrols Creme Chenille was mated to Turkuman Damar Pine Tree and produced Patrols Ali Bey, which was sold to Mr. Reg Floyd of the Ravelly Kennels. Mr. Floyd campaigned Ali Bey to become the first post-war champion dog and, a consistent winner. Ali Bey sired another champion for the Ravelly Kennels, Ch. Rajah Bey of Ravelly, which inherited his father's outstanding coat. These two dogs were brilliantly handled in the ring by Mr. H. A. Southgate. Ch. Rajah Bey also distinguished himself by eating the Minute Book of the Southern Afghan Club.

Also starting in the latter war years and emerging as considerable influences in the breed in the late 1940s and 1950s were the Khorrassan Kennels of Miss Eileen Snelling, and the Carloway Kennels of Mrs. Sheila Devitt. These two dedicated young ladies were destined to build up kennels of international repute, and to establish a formidable reputation as show winners, as well as a great personal rivalry.

Miss Snelling's Khorrassan Kennel was founded on the bitch Natara of Westover, purchased from Miss Matthews, and the dog Turkuman Pomegranite, owned by Mrs. Clarke.

The first champion, Ch. Moonbeam of Khorrassan, by Kassim of Khorrassan, out of Water Lily of Khorrassan, gained his championship title in 1951. This success was closely followed by another champion, Portrait of Khorrassan, a bitch by Chota Nissim of Ringbank out of Natara of Westover. Both these initial champions were creams, a colour made famous by this kennel. Many champions followed, outstanding among which was Cleopatra of Khorrassan, by Ch. Moonbeam of Khorrassan out of Sunrise of Khorrassan. A great show personality was Sirdar of Khorrassan, who won over 200 Best in Show awards and sired Ch. Bahia of Khorrassan out of Sunrise of Khorrassan, and her litter brother Montezuma of Khorrassan, who himself was a famous sire, producing Ch. Wild Iris of Khorrassan out of the bitch Zanella, and also Ch. Saleh Bey of Khorrassan out of Ajamais Amber Menthe.

The Carloway Kennels, owned by Mrs. Sheila Devitt, had as their initial stud force the famous dog Jalalabad Barwala of Carloway, purchased from Miss Ide. Barwala (known as 'Ba') although a potent and successful sire, was never shown in the ring owing to an injury sustained in his early life. His name, however, will be found in many pedigrees, and his influence on the breed was considerable. This kennel suffered a severe setback in its early days through an outbreak of hardpad, and some of its promising dogs were lost. Mrs. Devitt, however, with characteristic determination, was soon back in the ring, and the first Carloway champion was the bitch Ch. Carloway Charmain of Virendale, bred by Miss Trevitt by Barwala out of Shireen of Kenavon, which gained its title in 1952.

This initial success was followed by many famous champions including Ch. Yussef of Carloway, by Zog of Carloway out of Dana Khan of Carloway, Ch. Pasha of Carloway by Ch. Yussef out of Sheba of Carloway, and Ch. Waliwog of Carloway, by Ch. Horningsea Sheer Khan out of Ilexis of Carloway. Waliwog was exported to Mr. David Roche of Australia, where he continued his winning career. Ch. Yussef of Carloway is claimed to have sired more champions than any other English Afghan Hound.

Mrs. Devitt, in partnership with the late Mrs. C. Race, imported the American dog Wazir of Desertaire from Mrs. Kay Finch of the Crown Crest Kennels. Wazir, which is now owned by Mr. Bridges, became a champion in 1968, and has influenced the breed in this country by transmitting his soundness and his great show personality and temperament to his progeny. He was bred by Mr. and Mrs. Buchanan by American Champion Crown Crest Mr. Universe out of American Champion Zar-Kari of Shamalan.

Starting soon after the war the Horningsea Kennels owned by Mrs. M. M. Dods, were destined to emerge as one of the leading Afghan Hound kennels of the 1960s. Mrs. Dods has produced many champions, both in this country and overseas, including

America, Canada, and Europe. One of these exports became a Canadian, American, and Bermudian champion. He is Ch. Horningsea Tzaama, owned by Mr. and Mrs. Phillips of Toronto, Canada.

In this country, Ch. Horningsea Majid ('Spotter') by Horningsea Turridu out of Champion Marika of Three Streams was widely used at stud, and sired winning stock. Also owned by this kennel was the famous Champion Horningsea Khanabad Suvaraj, which became dog of the year in 1967. This great Afghan Hound, bred by Miss M. Niblock, was an influence on the breed through his stud activities. His most famous offspring was Ch. Rifkas Musqat D'Rar owned by Mrs. Race, and of which more will be said later.

The early 1960s saw the sudden reappearance of the brindle Afghan Hound in Great Britain, a colour that had not been seen here for many years. This was largely due to the progeny of Mrs. Dods's brindle Champion Horningsea Tiger's Eye, which is a son of Ajman Branwen Kandahar ('Smokey') owned by Miss P. Kean and Miss M. McKenzie, and bred by Miss P. Derasmo and Miss J. Goebel. 'Smokey' was by American Champion Chinah of Grandeur out of Suriyeh of Grandeur, and it is interesting to note that Chinah was line bred to Ch. Blue Boy of Grandeur, and Suriyeh's sire was a golden full brother to Blue Boy, which establishes a connection with the British 'blues'. Another contribution to the return of the brindles was made by the Khanabad Kennels when Ch. Khanabad Astrajid was mated to 'Smokey' and produced Khanabad Wadimango and Khanabad Wadimo.

Mention has been made of the Khanabad prefix of Miss M. Niblock. This kennel also emerged in the immediate post-war period, and has bred and exported widely, producing overseas as well as home champions. The first English champion was my own Ch. Khanabad Azravi of Vishnu, followed by his litter sister, Ch. Khanabad Astrajid, both being sired by Ch. Horningsea Majid out of Khanabad Azrar, a bitch bred by my wife and I by Khanabad Abdul Hamsavi out of our own Bletchingly Petula of Bleanhyrst. Azrar was the dam of many winners from this kennel, including the aforementioned dog of the year, Ch. Khanabad Horningsea Suvaraj, Ch. Khanabad Surasu, owned by Mr. and Mrs. Perdue,

American Ch. Khanabad Azreefa and, also, Khanabad Suredar, which died young at the outset of a promising career.

Latterly, the Khanabad Kennels have specialised in the breeding of blues, based on imported stock from Mrs. Cynthia Maddigan in Spain, and have pioneered this colour in Great Britain.

In addition to the larger kennels, there were many smaller breeders who supported and sustained the breed during the early post-war years. Among them mention must be made of the Barbille Kennels of Mrs. D. Hall, the Barakzai Kennels of Mr. Ali Hupka, my own Vishnu Kennels, the Brabourne Kennels of Mrs. Margaret Masters, the Shemsuki Kennels of Mrs. Violet Gilligan, the Khonistan Kennels of Messrs. Wilson and Walker, and the Ajman Kennels of Miss Patricia Kean and Miss Marjorie McKenzie, who started with the beautiful red bitch Netheroyd Chandibaba.

In the 1950s, the breed continued on an even course, neither gaining nor losing in popularity or in the number of entries at shows. During this decade many of those who, like myself, had started in the breed in the late 1940s, made their debut as judges.

I well remember one ambitious canine society at this time, having the ingenious idea of inviting the Afghan Ambassador to judge the breed at their open show. As a result, this charming gentleman, accompanied by a retinue of his countrymen, and wearing a slightly puzzled expression, gravely placed the exhibits in the order in which he considered they should be. It did not presumably occur to the organisers of the show that there was no more reason for the Afghan Ambassador to have expert knowledge of his native dog than for the British Ambassador in Afghanistan (if there is one) to be a judge of Bulldogs. It was, nonetheless, an enjoyable day.

There is a delightful story told of him when he visited Cruft's. Apparently, when walking round the benches, he is purported to have stopped in front of one that displayed a card with the exhibitor's prefix printed on it. With a look of shocked surprise on his face he remarked to his companion, 'I am sure they do not realise what that word means in Afghanistan'. Whether true or not, I think this little story points an important moral. When choosing romantic sounding eastern names for dogs or prefixes, make sure that their meaning is understood.

Also during the 1950s, many new prefixes made their appearance in the Afghan Hound world. Among these was the Davlin Kennels owned by the Rev. Ford and Miss H. Barnes, whose well-known Champion Aryana Shalym was bred by Mr. and Mrs. Robbins by Ch. Horningsea Khanabad Suveraj out of Sharima of Davlin. This dog was exported to Canada. Another champion from this kennel was Ch. Takabbor Tiaga by Horningsea Kublai Khan out of Ilexis of Carloway. Tiaga was bred by Mrs. B. Etheridge and was ultimately exported to Italy. Also from this kennel was Ch. Ophira of Davlin by Aryana Shalym out of Takabbor Sharaz, owned by Mrs. Woolley.

Mr. and Mrs. Pollock of the Tarril Kennels bred the well-known Ch. Kismati Khan of Tarril, who was by Ch. Wazir of Desertaire out of Chandi B'Har of Tarril. This dog was another Afghan Hound to distinguish himself by winning a Hound Group at Cruft's (1966) in addition to siring winning stock.

The Tarjih Kennels owned by Miss Pauline Leyder bred three champions, Ch. Khymn of Carloway and litter sister Enchantress of Tarjih, both by Ch. Yussef of Carloway out of Bletchingley Aurora, also Ch. Shere Khan of Tarjih by Tajammul of Tarjih out of Bletchingley Tara of Tarjih.

Mrs. Ruth Hughes's Kalbikhan Kennel at Banstead has produced several winners including Ch. Kalbikhan Ravi by Ch. Kalbikhan Ali Bey of Carloway out of Woodland Lassie, and my own Ch. Jali of Vishnu, by Ch. Khanabad Azravi of Vishnu out of Woodland Lassie. This kennel also produced the bitch Ch. Kalbikhan Kara by Ch. Ali Bey of Carloway out of Ch. Pina of Carloway, which was owned and exhibited by Mr. and Mrs. Severn.

Ch. Ali Bey of Carloway was bred by Mrs. Devitt by Ch. Yussef of Carloway out of Ch. Muphytt of Carloway before being acquired by Mrs. Hughes.

The Moonswift Kennels, at present resident in Ireland, are owned by Mrs. Bowdler Townsend. The first champion was the beautiful black and tan Conygar Janze of Carloway, bred by Miss Venn by Ch. Yussef of Carloway out of Conygar Gabel. The home-bred hound Int. Ch. Moonraker of Moonswift is by Ch. Horningsea Sheer Khan out of Indira of Carloway.

The Takabbor Kennels owned by Mrs. Barbara Etheridge bred, in addition to Takabbor Tiaga, mentioned earlier, Ch. Takabbor Golden Eagle, by Chandra of Takabbor out of Ilexis of Carloway. Mrs. Etheridge also bred Ch. Pina of Carloway by Anzari of Takabbor out of Narriman of Carloway.

The Bondor Kennels owned by Messrs Brooks and Swallow came to the fore with the two well-known home-bred bitches Ch. Bondor Lezah and Ch. Bondor Serenade. Lezah was by Ch. Pasha of Carloway out of Bletchingley Zuleika, and Serenade was by Ch. Wazir of Desertaire out of Yazeena of Carloway.

Mrs. Joan Wonnacott's Isfahan Kennels has produced fine quality stock and has kept the breed to the fore in the west country, as has also Mr. E. Dawson-Craven of the Khamora prefix.

The late Mrs. C. Race, one of the greatest of British Afghan Hound enthusiasts, founded the Rifka Kennels in 1950. In addition to other champions, Mrs. Race bred the famous twins Ch. Rifka's Tabaq D'Rar and Ch. Rifka's Musqat D'Rar. They were by Ch. Horningsea Khanabad Suvaraj out of Rifka's Rajeena of Carloway. The bitch, Musqat D'Rar, established a new record in this country by winning 20 challenge certificates, beating the previous record holder, Ch. Netheroyd Alibaba.

It is worthy of note that Musqat D'Rar received the challenge certificate that gave her the record from Mrs. Ida Morton who, as Mrs. Abson, was the breeder and owner of Ch. Netheroyd Alibaba, and who thereby deposed her own dog as record holder.

Mrs. Race's tragic early death robbed her of a great ambition, which was to judge the breed at Cruft's, an engagement she was due to fulfil in 1971.

The Kennel Club has given its consent to a special memorial trophy, presented by family and friends, to be awarded annually in her memory to the Best of Breed at Cruft's Show.

The Jagai Kennels, owned by Mrs. Daphne Gie, have many overseas as well as home winners to their credit. The home bred Ch. Rangitsinghi of Jagai by Ch. Waliwog of Carloway out of Amaduraya of Jagai and owned by Mrs. J. Holden was another to bring glory to the breed by winning the Hound Group at Cruft's in 1969.

The Badakshan Kennels of Mr. and Mrs. Adams bred the bitch Ch. Badakshan Rani, which was by Ch. Khanabad Azravi of Vishnu out of Rahane of Ladysmyle.

The Shanshu Kennels owned by Mrs. Betty Clarke were another addition in the 1950s, and their champion dog Horningsea Mitanni was sired by Horningsea Sheer Khan out of Horningsea Marue, and bred by Mrs. Dods.

Miss Stephanie Hunt Crowley's Chandara Kennels have exported widely and successfully, including overseas champions as well as importing the American brindle dog Chandara's Talisman Garlands of Camri by Javlin of Camri.

Mr. W. Kelly, who has been well known in Afghan Hound circles from pre-war days, started breeding in the 1960s under the Sherdil prefix.

The Ansari Kennels owned by Mr. and Mrs. Arthur Appleton are another northern source of quality hounds.

Mr. Denis McCarthy's Pooghan Kennels, owned Ch. Zaza of Khorrassan by Rajput of Khorrassan out of Ruanda of Khorrassan, bred by Miss Snelling, and home bred in this kennel was Ch. Tara of Pooghan by Ch. Pasha of Carloway out of Gina of Anzani.

In the 1960s many new kennels appeared, and it would be invidious to single out any for particular mention.

In 1959 the Afghan Hound Association invited an overseas judge to officiate at their championship show. Madame Deckers of Belgium, the owner of Amanulla Khan of Acklam was invited to officiate, and she awarded the dog challenge certificate to Mrs. Masters's Ch. Khrishna of Brabourne, and the bitch challenge certificate and Best in Breed to Mrs. Devitt's Ch. Muphytt of Carloway.

This procedure was repeated in 1961, when Madame Ch. Nizet de Leemans, also from Belgium, judged the Association show, awarding the dog challenge certificate and Best in Breed to my own Ch. Jali of Vishnu, and the bitch challenge certificate to Mrs. Home's Jahzah of Jasarat.

Throughout the late 1940s and 1950s the annual breed registrations remained fairly constant at around 250 to 300. The year 1960 saw the beginnings of one of those inexplicable phenomena that sometimes occur in dogs and other spheres of activity subject to the whims and vagaries of fashion. This breed, which for years had been the sole province of a limited number of dedicated enthusiasts, suddenly experienced an explosion of popularity that is destined to have a far-reaching effect on its future. At the time of writing (January 1970) the breed is still in the throes of this extraordinary happening, and it is therefore not possible to assess with any degree of accuracy what will be the final outcome of the situation.

A study of the annual registration figures for the breed included in Appendix A of this book will tell the story of this sudden up-surge of interest in the Afghan Hound. In the first half of the sixties the registrations rose slowly but surely from 250 in 1959 to 576 in 1965. By this time the situation had become known generally, and an influx of new breeders, anxious to climb on the bandwagon and supply this lucrative new market, sent the registrations rocketing in the four years following to 2,914 in 1969.

The results of popularity upon any breed of dog are many and varied, and certainly not all good. I am one of the many who view this sudden change in the fortunes of the breed with great apprehension.

On the one hand, entries at the shows have soared, and from the modest half dozen or so for each class to which we had all been accustomed for many years, they have risen to a point where twenty or thirty are not unusual, and at a recent championship show some classes boasted over fifty entries. The direct result of this is the increasing number of societies who are now including classes for the breed at their shows and also the improvement in classifications. Unfortunately, the size of the rings allotted to Afghan Hounds at most shows have definitely not increased in ratio with the entries, resulting in competitors being herded and huddled into ridiculously small areas, where movement is a virtual impossibility.

Judges, on accepting an engagement to judge the breed, now find themselves faced with entries running into hundreds and presenting a task that in some cases is too much for one person to accomplish efficiently, and certainly impossible to complete in the time allotted for the show. The situation has also caused a shortage of properly qualified judges.

The Afghan Hound Association took cognisance of this, and for the first time in the breed in this country appointed two judges for their 1969 show. This procedure, of necessity, calls for the services of an umpire, to give decisions in the event of differences of opinion between the two judges, in cases where both sexes are competing together, such as Best in Show. This method also calls for two rings, which may well make it impracticable where space is a major problem.

Nevertheless, opinion in the breed, while being somewhat divided when this experiment was first mooted, has now moved towards acceptance of it as the only obvious and workable solution to the problem, whose advantages so obviously outweigh its disadvantages.

The vast and ever-increasing influx of new Afghan Hound owners has provided a shot in the arm for the breed clubs, who, after years of comparative poverty, and the reluctant acceptance of show losses, now find that their bank balances have assumed a much more healthy appearance as a result of the large new membership and profits on shows.

A further and also inevitable result of the popularity of a breed is the large increase in the price of puppies, and a ready and assured market that would have been unthinkable only ten years ago. It is a truism that when popularity opens the door, commercialism creeps in. Or to be more precise, where there is a ready market there will always be a ready supplier.

Breeders are appearing who have little or no interest in the breed, and who owe no allegiance to any breed club or other organisation, and over whom neither the Kennel Club nor any other association has any influence or jurisdiction. In some cases the puppies produced are not even registered at the Kennel Club, the sole consideration being a quick cash turnover, and bitches are bought and used solely as breeding machines.

I once read an old dog book in which the writer drew a distinction between *bona fide* 'breeders' and mere 'puppy farmers', but I little thought that this distinction would ever be applicable to Afghan Hounds.

It must not be assumed that the practices about which I am complaining are confined to newcomers. Regrettably, many established breeders have presumably succumbed to the lure of the 'fast buck', and are breeding far too much, far too often, and with far too little thought and consideration for their animals and the future of the breed as a whole.

In the 1950s it was frequently difficult to dispose of puppies, even as gifts. Consequently breeders gave much thought and planned carefully before embarking on a litter. Today, not only is there virtually an assured market at a good price for individual puppies, but some breeders are indulging in the disgraceful practice of selling whole litters *en masse* to dealers for resale, with no questions asked, and obviously no thought for the possible fate of these defenceless animals.

Unfortunately, just at this stage (1969) when any form of control in the breed was more difficult than ever before, the discovery was made that hip dysplasia, a scourge from which British Afghan Hounds had so far been assumed to be free, was in fact present in some British dogs. The discovery was made by Miss Patricia Kean, who, acting promptly and responsibly, immediately made the facts known, not only to directly interested parties, but to all concerned with Afghan Hounds. Since then Miss Kean has devoted much of her time to collecting data and knowledge of the subject in the interests of the breed, and has made the results of her work available for inclusion in this book. These will be found in Chapter 11, and I earnestly hope that all intending breeders will study them.

After the first shock of the discovery, and the high sounding protestations of many breeders had evaporated, it became distressingly clear that some firm and decisive steps would have to be taken if this complaint was to be successfully contained, let alone eradicated.

The Kennel Club in conjunction with the British Veterinary Association offer an official scheme for testing by X-ray (*see* Chapter 11).

The argument has been put forward that because there are few clinical symptoms (at the moment) the situation can be ignored. This is very dangerous counsel, because if steps are not taken to combat the complaint a stage could be reached, as it has in some other breeds, where clinical symptoms will be evident and by then the time will have passed when effective action could have been taken.

Some while ago the Irish Setter breed was in danger from progressive retinal atrophy. It is now common knowledge how, by the concentrated efforts of the breeders in sacrificing their personal feelings and profits by refusing to breed from tainted stock, the danger was overcome. This is not an exact parallel to our hip dysplasia problem, but it does prove that concentrated effort and self sacrifice is possible by breeders in the interests of their breed. Is it beyond the bounds of reason to hope that Afghan Hound breeders will do the same as the Setter breeders in the long-term interests of their breed? Are we not all, in a sense, trustees of the breed while we are actively concerned with it, with a strong moral obligation to hand it over to future generations in the best possible order; and the older the breed the greater the obligation?

The upsurge in the Afghan Hound population has brought about the formation of three new breed clubs. In August 1964 the Midland Afghan Hound Club was formed with Mr. Denis Mc-Carthy as Secretary, and in April 1968 the Western Afghan Hound Club came into being, with Miss Linda Hammerberg as the first Secretary, and I shared the honour of judging at their inaugural show with Mrs. Joan Wonnacott. More recently, in February 1970, The Afghan Hound Society of Scotland was formed, under the secretaryship of Miss E. M. Holmes.

Most of the regional breed clubs produce a magazine or newsletter for their members, in addition to running shows. In 1969 the Northern Afghan Hound Association was granted permission to hold championship shows, and the first of these was judged by Mrs. Ida Morton, the Association's President, at the Corn Exchange, Leeds. The Southern Afghan Hound Club are to have championship shows beginning in 1971.

A significant event in the world of all the hound breeds was the formation of the Hound Association in 1962, with Mr. Douglas

Appleton as its first Secretary. This Association held its first show in the following year, 1963. The various Afghan Hound clubs and associations take turns in nominating a breed judge for this annual event of the hound world. Starting with the 1970 show, this Association is to adopt the two-judge system as pioneered by the Afghan Hound Association.

Reading through this chapter I am conscious of an air of pessimism concerning certain aspects of the breed's future. One fact, however, that augurs well for the future is the very high proportion of young people who have entered the Afghan Hound world, both as exhibitors and breeders. With this new influx of enthusiasts there is reason to hope that the many problems and difficulties that confront this rapidly expanding breed will be vigorously and efficiently dealt with.

(Eric Milward)

Ch. Rifka's Musqat D'Rar

(Thomas Fall)

Int Ch. Badshah of Ainsdart

(Len Tiernan)

Int Ch. Moonraker of Moonswift

Ch. Horningsea Khanabad Suvaraj

4

Standard and Conformation

THE standard of any breed is an attempt to express in words the concept and proportions of what is considered to be the ideal specimen of that breed. It could, in fact, be described as an attempt at the impossible, for however carefully and accurately the various measurements, weights, and proportions are laid down, such vital but imponderable factors as poise, bearing, balance, and most important in the great dog, personality, can never be adequately expressed in words.

Before 1947 the Kennel Club took no part in the formation or control of breed standards. This matter was left entirely in the hands of the breed clubs, an obviously unsatisfactory state of affairs which inevitably led to some extraordinary situations. Popular breeds, with many breed clubs (some had as many as twenty), found themselves with several different breed standards, all in use at the same time, causing grievous headaches to judges, who were obliged to judge to the standard of one club or another, thus causing a situation where judges who judged for one club could not in some cases judge for another. And when one considers the wide divergence of opinion that occurs today, when we are all, in theory at least, working to one standard, the trouble caused can well be imagined.

The early Afghan Hound enthusiasts, fortunately, did not have this problem to contend with. Numerically small, the first standard was written in 1912 but all copies have been lost. The first breed club was the Afghan Hound Club, formed in 1925. This organisation adopted a standard also, based on the famous dog Zardin described in an earlier chapter. This standard, which is reproduced here in full, was sometimes known as the Denier Standard and was comparatively short.

E

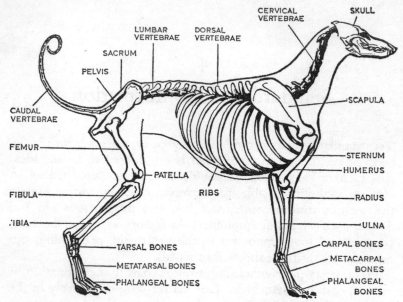

FIG 3   Skeleton of the Afghan Hound

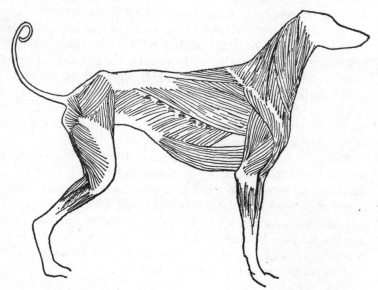

FIG 4   Superficial muscles

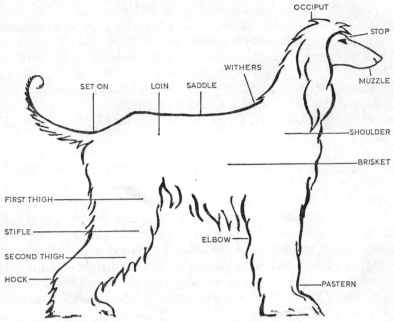

FIG 5 Points of the Afghan Hound

ORIGINAL STANDARD OF THE AFGHAN HOUND CLUB

Head. Skull oval with prominent occiput, jaw long and punishing, mouth level, ears long, eyes dark, little or no stop.

Neck. Long, strong, arched and running in a curve to the shoulder.

Shoulder. Long and sloping—well laid back.

Back. Strong, loin powerful and slightly arched, falling away towards stern.

Forelegs. Straight and strong—great length between elbow (which is straight) and ankle.

Forefeet. Very large, both in length and breadth, toes well arched and the feet covered with long thick hair, fine in texture.

Brisket. Deep and not too narrow.

Hindquarters. Powerful, well muscled, great length between hip and hock, which is low and strong. Fair bend in stifle.

Body. Well ribbed and tucked up under loins.

Coat. Hindquarters, flanks, ribs, and forequarters well covered with long thick hair, very fine in texture. Ears and all four feet well feathered. Head surmounted with topknot of long silky hair.

General Appearance. Strong and active looking, a combination of speed and power with a graceful outline.

Height (to shoulder). Dogs about 28 inches; bitches 25 to 26 inches.

The above standard was in force when the Afghan Hound Association was formed in 1927. This association drew up a new, fuller, and more detailed standard: a much more comprehensive work than the previous, rather sparse description of the dog Zardin. It would appear from a study of this standard that Mrs. Amps insistence on the short-coupled dog as the correct Afghan Hound had been successful. But the heights mentioned would seem to be more in keeping with the larger Bell Murray Hounds. This standard was in force in the breed until 1946 and is reproduced herewith.

STANDARD ADOPTED BY THE AFGHAN HOUND ASSOCIATION SOON AFTER ITS FORMATION

Head. Skull long and not too narrow, with prominent occiput. Foreface long, with punishing jaws and little stop, mouth level, nose usually black, liver no disqualification in lighter coloured dogs. Eyes: dark preferred, golden colour no disqualification. Ears long, heavily feathered, and carried close to the head, which is surmounted by long topknot of hair.

Neck. Long, strong, with a proud carriage of the head.

Shoulders. Long and sloping, well set back, well muscled and strong.

Back. Well muscled the whole length, falling slightly away to the stern. Loin: straight, broad, and rather short. Hip joints rather prominent and wide. A fair spring of ribs and good depth of chest.

Forelegs. Straight, well-boned, elbows rather straight.

Feet. Large. Toes very long, well arched and heavily feathered.

Hindquarters. Powerful and long, with plenty of bend to hock and stifle and well under the dog.

Tail. Set on low and carried 'gaily' with a ring at the end: sparsely feathered.

Coat. Long, of very fine texture on the ribs, fore and hindquarters and flanks. From the shoulders backward, along the top of the back, the hair is short and close. Hair long from the eyes backward, with a distinct silky topknot; on foreface hair is short as on the back. Ears and legs well feathered.

Colour. Any colour.

Height. Dogs 27 to 29 inches, bitches 2 to 3 inches smaller. The whole appearance of the dog should give the impression of strength and activity, combining speed with power.

The object of the dog is to hunt its quarry over very rough and mountainous ground in a country of crags and ravines. For this, a compact and well-coupled dog is necessary rather than a long-loined racing dog whose first quality is speed.

Expression. Dignified, aloof and intelligent. In motion his head and tail are carried high: springing gait.

In 1947 the Kennel Club, to end the existing unsatisfactory state of affairs, decided to bring the whole matter of standards under their control, and through the duly elected breed representatives to the Kennel Club Council of Representatives, drew up and issued one official standard for each breed registered at the Kennel Club. These standards, finally issued in 1950, were, and indeed are, binding on all breed clubs, who may not alter them without the permission of the Kennel Club. This permission, however, is usually granted where the reasons given are considered sound and necessary.

Before discussing the present standard in detail, it is well to pause and consider the real purpose of any standard. It is, I consider, wrong to look upon it as a rigid and inflexible formula into which every dog must fit in order to be considered a worthy specimen of its breed. It is rather a pattern to be aimed at—a framework within which a judge may work, while still leaving reasonable scope for individual interpretation. Any seasoned dog breeder or exhibitor will tell you that the perfect dog has not yet been born; it must therefore follow that the most successful champion in the show-ring must fall short of some points required by the standard. It is the relative importance of these points, in relation to the dog as a whole, that forms one of the most important and fascinating facets of the many duties of a judge.

It is also worth considering some important factors concerning the assessment of any thoroughbred animal. While the official standard of necessity takes the various points of the animal's anatomy one by one, the final judgment must always be from an overall picture; the individual parts being considered not in isolation, but in relation to one another as integral parts of the whole. Thus, the standard calls for a long neck, but it must be obvious that a certain length of neck that is correct on a large dog, would be quite out of proportion on a much smaller one, although both dogs may be within the permitted size limits of the standard. It must therefore be understood that while a thorough knowledge of the individual requirements of the standard is essential in assessing a dog, this knowledge must always be harnessed and subjugated to the overall picture that is presented. In judging a dog—as indeed in judging architecture, or a work of art—it is basically a question of balance, proportion, and rhythmic lines. The animal (or building or painting) that is correct in these factors will look pleasing and 'right', while when these requirements are absent, the result will be unpleasing and look 'wrong': much has been written on this subject down the ages but no one has, to my knowledge, been able to explain adequately why. It is interesting to note also that when a dog possesses the correct proportions and balance, it is invariably found to have its individual points conforming to the requirements of the standard.

The current standard was drawn up by a special 'Standards' Committee, appointed by the Afghan Hound Association in 1946, the composition of which was as follows: Chairman Mr. W. Riley, Mrs. Olive Couper, Mrs. Eileen Drinkwater, Mrs. Rothwell Fielding, Mrs. M. Sharpe, Miss Semple, Miss Simmons, Dr. Betsy Porter, Mrs. Bradshaw, Miss Ide and Miss Mathews.

There are those who do not consider the present Afghan Hound standard is sufficiently comprehensive, and therefore leaves too much open to the fads and foibles of the individual interpreter. I do not agree with this. While it is clearly not perfect, and is in some instances not full enough, it is none the less clear, devoid of unnecessary and muddling detail, and most important, free from the over verbosity and in some cases downright contradictions to be found in the more longwinded standards of some other breeds.

It is now time to consider in detail the current Afghan Hound standard and discuss more fully its application to the dog and some of the more frequently found faults that result from departures from its requirements.

CURRENT AFGHAN HOUND STANDARD
ADOPTED IN 1946—BY KENNEL CLUB IN 1950

Reproduced by permission of the Kennel Club

Characteristics. The Afghan Hound should be dignified and aloof with a certain keen fierceness. The Eastern or Oriental expression is typical of the breed. The Afghan looks at and through one.

General Appearance. The gait of the Afghan Hound should be smooth and springy with a style of high order. The whole appearance of the dog should give the impression of strength and dignity combining speed and power. The head must be held proudly.

Head and Skull. Skull long, not too narrow with prominent occiput. Foreface long with punishing jaws and slight stop. The skull well balanced and surmounted by a long topknot. Nose preferably black but liver is no fault in light coloured dogs.

Eyes. Should be dark for preference but golden colour is not debarred. Nearly triangular, slanting slightly upwards from the inner corner to the outer.

Ears. Set low and well back, carried close to the head. Covered with long silky hair.

Mouth. Level.

Neck. Long, strong with proud carriage of the head.

Forequarters. Shoulders long and sloping, well set back, well muscled and strong without being loaded. Forelegs straight and well boned, straight with shoulder, elbows held in.

Body. Back level, moderate length, well muscled, the back falling slightly away to the stern. Loin straight, broad and rather short. Hip-bones rather prominent and wide apart. A fair spring of ribs and good depth of chest.

Hindquarters. Powerful, well bent and well turned stifles. Great length between hip and hock with a comparatively short distance between hock and foot. The dew claws may be removed or allowed to remain at the discretion of the breeder.

Feet. Forefeet strong and very large both in length and breadth and covered with long thick hair, toes arched. Pasterns long and springy, especially in front and pads well down on the ground. Hindfeet long, but not quite so broad as forefeet, covered with long thick hair.

Tail. Not too short. Set on low with ring at the end. Raised when in action. Sparsely feathered.

Coat. Long and very fine texture on ribs, fore and hind-quarters and flanks. From the shoulder backward and along the saddle the hair should be short and close in mature dogs. Hair long from the forehead backward, with a distinct silky topknot. On the fore-face the hair is short as on the back. Ears and legs well coated. Pasterns can be bare. Coat must be allowed to develop naturally.

Colour. All colours are acceptable.

Weight and Size. Ideal height: Dogs 27 inches to 29 inches. Bitches 2 inches to 3 inches smaller.

Faults. Any appearance of coarseness. Skull too wide and foreface too short. Weak underjaw. Large round or full eyes. Neck should never be too short or thick. Back too long or too short.

SOME NOTES AND OBSERVATIONS ON THE STANDARD

Characteristics. The standard lays down very clearly the characteristics of the Afghan Hound and it requires little further comment. Any tendency away from aloofness, towards terrier or spaniel characteristics is not typical of the breed. An expression that is too sweet and kind, while lovable, is not correct for the

Afghan Hound. Excessive nervousness, or tricky temper, or other neurotic symptoms must not be confused with the natural breed aloofness and suspicion of strangers.

General Appearance. The springy, smooth gait called for in this section of the standard is most important to the breed. Any tendency towards terrier or 'hackney' movements must be avoided. The proud and dignified carriage here described is an integral part of the Afghan image. A rolling gait due possibly to overweight and lack of exercise is a fault as is also a cringing or 'scuttling' movement with tail clamped. Likewise any deviation from the straight line in the form of diagonal movement, or the throwing out of feet to the side.

Head and Skull. The head must be well chiselled and refined with no hint of coarseness, neither must it lack stop as in a collie, or have too much stop, resembling a setter. The foreface or nasal bone must be long with a slightly 'roman' shape, but not too long to balance with the skull. The mid point between occiput and nose is a point between the eyes (see drawing of skull). The foreface must have strength while not sacrificing refinement. Too much thickness through the muzzle tends to coarseness, while a weak or 'snipey' muzzle is equally undesirable. The 'dish face' as in pointers is a fault. The flews (lips) must not be pendulous as in gun dogs. The nose should have large nostrils to enable maximum air intake, and is preferred black although the standard clearly allows liver noses in light coloured dogs. It is interesting to note that some black-nosed dogs have seasonal changes to a lighter colour. The zygomatic arch (cheek bone) must be clearly visible but not too pronounced. It must be appreciated that bitches should always have finer heads than dogs. Doggy bitches or bitchy dogs are equally wrong.

Eyes. Eyes must be set slightly to the side of the head, and should be triangular in shape, and not too far apart. Expression is made up of the eye shape, placement, colour, and the set of head and neck. The Afghan Hound is far-sighted, and this tends to cause the head to be held back when looking at a close object, giving the aloof and arrogant expression so typical of the breed. Round and bulging eyes are a fault. Round eyes, set facing straight forward when, as they frequently are, combined with a heavy

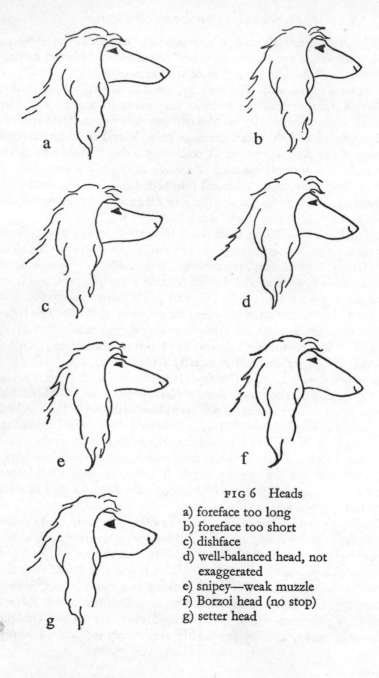

FIG 6 Heads
a) foreface too long
b) foreface too short
c) dishface
d) well-balanced head, not
   exaggerated
e) snipey—weak muzzle
f) Borzoi head (no stop)
g) setter head

muzzle, thick skull and too much stop, produce a setter-like head and expression quite foreign to the Afghan Hound.

Ears. Ears must never be set high on the head, and leathers should not be short. Long hair on ears of adult dogs is desired.

Mouth. The standard laconically dismisses this important feature with the one word 'level', yet almost every judge or breeder with whom I have discussed this point agrees that the scissor bite is the normal one for an Afghan Hound. The term 'scissor' is applied to the bite when the top front teeth meet, but slightly overlap

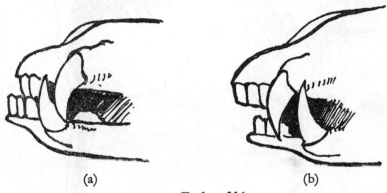

(a)   (b)

FIG 7   Faults of bite
a) undershot   b) overshot

the bottom ones. It is well to be wary of too level a bite in puppies, as the lower jaw tends to grow on after the top, and a jaw that starts level may well end up 'undershot'. Broken or single misplaced teeth, due possibly to accident, must not be confused with jaws that are undershot or overshot, both of which are, of course, faults.

Neck and Forequarters. These must be taken together as they are part and parcel of each other and can only be considered in relation to each other. Necks and shoulders are interdependent; a good length of neck is complementary to a good shoulder, just as a short neck is to an upright shoulder. The long neck facilitates the grasping of prey at the gallop; it also balances the dog. Any tendency to a ewe neck must be avoided.

The scapula (shoulder blade) should be well laid back with the humerus (forearm) set at such an angle as to place the forelegs well under the body. This will give what is described as front angulation. If the forelegs are in a straight line with the chest, the

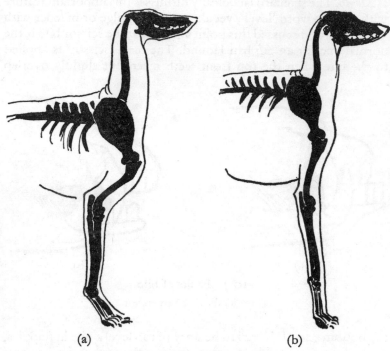

(a)   (b)

FIG 8 Faults of forequarters

a) Upright shoulder; neck badly set on, though head appears to be 'held proudly'; over-angulated elbow and pastern

b) Straight front—no shock-absorbancy or springing; upright shoulder; neck too short and badly set on

result will be a terrier front with the inevitable terrier action. This form of movement, while correct in terrier breeds is completely wrong for Afghans, and although eyecatching and attractive to the uninformed must be avoided at all costs. The exact angle to be aimed at between scapula and humerus is specifically laid down in some breed standards, but not in the Afghan Hound

standard, and I think it is right that it should not be. The observer
with an eye for a dog will have no difficulty in spotting the correct
angle when it appears, and equally the wrong one with its attendant faults.

The correct distance apart of the shoulder blades will naturally
vary with the size of the dog. They must be neither too wide

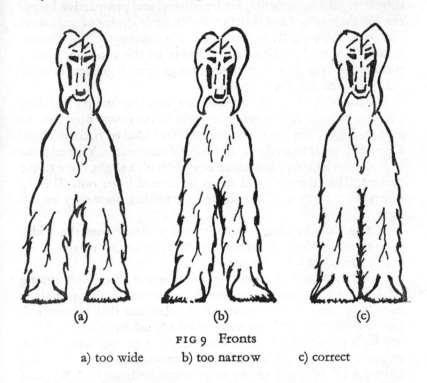

FIG 9   Fronts

a) too wide   b) too narrow   c) correct

apart nor too close together. If they are placed too wide apart,
the result will almost certainly be an upright shoulder. They must,
however, be wide enough apart to allow the necessary conver-
gence when the head is lowered. There was an astonishing fallacy
current, when I first began showing Afghans, to the effect that
the width between the shoulder blades was correct if one finger
could be placed between them, irrespective presumably of the
position of the head and neck, or the size of the dog. This piece of

nonsense has happily died a natural death, as I have not heard it in recent years.

It is impossible to assess the shoulders of a dog by standing over it and looking down. In addition to handling and feeling the position of the bones, it is essential to stand well back and observe the neck and shoulder placement from the side. Bad shoulders, like most faults, are hereditary, and prospective breeders will do well to bear this in mind in their choice of stud dogs and brood bitches. R. H. Smythe in his *Anatomy of Dog Breeding* states, 'It would be almost impossible to think of any feature transmitted by dog or bitch to their progeny with greater certainty than faulty neck and shoulders.'

The forelegs, viewed from the front, must be straight and dead parallel, with the feet pointing straight to the front. Bow legs, or legs that get wider apart towards the feet (due to narrow chest) are a fault, as are turned out, or Charlie Chaplin feet. Viewed from the side, the legs should also be straight with a slight slope to the pastern. The elbow should never be turned in or out. The leg bones must be strong but not coarse, neither must they be too light.

The size of the breast bone (sternum) determines the width apart of the forelegs. A narrow sternum produces a narrow chest with consequent loss of heart and lung room.

Body. No subject is more constantly under discussion among Afghan devotees than the merits and demerits of a long or short back, and the necessary amount of substance that is required. One bewildered exhibitor once asked my advice after her bitch had been penalised by one judge for being grossly overweight, within a few days of being told by another judge to take her bitch out of the ring and 'try to get some body on her'. So great then is the diversity of opinion between the supposedly well informed. Once again the true answer is to be found in common sense, and an ability to distinguish between fat and muscle. The body of an Afghan Hound must be muscular, but never fat. The ribs should always be able to be felt with ease, and the hip bones always prominent.

A dog is said to be short-coupled if the loin is short, i.e. the space between the last ribs and the pelvis. If the back is very short it is described as 'cobby'. If it is very long it is said to be 'long cast': over-rounded rib cages are known as 'barrel' ribs, and frequently accompany a shallow brisket. On the other hand, a very deep brisket may be found on a too narrow rib cage. This is known as 'slab' sided. A slab-sided dog such as this may

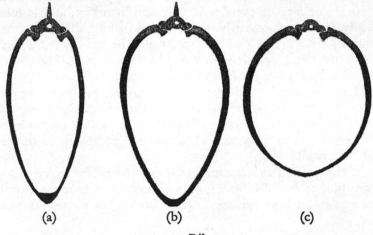

| (a) | (b) | (c) |

FIG 10   Rib cages

a) slab-sided—legs too close together in consequence, also elbows probably 'tied' in, looking as if both legs 'come out of one hole'. Feet probably turn out to preserve balance

b) normal

c) barrel—plenty of lung room, etc, but elbows pushed out causing forelegs to be very wide apart. Otherwise forelegs may converge at the pasterns which then twist so that the feet can preserve balance

look very well from the side, where the deep brisket shows to advantage, but will be less impressive when viewed from above. Wide 'barrel' chests interfere with the elbows, affecting movement and stance. The correct rib shape, seen in section, could best be described as 'pear-shaped'—that is, the fair spring of rib called for in the standard, going down to a good depth of brisket (approximately down to the elbow). Layers of fat on the sides of a slab-sided dog are not, I am afraid, a substitute for a good spring of rib.

If the back is too short, the hind legs will be too close to the fore legs, and therefore be inhibited in their movement. This may cause short, restricted strides, and possibly a tendency to throw out the hind feet to avoid the forefeet.

The top-line, that is the line running from the withers to the hip bones, must be level. A sagging or 'dippy' back due to either heredity or lack of exercise is ugly and incorrect, and is more likely, but not necessarily, to be found in long-cast dogs. Any sign of roaching in the back must also be considered a fault. Backs that slope 'uphill' or 'downhill' are also wrong. The withers must be on the same level as the hip bones.

The loin must be well muscled and strong, but narrower than the rib cage, and never arched as in a whippet. Opinions vary considerably as to the correct length of loin. The answer again is to be found in balance and proportion compared to the rest of the animal.

Hindquarters. The Afghan Hound must stand foursquare, with well bent stifles. The hocks, either standing or in motion, must be straight, neither turning in (cow hocks) nor turning out (toe

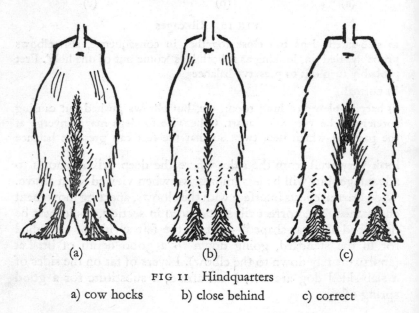

(a)　　　　　　　　(b)　　　　　　　　(c)

FIG 11 Hindquarters

a) cow hocks　　　b) close behind　　　c) correct

(C. M. Cooke)

Ch. Taj Achmed of Chaman

Ch. Pasha of Carloway

(C. M. Cooke)

Ch. Netheroyd Alibaba

Ch. Bletchingley Zara

in). Cow hocks can be inherited, or may be the result of faulty rearing. They can also be caused in young puppies by too much standing on the hind legs peering over doors or fences. Reason-

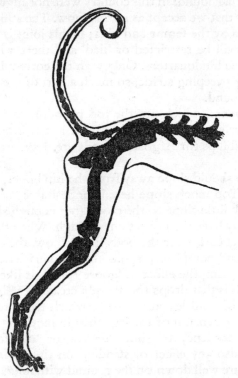

FIG 12   Faults of hindquarters

Badly set tail, held too far over rump; no slope-away; short second thigh, giving hock appearance of being too high and also causing a straight stifle

able angulation of hindquarters is essential both for aesthetic reasons and for good movement; without it the correct amount of thrust is impossible. The Afghan Hound, however, must not be overangulated. There is a tendency in the show-ring to place too much emphasis on this important feature, with the result that dogs are appearing with stifles so bent that they seem almost to

F

be kneeling. Like all points when pushed to extremes, this amounts to a weakness, and therefore a fault, and it must be guarded against. From the study of old pictures it would appear that the original hounds in this country were not angulated behind to the extent that we accept as normal now. The stifle joint is the angle formed by the femur and tibia; if this joint is straight, the hind action will be restricted or 'tied' and there will be lack of drive from the hindquarters. Only with the correct bend of stifle will the long sweeping stride, so much a part of the true Afghan Hound, be found.

The hip bones, which are the top prominence of the pelvis, must be clearly visible, and fairly wide apart. Stories claiming special swivel hips for Afghan Hounds are, I am afraid, without foundation.

The croup should slope away from the hip bones, with the tail set on low. Too much slope here is undesirable, as is too little. The dog with little slope to the croup (not enough slope behind) will frequently have the tail set on too high. When this combines with a tail that curls over the body like a chow, the effect is most unpleasant, and completely spoils the hindquarters. Too much slope away, giving the effect of 'goose rump', is likewise a fault, because a pelvis that drops too sharply creates a restrictive angle at the point of hind leg attachment, which tends to curtail the possible back extension of the leg when in motion.

Feet. Any tendency to short 'terrier' or 'cat' feet must be avoided, as also any effect of standing on tiptoe. It is essential that the feet are well down on the ground with long, arched toes, which give great braking ability, especially on rough ground.

Tail. Straight tails, while not a serious fault, do not set off the hindquarters as do the correct ring tails. Standing, the tail should rest on the hocks, and only in action is it raised, but never too high. The tail that curls over the body as in a chow, giving the effect of a 'teapot handle' must be avoided at all costs. The tail is an extension of the spinal column, and must therefore protrude from the body in a way that is in accordance with this fact.

Coat. The original Afghan Hound distribution of coat, so strikingly individual and unique to the breed, has in the last twenty-five years virtually disappeared. This must be blamed on the influence of the show-ring with its over-emphasis on glamour. There has been no alteration to the requirements of the standard, which still proclaims that bare pasterns are allowed and that the coat should be short on the shoulders and saddle. When a dog with the true Afghan Hound distribution of coat appears in the

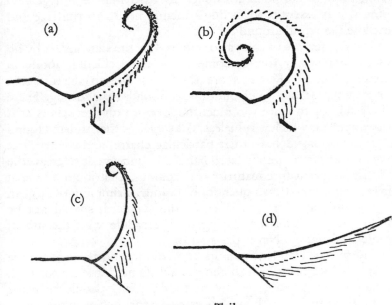

FIG 13 Tails

a) correct set on and carriage
b) undesirable: 'teapot handle'
c) undesirable: too high set and carried too high
d) undesirable: straight

show-ring today, it looks completely alien among the remainder, who are invariably sheeted in coat from head to foot. Many people refer to it as the 'old type' in a somewhat condescending manner. My own feelings are that the breed has lost much of its personality and individuality with this change. Moreover, when too much coat is present much of the outline is lost to view. The pursuit of coat at all costs is the cause of many dogs being flabby and under-exercised. To preserve the precious coat some owners never allow their dogs out in the wet, or permit them to run free on rough ground. In fact, one hears hair-raising stories of show dogs who are permitted no exercise at all, but are shut up in a very limited space in what is virtually solitary confinement. Apart from physical considerations such as hard muscle and general fitness, it is essential for a dog's mental health to run free and explore the world around it.

The fine texture of coat, also required by the standard, is by no means universally found. Some coats are decidedly woolly in texture. These differences are doubtless due to the different original types from which our present hounds have sprung. There is a tendency to place too much importance on precocious coat development, which is valueless. All stages of the Afghan Hound coat development have their particular charm, and to strip out the very attractive puppy facial hair, in an endeavour to create the illusion of premature maturity is ridiculous. Distribution of coat is more important than quantity or colour. Trimming of Afghan coats, although not mentioned in the standard, should not be indulged in apart from tidying up the saddle with the use of finger and thumb. Never use a stripper.

Colour. The standard permits any colour, and there is a wide range today from which to choose. White markings on the face, although not a fault, are not desirable. Many people have the impression that a black mask is essential for success in the show-ring. While some judges do seem to have this bias, it is quite unjust, as self-coloured faces are perfectly permissible and can look very attractive if the face is well chiselled and refined.

Size. The over-large dog may stand out in the show ring, but it is seldom well balanced, and probably coarse. Likewise, the oversize bitch will tend to lack femininity. Undersize Afghan Hounds are clearly not up to the job for which this breed was designed, and will probably appear 'pretty pretty'.

To be over or under the size laid down by the standard is a fault like any other, but not necessarily a disqualification; it is a matter of degree, and must be weighed in with all the other points, when assessing the dog.

Although the standard calls for a long neck and well bent stifles, it must not be interpreted as meaning 'the longer, or the more bent, the better'. Too much neck, like too little, is a fault, as is over-angulation. The best dog in the ring may not excel in any one point, but may none the less be sound and of correct proportions.

It must be emphasised that the British official standard is not the only one in the world, although it has been adopted by most European countries. Shortly after the Second World War an attempt was made in America to set up an international breed council with the primary object of drawing up a standard to be accepted in America, Europe, and parts of Asia. This rather over-ambitious venture, although meetings were held, did not bear fruit. The American standard, adopted in 1948, will be found in Appendix D.

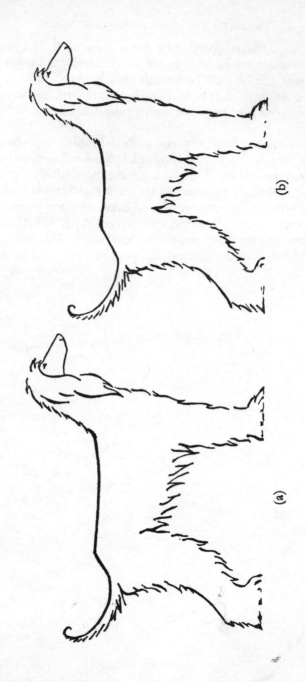

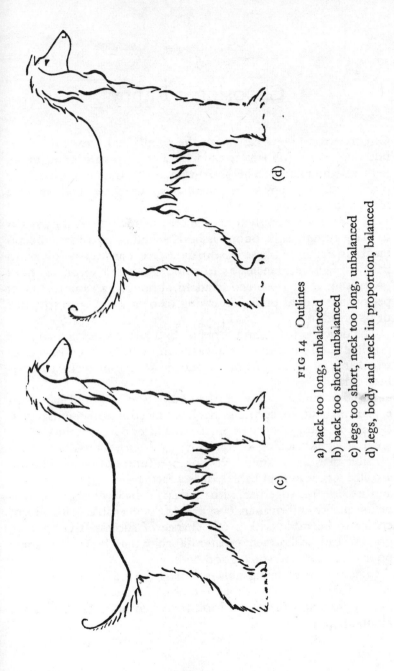

(d)

(c)

FIG 14 Outlines

a) back too long, unbalanced
b) back too short, unbalanced
c) legs too short, neck too long, unbalanced
d) legs, body and neck in proportion, balanced

5
Choosing a Puppy

CHOOSING a puppy can mean the simple and pleasant task of selecting a small Afghan Hound to be a house pet and companion, with no thoughts of the show-ring, or it can imply carefully picking out a puppy as a potential show winner and possible foundation for a breeding kennel.

In choosing a pet, the only concern of the potential owner is to make sure that the puppy is healthy and of pleasing temperament. Apart from these essentials a free rein can be given to personal fads and fancies as to colour, size and so on, without giving thought to the breed standard, although I assume that most pet owners would prefer their dog to be a good representative of its breed.

The decision to acquire a puppy as a show specimen and for possible future breeding is a vastly more difficult undertaking, whether it be chosen from an outside source or from a home-bred litter.

Lest I should be accused of presumption, I would hasten to explain that I do not consider that I, or indeed any other individual, can choose a top quality puppy from a litter with certainty, quite apart from instructing others how to do so. This is no more possible than the accurate selection of a future Miss World from a collection of human babies. It is a fact, however, that practise and experience, together with perhaps a little of that hard-to-define quality known as an 'eye for a dog' will enable an intelligent choice to be made with a fair chance of success. Even litters, good or bad, will present greater difficulty than litters with some poor specimens and some good ones.

In the hope of being able to assist the novice in this vital choice I shall attempt to explain some of the physical and psychological characteristics that I look for when selecting an Afghan Hound puppy.

When choosing from a home-bred litter the choice will have to be made early to enable the other pups to be offered and sold. The temptation to run the litter on too long as a result of indecision, or in the hope that one will suddenly become outstanding, is to be resisted, otherwise, when it is too late, the breeder is saddled with several fully grown and hungry Afghan Hounds.

If the choice is to be made from a litter bred elsewhere, the prospective purchaser may be able to postpone a decision until the puppy is much older, and can be more accurately assessed. Indeed, it is possible to buy a puppy that has already had some success in the show-ring. This reduces the odds against failure, but greatly increases the price. Most people prefer to buy a pup while it is young, to facilitate training, and to ensure that it settles readily into the new home.

When buying from a breeder make sure that the kennels and surroundings are clean and in good order. If they leave any doubts, be very cautious about buying. Malnutrition and lack of care in the early, formative period of the puppy's life can seldom be rectified later.

Most breeders attempt to scale their prices in accordance with the merits of the puppy, but this is not always a reliable guide, as they are no more foolproof than anyone else in making a choice. Although I would always consider that the breeder has an advantage in selecting from home-bred litters, both because he knows what to look for in his own strain and also because he can observe the pups constantly, the visiting purchaser must make the assessment in a limited time. The achievements of the parents can also influence the price of the offspring, irrespective of its own merits.

Very young Afghan Hounds can be a shock when seen for the first time. With their squashed in muzzles, short coats, and short legs, they little resemble the finished picture of the adult dog. Newcomers can be forgiven for imagining that they have been sold a mongrel.

If the selector is very inexperienced, it is much to be recommended that a more knowledgeable friend is present to assist in the choosing. Always ask to see the mother (father, and relations also, if possible). Although she may appear somewhat scruffy after producing and nursing a vigorous litter, she should nevertheless be friendly, temperamentally sound, and her coatless condition will reveal her basic conformation.

A knowledge of the breed standard is imperative, not so much for direct application to the small, immature pup but for an informed appraisal of the parents and other relatives.

To assess the potential of any young puppy some knowledge of the development characteristics of its particular strain is necessary. Different strains develop along different lines and at differing speeds. Most experienced breeders with a characteristic kennel type will know from long usage what produces what in their own particular strain, but will be aware that other strains will develop quite differently.

Make sure that the pups are sturdy, outgoing, and friendly. Resist the attractions of the biggest in the litter; this one may well end up coarse. Likewise, be wary of the sentimental appeal of the very small and undersized: these may never make the grade, although some pups, undersized at birth, have been known to catch up and turn into winners. Generally speaking, birth size is not an indication of ultimate adult size. Do not be dazzled by the black mask. More inexperienced enthusiasts have picked the wrong puppy in this way than for any other single reason. In addition to a sturdy body, look for firmness but not fatness, and a well-defined brisket and rib cage. The shoulder should be well laid back from the neck, and also form the correct angle. Shoulders and front angulation can be seen in the young puppy, but it requires some experience. These points, if not correct in the puppy, will not improve with time. Hip bones should be prominent, and although in a young puppy the slope-away will not yet have developed, the set of the tail in relation to the hip bones can be seen. Puppies that later will have a pronounced slope-away may appear long backed, but always remember that the length of the back is from shoulder to hip bones only. What is behind the hip bones will drop to form the slope-away.

Front legs should be straight and well boned, with feet pointing directly to the front. Beware of any sign of feet turning in or out. Because perfectly sound puppies can sometimes stand in peculiar ways, which may give the impression of twisted legs and feet, make certain that the assessment is made while the puppy is standing (or moving) naturally in accordance with its conformation.

Hind legs on the very young puppy will be wide apart, but should give signs of angulation and length between hip and hock. As the pup grows, and rear legs lengthen, stifles will become straighter, but will develop a bend again as maturity approaches.

Feet should be large—compared to the size of the pup they should appear too large—but this is an indication that it will reach a good size eventually. Joints should also be prominent and knobby. In fact, as the puppy grows it will undergo a lanky, coltish period which is both charming and disconcerting when attempting to assess its merits.

Choose a short loin. Two pups may have the same length of back, but one may have a short rib cage and a long loin, while the other has a large rib cage and a short loin. Always choose the latter.

The head is probably the most difficult part of the immature Afghan Hound to assess. The squat muzzle will bear little resemblance to its ultimate length and shape, although experience will teach the signs to look for. In this case, more will be gained from an examination of the head of the mother and, or, father. Always choose a slightly roman nose. This will be indicated by what appears to be a slight bump on the foreface. Without this, the final foreface may be too straight or, worse still, dishfaced, which is a way of describing a concave foreface.

The foreface should be deep rather than broad, and the head oval, with pronounced pointed occiput. Avoid any sign of a round or 'apple' head. There should be little indication of a stop.

Mouths should tend towards being overshot rather than undershot. The overshot mouth in a puppy will almost certainly rectify, while the undershot mouth will tend to get worse.

Eyes must be small, dark, and not too wide apart, also healthy and free from any suspicion of discharge. All very young puppies have dark eyes in the early stages, with a bluish tinge, but these may alter later. Eyes that show very early signs of lightening will in all likelihood be yellow.

Ears must be low set and well furnished with hair. At around ten to twelve weeks the leathers will be longer than the foreface, but the muzzle will protrude later.

The neck should be of good length and show signs of the desirable arch. The long neck will be apparent at around eight to ten weeks, but will tend to become obscured by flesh and fur during certain periods of the puppy's growth, to emerge again with the approach of maturity.

Inevitably, we now arrive again at my particular 'hobbyhorse'—movement—and I make no excuse for this. At ten weeks or so, the Afghan pup should be well up off its hocks and be standing and moving properly on its feet. From this time on, the style and quality of movement should be apparent, and this is the surest indication of the true quality of the pup. The springy flowing carriage, and the proud way the head is carried on the neck will reveal much that is to come. Note that the stride is uninhibited; that is, that the forelegs do not interfere with the free and extended movement of the hind legs. When the pup is coming and going there must be no deviation from the straight path, and no tendency to throw feet out or indication of cow hocks, or toeing in. The true, shock-absorbing, springing gait, causing the back to sail along without jerking or jarring, should be evident, even in the young puppy.

Tails should be set low. Their development will vary in different strains, some pups of eight weeks will have clearly defined rings to the tail, others may not give an indication of this desired feature until much later. It is fair to say that the excessively limp tail, or the tail carried up over the back, should be avoided. Take particular note of where the tail is set on the body. A high set tail is always wrong, although it may accompany a form of cocky showmanship that could impress the uninitiated.

Colour should be the last consideration in assessing the merits of a future show winner. Remember that the standard permits all colours. No judge worthy of the name should ever give awards to a dog on colour. I would only make one qualification to this: that is, the dog with white markings on the face—this is not desirable in a show specimen.

Finally, coat. There is no ready-made or foolproof method of assessing ultimate coat. Some strains are very lightly coated when young, only to be heavily endowed in later life: others carry heavy puppy coats but may lose them later. Here again, knowledge of the particular strain will be necessary to make a truly sound forecast. Some breeders put great store by the heavy puppy coat and monkey whiskers, and they may be right for their particular strain. Others are content with a sparse puppy coat, confident that the final result will be a fully coated adult. I am sure that all these experts are right for their own types.

Speaking in general terms, I would look for a fairly rough-looking short coat as being quite satisfactory in a young Afghan Hound. Avoid a very shiny short coat, or the too premature saddle that may extend down the sides of the pup until it virtually meets under the body, or to put it crudely, the pup is bald.

The saddle, so desirable in my opinion, and called for in the standard, should not appear until the dog is adult, say from eighteen to twenty-four months.

So far, this chapter has been confined to the physical characteristics of the puppy. The psychological make-up must not be overlooked. Correct reflexes, a quick reaction to stimuli, and a friendly disposition, are desirable for the pet as well as the show dog. There must be no indication of neurosis, any symptoms of fear, shaking or running away to hide may be signs of a nervous, unshowable and unhappy adult dog. Do not seek the aloof and far away characteristics so much part of the true adult Afghan Hound. These will come later. In a puppy, the friendly, completely outgoing approach is the one to look for.

The advice given in this chapter is fairly general as it is not known at what age the puppy is to be chosen. The everchanging development of the Afghan Hound puppy, so much a part of its charm, calls for different points to be looked for at different ages. I have assumed, however, that most choices will be made when the puppy is young.

6

Management, Feeding, and Training

OF all the aspects discussed in this chapter nutrition is almost certainly the most important. There was a saying among old-time dog breeders to the effect that half the pedigree goes in at the mouth. This was merely another way of saying that however good the hereditary factors might be, they were of little value unless the nourishment and rearing of the dog were equally good. Not only is this true in respect of the final size and conformation, but it is also the basis of good health and freedom from disease.

Food can be described as the basic fuel taken in by the body, where it is broken down into readily absorbable forms to be utilised in the process of growth, replacement, and maintenance, and, of course, reproduction.

The main divisions of the basic foods are protein, carbohydrates, and fats, with certain vitamins and minerals, including trace elements. Protein is provided by such foods as meat, fish, fresh eggs, and cheese, and carbohydrates in biscuit, meal, and wholemeal bread. Vitamins are substances required by the body in very small amounts. They are found in natural foods or are synthesised in the animal's body. The correct quantities of these substances are essential to maintain proper health, and deficiencies can cause malnutrition and certain specific diseases.

Vitamin A is found in fish liver oils, butter, liver fat, and some green vegetables. It provides resistance to infection, helps the growth of tissues, and is important for night vision. I recall that night fighter pilots during the war were encouraged to eat carrots for this reason. Deficiencies of vitamin A can cause poor growth in young animals, deafness and night blindness in dogs, and can even interfere with the reproductive process. Vitamin B, or thiamin, is found in wheat germ and cereal grains, liver, and egg yolk, and comprises a complex series of chemical substances. Brewers yeast is a good source of this vitamin. Vitamin C, essential for preventing scurvy in human beings, is usually synthesised by the dogs themselves. It is found in fresh fruits and green vegetables. Vitamin D is formed in the skin by the action of the sun's light, and is found in fish oils, eggs, and butter. It is necessary to assimilate lime and phosphorous, as explained in Chapter 7, on puppy rearing, to produce good bones and teeth, and to prevent rickets. Lack of this vitamin retards calcification of bone. Vitamin E is found in wheatgerm oil: a deficiency of this vitamin leads to muscular dystrophy in dogs, sterility in male rats, and infertility in female rats. Vitamin K is necessary to help stop the bleeding of cuts and wounds. Lack of vitamin K increases the clotting time for the blood.

The necessary minerals to maintain health are the aforementioned lime and phosphorous, also manganese, iron, and other trace elements such as zinc, cobalt, and iodine.

The dog is essentially a carnivore, or eater of flesh, and this is its natural food. The formation of jaws and teeth and the digestive system are designed for this diet.

The dog in its wild state will kill and eat its prey, fur, feathers, bones, viscera, and the contents of the stomach, in addition to the flesh. In fact, after the kill, the dog will usually go for the stomach, offal and entrails first. In this way a perfectly balanced diet of protein, carbohydrates, fats, vitamins and minerals will automatically be obtained. In captivity, however, it is all too easy for the diet to become deficient in some of these elements, however kind and well intentioned the owner may be. Pet dogs that depend to a large extent on the leftovers from the owner's table, are particularly vulnerable in this way, and may suffer deprivation of some essential food elements, depending upon whether or not their owners indulge in a diet suitable for dogs.

Whereas the ruminant is equipped with four stomachs and the ability to bring up its food for additional chewing, the dog is endowed with very powerful gastric juices, strong in hydrochloric acid, which can break down and cope with large pieces of raw meat, fur, feather, and bone. As a result of this the dog does not normally chew its food to any extent, but rather gulps it down in large chunks and leaves it to be dealt with by these strong gastric juices. It will also be apparent from a cursory glance at the teeth and jaws of the dog that it is equipped for tearing rather than careful chewing. It is not always appreciated, however, that the strong gastric juices of the dog, if not given sufficient work to do, will be a source of trouble. Many dog owners, with the best intentions, attempt to refine the dog's food far too much, cutting the meat into unnecessarily small pieces, and painstakingly removing all gristle, bones and even fat, forgetting that they are involuntarily imposing human standards of digestibility on the dog, whose needs are quite different. In fact, all these items, so carefully eliminated, are vitally necessary for good digestion, which, in turn, is essential for growth, health, a sound nervous system, and general joy of living.

In addition to the ability to digest such formidable items of food, the dog is also endowed with a very large stomach, which enables it to go for long periods between meals. In the wild state, following a kill it will eat its fill and possibly not eat again for a considerable period, in fact until the next kill takes place. This is why most dogs are happy with one meal every twenty-four hours, and owners who fuss because their pets will not conform to human standards and accept three meals a day are failing to understand the basic difference between the needs of dogs and those of human beings.

The diet of every dog should contain a fair percentage of good red meat, given raw if possible, but slightly cooked if the dog will only accept it this way. A certain amount of offal (liver, heart, tripe, and paunch) are also good. Tripes, which are not suitable for puppies, must be undressed, direct from the slaughterhouse, not the bleached and refined version sold in butchers' shops for human consumption. These tripes, when collected from the abattoir are revolting to the human eye, containing as they do partially digested food and many other items that presumably appealed to the cow. The part digested food is beneficial to the dog, but the contents and walls of the tripe must be carefully examined for anything harmful; nails, small pieces of barbed wire, and even a penny piece I have found in this way, and while they may not have done much harm to the cow, they would be very injurious if inadvertently swallowed by a dog. Sheep paunches can be given—again, not to puppies—but these must be cooked as a precaution against tape worm.

Fish is an excellent variation to meat as a protein food, herrings and mackerel being especially nutritious. It is also excellent as a light diet for invalids, old dogs, and bitches immediately after whelping. But fish must be carefully boned, because fine bones can become lodged in the throat. Never give dried salt fish, particularly to puppies. Other desirable protein variations are eggs and cheese. Breasts of lamb, which are cheap in the butcher's shops, are very beneficial to Afghan Hounds on account of their fat content, and the soft crunchy bones will be particularly enjoyed. These must not be given too often, because the fat so beneficial to the Afghan Hound coat in reasonable amounts, will upset them if given in too great a quantity. While variation is desirable in any diet, never allow the intake of good red meat to fall too low.

In addition to the protein foods described above, the diet must contain carbohydrates, and the usual form is a good brand of meal. This can normally be purchased in pieces of a size to suit the age and size of the dog. Brown, or wholemeal bread, is another form of carbohydrate; do not give white bread. I give my hounds their meal dry, mixed with the meat. On the whole, Afghan Hounds prefer their food fairly dry. Some breeders keep a stock-pot and moisten the meal with its contents. If this is done, allow the meal to soak thoroughly before serving, for if the meal swells it is better that it takes place outside, rather than inside, the dog. If the dog is disinclined to eat the meal, preferring the more appetising meat, then it is best to give the meal first, when the dog is hungry, and follow with the more attractively flavoured meat after the meal has been consumed.

Vegetables are a good, if small, part of the diet of the dog, and they are best given raw. Left to themselves, and given the opportunity, most dogs will seek out potatoes and peelings, swedes, turnips, parsnips, carrots, and will devour them in reasonable quantities with relish. I have also known them to find fruit and eat it in limited quantities. Coarse grass, which should always be available, is frequently eaten, and not always for the purpose of inducing vomiting, although this is its usual function. Cabbage and lettuce should be finely shredded and mixed raw with the rest of the feed. Peas and beans are a source of protein and can

G

be given occasionally. Dogs will seldom relish cooked vegetables, which shows their extreme good sense. Only human beings choose to cook their vegetables, thereby destroying the vitamins, and washing away the mineral salts, leaving only a sludge of fibre and water to be eaten. There are some exceptions to this, however; kale and turnip tops, which are rich in iodine, are best given cooked. The onion family (which includes garlic, valuable as a worm deterrent) are very beneficial when grated or cut small and given in limited quantities with the main feeds.

The above-mentioned foods, given with a plentiful supply of clean, fresh water, which should always be available, should provide an adequate and comprehensive diet containing the necessary protein, starch, fat, vitamins, mineral salts and water, and supply the 'builders', 'warmers', and 'energisers' required by the fit dog.

Many owners give additional vitamins and minerals in the form of brewers yeast or similar products. Cod liver oil or halibut liver oil are also beneficial and, in some cases, extra calcium; for special reasons such as teething, pregnancy, and nursing, calcium is essential. As a general rule, however, correct feeding in the first place is the best, for if it is correct, few supplements should be necessary. Guard against becoming a 'pill' fanatic, cramming your dog full of every proprietary veterinary product claiming to transform your Afghan Hound into a super dog. In all probability they will cancel each other out, or worse still, produce unwelcome side effects, or interact with each other to produce actual harm. Your veterinary surgeon should be the ultimate guide in this matter. I am a firm believer that with animals, as with humans, a sensible, balanced diet should obviate the necessity for additional pills and patent medicines. This observation naturally refers to the dog in normal health. Medicines and remedies for the sick dog are another matter.

Some general observations on points of feeding may be of some help at this stage. If bones are given, and they are certainly good, they must be of the marrow-bone type. The butcher will always oblige with some beef rib bones or leg bones. These will keep a dog happy for hours, but beware of fights if the dog is not alone. Bones are also good in keeping the teeth free from tartar, and gnawing stimulates the gastric juices. The trouble with Afghan Hounds is that when they are gnawing bones, the coat on the forelegs frequently becomes chewed as well. For this reason many Afghan Hound owners are against giving bones to their dogs. My own feeling is that it is unfair to deprive them of an obvious pleasure on such selfish grounds, and I frequently take a chance with the coat. Never give poultry or rabbit bones or indeed any other form of bone liable to splinter. It was for this reason I purposely omitted poultry and rabbit in the previous paragraphs on diet; both poultry and rabbit meat are excellent foods if they are free from bones.

Afghan Hounds allowed free running in the country will sometimes catch and eat hares and rabbits. If this occurs, one can only hope that the bones that will be consumed along with the fur, viscera, and flesh will not become lodged in the intestine. Another hazard is that most rabbits are alive with fleas and, also, likely to be infested with tapeworm.

There are many brands of tinned dog meat on the market, many of them good, that will make yet another alternative to the protein foods; they are also useful in saving the time and effort needed in cutting up and preparing other foods.

Beware of proprictary foods claiming to provide a complete and balanced dog diet on their own at low prices. This just cannot be done, and the various concoctions, while containing some meat or offal will be made up with much that is pure waste. Lights are sold in shops as dog and cat food, but they contain little nourishment, and are not recommended.

A dog may sometimes display what is called a depraved appetite. That is, it will eat excessive quantities of manure. This is not as disgusting as it may appear. It merely denotes that the dog's diet is deficient in certain minerals, and the wise owner will take steps to rectify this by adjustments in the feeding programme.

When a puppy is first acquired make sure that the breeder supplies complete information about the way it has been fed. It is most important that there should be absolute continuity of diet when a puppy changes homes. Variations, if too sudden, are bound to cause stomach upsets and diarrhoea, with consequent loss of progress. Some puppies settle in new homes without any signs of unhappiness and little or no loss of appetite, but others may be intensely miserable for some days, and in all likelihood refuse all food.

I have stated in an earlier chapter that I do not agree with the sale of Afghan Hound puppies before the age of ten weeks. Many breeders do, however, dispose of young stock at eight weeks or so. For this reason I have started the following specimen diet sheet at that age. I must emphasise that this is a diet programme I personally have found to be efficient and successful. It does not mean that other people may not have different but equally good ones. It is offered as a basis on which breeders may evolve their own particular ideas on feeding.

DIET SHEET

This diet sheet is based on a puppy of eight weeks. The quantities to be increased as the puppy grows.

Where milk is mentioned, it refers to goat's milk, or a good brand of puppies powdered milk.

Breakfast   Farex or porridge mixed in ½ pint of milk, plus one teaspoonful of glucose or golden syrup or honey. One egg beaten into breakfast, either daily or every other day, according to preference.

Midday   4 to 6 oz cooked meat, grated vegetables, one thick slice of wholemeal bread crisped in oven, and broken up. One dessertspoonful of flaked maize, ½ teaspoonful steamed bone flour mixed with a little gravy to absorb it. A small drink of milk.

4 p.m.   Milk.

Evening   As midday, but without bone flour.

Late night   Milk.

Daily   One capsule, or one teaspoonful of cod liver oil. One Lakovel tablet per 10 lb weight of puppy. Water always available.

At ten weeks, the pups will need about 8 oz for the main meals at midday and evening.

Continue in this way as the puppy grows, gradually increasing the meat until it reaches about 1 lb a day, and also increasing the meal accordingly. At around twelve weeks the number of feeds can be reduced to three a day, and at six months they can be further reduced to two a day, with a final reduction at nine to twelve months to one a day.

The normal average feed for an adult Afghan Hound is $2\frac{1}{4}$ to $2\frac{1}{2}$ lb weight of food a day, made up of $1\frac{1}{2}$ lb of meat or similar protein food, and the remainder in meal or other carbohydrates. The healthy growing puppy, towards the latter part of puppy-hood, may need more than this, and within reasonable limits it is difficult actually to overfeed a vigorous growing puppy. In spite of this, the owner must be on guard against the overweight puppy, and be prepared to deal promptly with the problem if it should arise. During puppyhood the bones are soft, and excess weight may cause bow legs or cow hocks, thereby ruining the dog as a future show specimen. These deformities, once acquired, cannot be cured in the adult dog.

Afghan Hounds, generally, are not greedy feeders. I have owned some who were a constant source of anxiety because of their finicky feeding habits and poor appetites. Others have reached the other extreme, and appeared to be eternally ravenous and would, if allowed, have become grossly overweight. Much depends on the character and disposition of the individual dog. Those who spend their days sleeping and lying around use up little energy and, therefore, need less food than the energetic dog who is perpetually on the move. Pet dogs who live in a well-heated home will also need less than those living in possibly harder conditions in outside kennels. Dogs, which are considerably larger than bitches in this breed, will naturally need slightly larger meals, and both dogs and bitches that are heavily exercised will need more food than those seldom exercised.

From the foregoing it must follow that the diet sheet and weights and quantities I have included in it, must be taken as an average, to be used as a foundation for the guidance of the breeder, who must, in the final analysis, make individual variations to them, based on observation, experience, and common sense. If there should be cause for concern about the feeding of any dog, veterinary advice should be taken. One point must be stressed again, at the risk of becoming monotonous: a fat dog is not a healthy dog, even though it may be a reasonably happy one, and look pleased when it receives yet another titbit. Obesity places a strain on the heart and restricts other important functions, thereby shortening the life expectancy of any dog.

The problem of underweight dogs is one that may have to be faced. Should a dog persist in eating so little that its body is being deprived of the basic minimum of nutrition, then steps must be taken to remedy the situation and, if possible, stimulate the flagging appetite. Initially it is imperative that an accurate diagnosis be made to establish the cause of the trouble. If there is no actual ailment causing the loss of weight, and the dog is free from worms and other parasites, the cause may be a nervous temperament. Nervous dogs, in my experience, although frequently thin, usually have normal appetites. It is simply that however much they eat, their weight remains the same. They never relax and seem to be perpetually tearing themselves to pieces mentally. It must be realised that at certain periods of growth the young Afghan Hound looks extremely thin to the inexperienced eye, although in fact it may be in perfect health and condition. In the same way the normal and correct Afghan Hound body with its prominent hip bones causes concern to new owners, whose eyes and experience have been accustomed to more rounded breeds. If the underweight dog is a good feeder, his meals can be increased in quantity and content, with additional fats and milk if they will be taken.

If the dog is a poor feeder, then it can sometimes be encouraged to eat by being fed in the company of another dog who eats normally. The introduction of the competitive element will in all probability cause the poor feeder to eat in order to deny its food to the greedier companion. A tonic from the veterinary surgeon can also do good here.

The danger in trying to tempt poor feeders lies in the extra attention they are given; the additional service is enjoyed by the recipient and is soon demanded as a right. Afghan Hounds, like all dogs, only need a course of action to be repeated twice for it to become an established habit. I had one dog who would eat his meal only while I stood and talked to him. If I moved away he would stop eating until I returned. I have known children who refused to eat their meals in order to draw attention to themselves, and because they enjoyed the extra fuss and concern given to them by their frantic parents endeavouring to coax the food down. Dogs do this for precisely the same reason. As a general observation it must be accepted that with dogs, as with human beings, some are naturally thin, while others tend to rotundity. It is a matter of individual metabolism and not necessarily a sign of ill health.

Obesity

The over-fat Afghan Hound is one of the worst problems for the breeder, causing, in addition to heart strain and other health hazards, infertility in dogs, and whelping difficulties, and failure to conceive in bitches. As in the underweight dog, first ensure that there is no organic cause. (Thyroid disease is a common cause of obesity.) This being ascertained, the most likely cause, as with human beings, is overeating, or too much food of the wrong sort. As stated, the temperament and metabolism of dogs will vary, and so will their tendency to lose or put on weight. I have known dogs who, although very active, and on reduced diets, still persisted in remaining overweight.

In reducing diet to combat weight, cut carbohydrates rather than the meats and protein. Carrots are a source of non-fattening protein, if they will be accepted, as also is cottage cheese. When reducing a dog's diet to curtail weight, great care must be taken not to reduce the food intake so much that the animal receives less than that necessary to maintain normal health.

Exercise is of vital importance in weight control, and must be taken in conjunction with diet. If all efforts in dietary control and exercise fail to remedy the trouble, consult your veterinary surgeon.

Exercise

After nutrition, I would place exercise next in order of importance. The perfect balancing of exercise and feeding should produce perfect condition, assuming that it is supported by correct housing which is dealt with in the next section. Correct exercise stimulates muscles and body functions dependent on muscular action such as bowel movements and breathing.

In the first few months of life the puppy will obtain all the exercise necessary in the communal play with brothers and sisters. It is essential that they have adequate space for free and vigorous play, which is, apart from physical and practical considerations, the birthright of all young living things, a factor ignored by many advocates of intense farming and livestock breeding.

When the young Afghan Hound leaves its brothers and sisters to take up an independent life, proper and adequate exercise must be a prime concern of its new owners. Occasional walks on a lead, ambling along beside the owner are inadequate for this vigorous, active, galloping dog, bred for speed and agility over rough and irregular terrain. Free running in an open space is an absolute essential, so that in play, with its jumping, dodging and turning, all muscles can be exercised and developed to produce perfect overall condition, as well as a happy and contented mental state. For this to be achieved there must be adequate open space available, either an enclosed field or paddock, or a fair sized garden. Wherever these hounds are permitted to take their free exercise, the area must be securely fenced in. If they escape in towns, they will probably end as casualties on the road. If they escape in the country, they will chase and kill poultry, worry sheep and cattle, and probably be shot. At best, a day out (or even a few hours freedom) in the country will end with the owner running round the neighbouring farms with cheque book at the ready, hastily pacifying and recompensing irate and bereaved owners of live-stock and poultry. I decided very early in my association with this breed that it was cheaper to spend several hundred pounds on good chain link fencing, than to pay large bills for defunct poultry, quite apart from the mental anguish of not knowing what my escaped dogs were doing, or how they were faring.

It is a mistake to assume that all types of exercise are necessarily beneficial to the Afghan Hound. Young puppies that over-indulge in jumping up on their hind legs, possibly to see over the fence, are likely to end up with low hocks. Adult dogs, if confined in too restricted a space, may use up their energies in swivelling

round and round and generally overdoing the twisting movements as opposed to the extended galloping and free movement
so imperative to dogs of the greyhound family. Puppies must also
be protected against over-exercising. Like children they are
possessed of seemingly limitless reserves of vitality, and must
therefore be forced to take adequate periods of rest. This apparently inexhaustible energy, if not checked, will end in overtiredness
and even hysteria, particularly during the teething period. The
enforced siesta is a good way of dealing with this problem. Shut
the pups up in their kennel for 1½ to 2 hours in the middle of the
day. Even if they don't all sleep, they will be virtually forced to
take some rest.

In the realm of exercise, single-dog owners will have more of a
problem than the owner of several dogs. Afghan Hounds, in
addition to their need for human companionship, also enjoy and
thrive on the company of their own kind. Several, or even two
together, particularly if of similar age, will play and exercise
themselves without help or interference from their owner. One dog
alone, however, if turned loose in a large paddock, will frequently
sit in one spot, usually near the gate, looking miserable and clearly
waiting to be brought indoors. The paddock may be of several
acres, but the dog will utilise only one square yard.

In these circumstances the owner will have to devote time and
trouble to ensure that proper exercise is taken, and to my knowledge there is only one way this can be achieved. The dog must
be played with. There are many 'toys' or aids to play; hard rubber
rings or balls, lumps of wood and other improvised aids can be
used to encourage the dog to exercise itself. Don't expect your
Afghan Hound to retrieve. It is an instinct foreign to the breed,
and while I know that some enthusiasts have achieved a measure
of success at this game, for all practical purposes the owner will
not only have to throw the object, but retrieve it as well. Some
dogs will enjoy a tug-of-war, and an old tyre or something similar
does well for this purpose.

If the owner makes no effort to exercise the dog its energy will
find an outlet in less pleasant ways. A dog described as 'impossible'
in the home, destructive and prone to dashing round the house,
scattering furniture and ornaments and chewing carpets and

curtains is almost always one that has had too little exercise out-side the house. I have never known a dog who was well exercised being a menace in this way. I am, naturally, referring to adult dogs; puppies will inevitably pass through a destructive period as a normal phase of growing up, and at this time house dogs must be confined to rooms where they can do a minimum of damage.

In wet weather, exercise must still go on, but do not allow the dogs to sit around in the wet. After a good run bring them in and dry them thoroughly. An electric hair drier is excellent for this purpose, but a good dry, rough towel will do the job as well. The possession of a large barn, or some other building that can be adapted to form a covered run is a godsend to any Afghan Hound owner in the wet weather, but few of us will be as fortunate as this. Wet is a potential enemy of a good coat, which brings the interests of the dog's health and the requirements of the show-ring into direct conflict. Many otherwise kind and considerate owners tend to keep their show dogs inside during spells of wet weather, to preserve the quality of the coat, but the dogs can suffer if deprived of exercise for too long. As in most animal management, common sense must be the guide. Clearly, when the weather is wet on the day prior to a show, and the intended exhibit has been bathed and groomed, it is stupid to allow it out to become filthy. One day, without free running, cannot harm a fit dog, particularly if there is a small concrete yard or run available for a quick leg stretch and an opportunity to answer the calls of nature.

Road work is an important part of the exercise programme, although in my opinion sometimes rather over-emphasised. It must never be assumed, or allowed, to take the place of free running. Dogs of the greyhound family have more need of road work than some other breeds, and this must be included in their curriculum in order to achieve first-class condition. Every Afghan Hound has its own particular, individual pace, i.e. the pace at which it is trotting out fully extended, yet not overpacing. This form of exercise can be carried out with the owner on foot and the dog on the lead, which is as beneficial to the owner's muscular condition as to that of the dog, but it can also be done with the owner on horse or bicycle. In the latter two methods, be careful not to overtire the dog. Two to three miles are usually enough for road work.

It is during these trotting sessions that a close and unhurried check can be carried out on the finer points of the dog's construction and movement. Weaknesses and faults that have not been apparent in the limited movement and restricted space of the show-ring are accentuated, and more easily spotted when the dog begins to tire. Not all faults can be cured by toning up the muscles, but sometimes slack backs, dragging feet, throwing out feet or sloppy movement generally can be cured in this way. Short road walks can be started at about four to five months, increasing gradually in length as the puppy grows. Road walks are also invaluable in keeping the nails worn down to a reasonable length.

Do not become an exercise fanatic. Dogs need sleep and rest as much as exercise. Make sure that the natural rhythm of eating, sleeping, and exercising is evenly and properly maintained.

Housing, Kennelling and Runs

The pet owner and small breeder will have little difficulty housing a dog or dogs. If the dog does not live *en famille* either in the kitchen or even on the bed, then most houses have spare rooms, outhouses or stabling that can be easily and cheaply adapted as suitable living quarters for Afghan Hounds. It is a fact that dogs who live in properly equipped kennels with adequate runs tend to live longer and be more healthy than those who live indoors, because they are saved from the overheated rooms and frequent and usually unsuitable titbits that are the normal hazards of the average house pet.

Many reputable firms will supply single kennels or whole ranges to practically any specification, but these are of more interest to the larger breeding establishment. If these made-to-measure ranges are used there will inevitably be some choice in their siting, so make sure they are sited on well-drained ground that will ensure maximum sunshine.

Most beginners, however, will have little choice in this respect as they will be obliged to make the best arrangements possible with existing buildings.

Brick buildings, with concrete floors, are indubitably the best, being warm in winter and reasonably cool in summer, and completely weatherproof. The concrete floors are easy to hose down and keep clean. Wooden buildings, if suitably weatherproofed and free from draughts are also good, but I do not recommend wooden floors, which tend to become soaked in urine and, if frequently washed and scrubbed, will be hard to keep dry and will almost inevitably smell. If existing stabling is to be adapted, the overall requirements are warmth, freedom from damp or draughts, adequate space and fresh air, and reasonable ease in keeping clean.

Whichever type of building is finally chosen as kennelling, lighting and heating must be installed. Electricity can be laid on from the house at a reasonable charge. To attempt to struggle on without light is most frustrating, particularly during the early evenings of winter, and blundering around with oil lamps and torches during an emergency or night whelping is not to be recommended. Heating is also best carried out by electricity. The exact type of heater used will depend on the type and size of the building. In my own kennels I have a strip heater, of the type used in bathrooms, fixed high on the wall and I find it most efficient and well out of reach of the dogs. Other methods of heating can be used, but they are not, in my experience, so effective, safe or trouble free as electricity. If paraffin oil heaters are used, great care must be taken to keep the wicks correctly trimmed, and when they are extinguished, check carefully by turning up the wick again to ensure that they really are out. I am one of many who have had narrow escapes from fires in my kennels due to this type of heater. They are also difficult to site out of the way of the dogs, who must not be able to knock them over. I cannot really recommend this form of heater. A large kennel building, such as a converted Nissen hut, can be efficiently heated by a centrally placed stove, but it must be firmly fixed and guarded. This type of stove must have an efficient chimney and ventilation, as fumes can be harmful and even lethal, particularly coke fumes. I had a narrow escape with this type of stove, which blew back and opened the front, allowing the fumes to permeate the room instead of escaping up the chimney. I found my dogs lying unconscious on the floor and was only just in time to drag them out into the air, where they eventually revived. With good reason, therefore, I recommend electricity.

Do not site your kennels too far from the house. I made this mistake when I started an Afghan Hound kennel. Hoping to keep the attractive vista from my windows, I sited the kennel buildings out of sight, some distance from the house. After many nocturnal trips in my pyjamas in the depth of winter, I now have my kennel and yard adjoining the house and visible from my bedroom window, whence I can not only see, but speak to my dogs.

There is really no need for the kennels to be an eyesore if they are kept clean and sweet-smelling and decorated in harmony with the house. In addition to the buildings to house the dogs, there must be a separate apartment for whelping and possible use as an isolation or sick room. Finally, a shed or large cupboard is needed for the necessary equipment such as brooms, brushes, buckets, disinfectants, spare bedding, and the countless other items required for the kennels.

I have found it invaluable to have a separate kennel kitchen for storing and preparing food and for washing up utensils. This facility may not always be possible for the small breeder, but if there is a suitable room available in which to instal running water, a sink unit and, possibly, a fridge and cooker, then the extra expense will be well worth while over the years. An outside water tap is also useful. Sited in the vicinity of the kennel yard, it facilitates hosing and cleansing generally.

Inside the kennel some form of bed or bench must be provided on which the dogs can sleep and rest. If normal type dog beds are used, there will be no problems, but benches or bunks must be fitted with a board along the front to contain the bedding. Benches and bunks will normally be quite clear of the floor, but beds must be raised from the floor to avoid damp. Make sure that the beds are big enough for the dogs to sleep on comfortably. Different breeders advocate different types of bedding: some use straw, others wood-wool, but I prefer sacking, which is easy to wash at frequent intervals and is warm and comfortable. Hay and straw tend to encourage fleas and are not very suitable for long-coated dogs as they get into the hair.

Sawdust on kennel floors is another controversial subject; it certainly soaks up moisture, but also gets into everything including the food, and for this reason I no longer use it, as it is harmful to dogs if eaten. Afghan Hounds, being a naturally clean and fastidious breed, do not like fouling beds or kennels. If they are let out regularly for exercise and spend only limited periods and nights in their kennel, there will seldom be any cleaning up of faeces or urine to do. All kennels, however, must be cleaned daily to minimise risk of parasites etc.

Exercise runs are of vital importance in the general care of Afghan Hounds. If they can be sited to adjoin the kennels this will be ideal, but most breeders have to be content with the small concrete runs or yards leading out from the kennels and a paddock or larger grass run situated a little farther away. The concrete runs must be equipped with a gully and drain to facilitate hosing and cleansing and to ensure reasonable drying. Never allow your dogs to lie around on wet concrete or damp ground.

The grass runs or paddocks must be large enough for the dogs to extend themselves at the gallop. They must also, if possible, be on well-drained soil. Pools of urine and sour ground are health hazards, as well as being unsightly and offensive. Ideally, these larger runs should contain some trees or bushes to afford shade, and a few obstacles to encourage leaping and turning, and thus, as far as possible, recreate the natural, uneven terrain over which these dogs are bred to hunt.

I would also strongly recommend permanent benches in all grass runs to allow the dogs to sit out of the damp when they are not actually moving around. These benches, as well as providing escape from the wet ground, are very popular with Afghan Hounds, which seem to enjoy sitting on a raised platform and surveying the countryside. They also provide another stimulus to play and exercise, and can be easily constructed from planks, with legs firmly sunk into the ground; but make certain that they are rigid and strong. Wobbly benches seem to frighten Afghan Hounds.

The grass on runs and paddocks should be kept short, not only because it looks better, but because it dries quicker than long grass, and therefore does not cause such wet coats. Short grass also does not seed, and keeps free from troublesome ticks.

Of all the varied types of fencing available, the chain link is the only complete deterrent to Afghan Hounds. The various techniques used by this astonishing breed in their efforts to break out of their enclosures should not be interpreted as a sign that they are unhappy in their homes, or that they want to go anywhere in particular. It is, I am convinced, a manifestation of their complete independence. I have noticed that when my own dogs have managed to gain freedom they do not usually go very far, but tend to run around in neighbouring fields, using all their skill to evade recapture. It is as if they are saying 'I do not want to leave you, but I want it understood that I could if I did'. Some however, will wander farther away.

Fundamentally, Afghan Hound 'escapers' fall into three categories: the 'jumpers over'; the 'diggers under'; and the 'pushers through'. The last-named group are the easiest to combat, as any stout fence of reasonable size will efficiently contain them. The 'jumpers over' are a more difficult problem. My first Afghan Hound, a bitch, was in this group, and I actually saw her negotiate a five-foot chain-link fence. It was therefore necessary to increase the height of the fence to six feet and to fix an eighteen-inch overhang on the inside. This obstacle has not been negotiated to date. The second group, 'the diggers', present the most difficult problem of the three. While there is, of necessity, a limit to the height any dog can jump (even an Afghan Hound), there seems to be no limit to the depth to which a determined member of the breed can dig. It is clearly not possible to sink the fencing some three feet into the ground. I have found, however, that if it is sunk about six to twelve inches into a concrete strip in the ground along the bottom of the fence, then the dogs will be successfully contained.

There is one more type of Afghan Hound escapologist worth mentioning. This is the 'darter through open gates'. This type will observe the habits of its owner carefully and, over a period of time, take note of any careless tendency to leave a kennel door ajar, or a run gate open, even for a moment. Such dogs show great patience and apparent unconcern until the owner is lulled into a sense of security and carelessness, and then one day, in a flash, they are through and away. The moral to all this is, surely, never relax precautions, however docile and disinterested your dog may appear, and never underrate the intelligence of your dogs.

Runs must be kept free from faeces. I advocate clearing up, with a bucket and shovel, at intervals, according to the number of dogs kept. Disposal can be carried out by incineration, or by digging deep pits in some unused and out-of-sight corner of the garden. These pits will serve for a long period, and when nearly full, earth can be shovelled back and a fresh pit dug. If this essential job is not done, and faeces are left all over the runs, the ground will become foul, and infested with flies.

Finally, make sure that runs always have ample supplies of clean fresh water. Do not, however, leave the drinking water in the runs when the dogs are not there; rats may use it, and disease is spread in this way.

If it can be avoided, do not kennel dogs alone, merely taking them out for an hour or so before returning them to their solitary confinement. Dogs kept in this way appear dull and lacking in intelligence, which has given rise to the idea held by some people that kennel dogs are 'dim', and less intelligent than their luckier brethren who live as house pets. By nature lively and sociable, needing both human and canine companionship, dogs sentenced to what is virtually solitary confinement will give this impression, just as a human being treated in a similar way would. When a confined or chained dog is let free, it will tend to act in a crazy manner and even become hysterical. This form of treatment, which is very cruel, can produce a vicious dog from one that was perfectly normal.

Some single-dog owners may think the foregoing advice lacks an understanding of their particular problem, but it doesn't. A kennelled dog should be taken out frequently during the day, preferably in the company of the owner, either around in the car or down to the supermarket or pub. Somehow it must be given the companionship that is so desperately important to it. Sleeping alone at night does it no harm; there is no need to carry things too far and endure a bony Afghan Hound as a bedmate.

If there is no paddock or enclosed field for free running, then use must be made of parks and recreation grounds. Here difficulties will be encountered, as Afghan Hounds with their customary disobedience, once loosed, may well run off and perish on the roads, or become a nuisance by chasing smaller dogs. In my very early days with these dogs I let a bitch of mine off the lead for a free run on some rough open country adjacent to a golf course. She immediately bolted and I finally caught up with her in time to see her walk on to one of the greens and pick up a ball just as a player was about to make his putt. She walked off calmly with the ball in her mouth and a look of fiendish joy on her face. The ball was never retrieved and I have never faced up to a more uncomfortable and embarrassing situation. My profuse apologies, interspersed with painstaking explanations and descriptions of the rare qualities and charming, if disobedient, nature of the Afghan Hound fell on very unsympathetic ears. I sometimes think that an anthology of horrific situations inflicted by Afghan Hounds on their owners would make an amusing addition to the breed literature.

Yet, if use is not made of public open spaces, what alternative is open to the owner without garden or field? Some while ago I spoke to some people in a nearby town, who owned an Afghan Hound as a house pet. They explained that the dog was never let off the lead as 'he wouldn't come back when called'. This dog, bred for freedom and galloping, literally never had a free run. It's owners were kind, and they obviously loved their dog, but they were subjecting him to intense cruelty. The truth must be faced. The Afghan Hound is not a suitable dog for a town house or flat, unless there is safe enclosed space available large enough for it to have adequate exercise, and the owner can spare the time to take it there with reasonable frequency. Many Afghan Hounds, living in town houses are loved, happy and in fine condition, due to the selfless devotion and dedication of their owners. Others, I fear, do not fare so well, and are soft, and, generally, in poor shape.

Character and Training

The dog which in its distant, wild state was a pack animal, giving allegiance to the pack leader and obeying the laws of the pack, when domesticated and separated from this group existence needs a substitute as a focal point for this inborn allegiance.

Fortunately, the submissive attachment shown by wild dogs to the leader of the pack is readily transferrable to the human master.

The origins of the domestic dog's fidelity to its human master are basically two in number. First, the inborn allegiance to the pack leader already mentioned, and second, the strong tie that binds the young wild dog to its mother until it becomes adult, but which, in the domestic dog is retained throughout its life, and focused on its human owner. To assist the dog in this process some form of basic training is required, which means that it must be given a code of behaviour and a set of rules to help it substitute the owner for the original pack leader. Dogs deprived of some form of training or ordered existence will not be happy or mentally well adjusted.

The word 'training' is used in a general sense, that is, teaching the dog to be clean in home or kennel, to come when called (as far as it is possible with an Afghan Hound), and to respond reasonably to the owner's simple commands, so that life for both owner and dog can be smooth running and enjoyable. Obedience training, which calls for a high degree of subservance and instant compliance to the slightest command or sign, together with an ability to retrieve, while suitable for certain breeds of dog, is not in my view suitable to the Afghan Hound temperament. The whole ritual of the obedience test is foreign to the nature of these dogs, who are sight hounds, bred for the chase, with an aloof and suspicious nature and totally lacking in the instinct to retrieve. In some countries some success is achieved in the obedience ring with Afghan Hounds, but this proves very little. All animals can, under certain circumstances and to a certain degree, be trained to carry out tasks or rituals that are foreign to their natural instincts and normal behaviour patterns. I have, however, always felt slightly unhappy when witnessing this. The ultimate in this field is the ghastly spectacle of elephants carrying out dance steps and bears on roller skates, seen in some circuses, a sight that fills me with nausea.

As already stated, the Afghan Hound is not by nature an obedient dog, and the instantaneous and almost servile response to the commands of the owner displayed by many breeds is foreign to the Afghan Hound temperament. This must not, however, be confused with lack of devotion or loyalty. This breed, which seems, to the uninformed, to be haughty and sometimes indifferent to their owners is, in fact, capable of a fanatical devotion which on occasions can be detrimental to themselves. Afghan Hounds separated from their owners will sometimes refuse food, pine, and lose condition to an alarming degree. The famous American Champion Rudiki of Pride's Hill is said to have died of a broken heart when his owner, Mrs. Marion Florsheim, was forced to leave him behind when she left for Europe in 1947. I know that there is no official medical recognition of this complaint as such, but all who have had long experience of this breed will recognise it.

This intense and unswerving devotion, of which more will be said in the ensuing paragraphs, places an immense reponsibility on the recipient; a responsibility that is too often shirked.

The Afghan Hound has retained to a marked degree many of the characteristics of its wolf ancestors. Unlike many breeds which display few pack instincts, and give an almost fawning devotion to their owners (and others), as well as instantaneous obedience, the Afghan Hound has a strong pack instinct, with all the loyalty and other attributes that this implies. Such dogs, according to Dr. Lorenz, display a 'strong manly loyalty far removed from obedience', and when taken for a walk, will not walk to heel, as do more subservient breeds, but 'keep loose contact giving their companionship now and again' and when called 'comes not at all, but seeks to appease you from a distance with friendly gestures'. The loyalty of such dogs is given on a basis of equality, as between friends, and is quite devoid of servility. Dr. Lorenz sums up the outlook of this type of dog perfectly in the following words, 'He is ready to die for you, but not to obey you.'

I do not decry the breeds that display more obvious signs of sentimental devotion or instant obedience, for I accept that there is a breed to suit every human need. It would also be wrong to give the impression that the Afghan Hound cannot behave as sentimentally or effusively as any other breed, but this behaviour is not automatic, neither can it be produced to order as a right;

rather is it bestowed as a favour on selected individuals when the dog feels inclined, and is all the more valuable for this.

In addition to its naturally independent spirit, the Afghan Hound has been bred to act on its own initiative, and to formulate its own plans when hunting, as opposed to obeying the whistles or commands of a human master. It must follow, therefore, that those who expect the same behaviour and reactions from an Afghan Hound as they would get from a terrier, gun-dog, or poodle, are going to be disappointed. Breeders have a great responsibility to point these facts out to prospective purchasers of puppies. It would be foolish indeed to pretend that the highly individual character of the Afghan Hound, while appealing strongly to the dedicated devotee, could be other than a source of trouble, bewilderment, and frustration to the owner whose requirement was a docile and obedient little family pet to trot unobtrusively to heel, and give no trouble.

It has been claimed that the Afghan Hound has a sense of humour, and there have been occasions, when I have believed my dogs were laughing. Nevertheless, viewed dispassionately, it is an extravagant claim. I think it is safer to say that they have a very pronounced sense of fun which provides a delightful contrast and compliment to the aloof and unapproachable facets of their character. Sceptics have asked how it is possible to be 'aloof, dignified, and suspicious,' and also 'playful with a sense of fun'. The answer is that they are not all these things at the same time. It is the incredible range of the Afghan Hound's character that enables it to encompass these apparently incompatible extremes.

It would be a tragic thing if the breed were ever to lose its highly individual character and temperament, difficult as this can sometimes be, but I fear there is a real danger of it. I would go so far as to say that an instantly obedient, subservient Afghan Hound is not, in fact, a true Afghan Hound, whatever its physical appearance might be.

The Afghan Hound gives its loyalty to one person, and having done so, it remains for life. This does not mean that it will not live happily and affectionately with all members of the family. It is difficult to be precise as to the exact moment when this loyalty is bestowed, but it is around five months, and anyone who is with the pup at the time can be selected for this allegiance.

The dog may make the best of new homes and owners to a greater or lesser degree, depending on its temperament, but the person on whom the loyalty was first bestowed will always be first. Afghan Hound owners have seen this demonstrated when a judge in the show-ring has been confronted with an adult dog he sold as a youngster, and has not seen since, displaying transports of delight, and giving such a show of affection, that cynical ringside observers could be excused for believing that the judge had been entertained by the owner the night before.

This whole question is a disturbing one for those who care, and are genuinely concerned, for the happiness and mental well being of their dogs. It should certainly make owners think carefully before disposing of adult dogs, and make sure that puppies are sold before they reach five months. Intending owners should also be sure, before they decide to buy an Afghan Hound, that they really want it and can keep it permanently and that the puppy is young enough to buy. I have known Afghan Hounds which, starting with a friendly and amenable temperament, after passing from one owner to another have ended up savage and unapproachable, and had to be destroyed as completely unmanageable.

Dr. Lorenz informs us that in extreme cases dogs of this type, when they are separated from the owners to whom they have given their allegiance, may become literally unbalanced, and sink morally in their grief to the level of the ownerless dog or street cur.

My wife and I have a simple rule. If we decide to keep a puppy, we keep it for life. Having made our choice, if it fulfils our hopes in the show-ring we are delighted. If it does not, then it remains in the kennel as a pet. After all, it is not the fault of the dog if we make a mistake in our selection.

It is no accident that character and training are linked together in this chapter. Without a thorough and accurate understanding of the character and temperament of a dog it is impossible to train it successfully. Too often, dog owners apply techniques, rewards, and punishments based on human rather than canine psychology. The late Count Max Thun Hohenstein, carrying out experiments with monkeys, found that they did not react to a beating after a misdemeanour, but were much more impressed by a nip with the teeth, the reason being that hitting is not associated in the monkey mind with chastisement, while biting is the normal punishment expected by one monkey from another. The same theory has been applied to some extent to dogs, and it is claimed that a dog understands a bite, which he might receive from his pack leader as a punishment, but does not so readily recognise a blow, which is a human rather than a canine form of chastisement. I do not, however, suggest that these scientific findings should be applied too literally by Afghan Hound owners; I would not fancy my chances in a biting contest with any of my Afghan Hounds. It is also suggested, as a result of experiments, that to pick up a dog by the scruff of the neck and give it a good shake, as the pack leader would do, is a more understood punishment than a beating, but once again this is not a practical proposition for Afghan Hounds.

It has been said that all training is a matter of reward and punishment, and this is largely true. Neither reward nor punishment, however, is of the slightest use unless it is associated by the dog with the appropriate deeds. A reward given some time after a good deed will be enjoyed, but not associated with the deed. Likewise, a smack given even a minute after the pool has appeared on the floor, will not be connected with it in the mind of the dog, and therefore only lead to bewilderment, and defeat its purpose. I would not rule out corporal punishment but, as with children, it should be administered only by someone who loves the recipient. It must in fact always hurt the giver as much as the receiver. Without this very necessary safeguard I would consider it highly suspect and undesirable. I am strongly opposed to the use of a stick, whip, or any other weapon (even the oft recommended rolled newspaper). Chastisement must be administered by hand only, as the effect must be more psychological than physical. The justifiable claim that it is nearly impossible to hurt a dog of any size with a blow from the hand is a good safeguard, and I can personally vouch for its veracity. I well remember the first occasion that I had to slap a young Afghan Hound. The effect on the dog was nil, but my hand was numb for the rest of the day.

All this brings me to the point that I wish to emphasise. The control of a dog should be by voice. Not that the actual words must be understood, although this is quite feasible, but Afghan Hounds are sensitive to tone and inflection and can readily differentiate between a 'cross' voice and a 'pleased' voice, and various shades between. I find that my own dogs will readily recognise admonitions given in an angry tone, seeming to realise at once that they have transgressed, while a pleased or congratulatory tone is equally understood. So effective have I found this method of control that I cannot remember when I last found it necessary to chastise an adult dog. I would certainly claim that after the usual, necessary slaps of puppy training, there should never be occasion to hit an adult Afghan Hound if training has been correctly carried out and maintained.

One final word on punishment. It is imperative to take into consideration the temperament of the individual dog before meting out punishment. As sensitivity to punishment varies considerably in different dogs, it must follow that a relatively light slap may mean more to a sensitive, impressionable dog than a severe thrashing to a more robust and insensitive one. Dr. Lorenz points out that 'canine punishment is effective less by virtue of the pain it causes than by revelation of the power of the administrator'.

Thoughtless and excessive punishment administered to a highly strung or sensitive dog can ruin it psychologically, taking away its joy of living and turning it into a timid, cringing creature.

House training is the first step towards making the young puppy an acceptable member of the family. The natural fastidiousness of the breed provides a good foundation for this task. For kennel dogs, it is desirable they should be clean because it reduces work, but for the house dog it is essential. The young puppy, when first brought into the home should be kept in one room, where there is direct access to the garden. It is most important that it should be put outside at regular and frequent intervals so that it may relieve itself, particularly after meals. At first, these excursions will not be understood, but with perseverance and after much petting when the pup obliges, with mild scolding when a puddle occurs inside, success will eventually be achieved.

The ideal is to spend several hours with the new puppy when it first arrives, and the moment it shows signs of relieving itself, to whisk it outside. In this way it is remarkable how soon the idea catches on. Always use the same exit so that the puppy knows which door to go to when it wants to go outside. The use of different exits will confuse and prolong the training.

Puppies and even older dogs will, on occasions, crouch down and urinate after a chastisement. This is a deep-seated instinctive act of submission and must not be treated as a lapse in house training, and on no account must it be followed by further punishment.

In this category is the habit displayed by male dogs of urinating in various places around the boundaries of their runs or kennels. This has nothing to do with a desire to empty the bladder, but is a manifestation of a strong instinct inherited from their wolf ancestors. It is the marking out of territory by boundary marks, which are respected by other members of the species.

Farley Mowat, in his book *Never Cry Wolf,* describes an experiment he carried out while studying wolves for the Canadian Wild Life Service. Establishing his camp in the 'territory' of a wolf family, he marked out his own territory, deliberately impinging on that of the wolves, over an area of approximately three acres (a feat he claims took the whole night and the consumption of large quantities of tea). As a result the wolves re-marked their own boundaries, outside his.

I have a dog that has this instinct to a marked degree, although very obedient and trainable in every other way, and I am convinced that any attempt to stop him by punishment would be cruel.

Contrary to what one might expect, I have found bitches more difficult to house train than dogs. The main point to remember is that scolding or chastisement if it is to be effective, must take place during or immediately after the misdemeanour, likewise any demonstration of pleasure or reward must be equally coincident with the deed.

Lead training, to some degree, is a necessity for all dogs, but is of particular importance for the show dog. For this reason I deal with it in Chapter 8, on showing.

This leaves the all-important but, for our breed, touchy aspect of training, teaching young Afghan Hounds to come when called. Whereas in house or kennel training the fundamental breed temperament is definitely on the side of the trainer, it is an entirely different story when an attempt is made to instil any form of obedience. Afghan Hounds will vary in their adaptability to this aspect of training, and indeed, some lucky owners with one or two very amenable dogs will know little of the frustration that many of us have endured. Most Afghan Hounds will come to a call when it suits them, and in this way may build up in the owner an entirely false sense of achievement and security. Such complacency will soon be dispelled when the dog decides not to conform. The main aim must be to associate the dog's compliance to the call with some form of pleasure. Encourage the puppy to come to you by using a coaxing voice and actions, and follow up, when the call is answered, with a small reward that is psychological, in the form of petting, and practical, in the form of a titbit. But above all, when a puppy does answer a call, make much of it and let it know beyond any doubt that you are pleased. Never chastise a dog who has finally been caught after persistent refusal to answer a call. The act may well relieve the pent up emotions of the frustrated owner, but will inevitably be associated in the dog's mind with the return, and not the running away, thereby ensuring that there will be less likelihood of success next time. Above all, never lose your temper.

Dr. Lorenz in one of his books mentions the difficulty in curing this form of disobedience in dogs. He suggests that the only logical and therefore possibly successful way that chastisement could be used in this context, is for the owner to be armed with a catapult and, immediately the dog starts to bolt, to sting it with a well-aimed pellet. This suggestion, while admittedly logical, is of doubtful practical value as it calls for a high degree of skill on the part of the owner, particularly with an Afghan Hound, whose speed off the mark and ability to turn is legendary.

I have come to the conclusion that in this particular aspect of training the Afghan Hound owner will generally have to be content with only comparative success. If my dogs come to me eventually when called I am content, and accept the fact that if anything more interesting turns up, then I may have to wait until they are ready. My old Champion Jali of Vishnu insists that I chase him round the bushes for five minutes before he condescends to come to me. If this ritual is not observed he refuses to be caught, but after it he will come willingly and happily. I have had many Afghan Hounds who insist on playing hard to get for a few minutes before giving themselves up, and I am convinced this is done to establish their basic independence.

All this can be exasperating, and I fully accept that it would not do for many dog owners. But if you are not prepared to tolerate it, then my advice is not to keep Afghan Hounds.

The basic training I have outlined may seem scant and inadequate to the obedience enthusiast, but it is sufficient to provide an adequate substitute for the pack allegiance and obedience inherent in the dog, and at the same time make the life of dog and owner amenable and smooth running. Some owners may enlarge on the programme suggested and carry it further, while large kennels may not be able to spare the time to carry out even the bare essentials, which is understandable but regrettable. Dogs who are not afforded some training may well appear difficult, even on occasions biting their owners and others, which can be as much a symptom of bewilderment as of hereditary instability.

Always remember that the essence of any training is consistency. The same sequence of events must always be followed, and the same causes must produce the same effects. Lessons must be constant, and given regularly. Spasmodic bursts of intense effort, followed by long periods of no training at all, are of little value, while an inconsistent, constantly varying programme will lead to bewilderment, the most usual cause of training difficulties.

Do not attempt to train a puppy before the age of three or four months. Very young animals, like very young children before they are sufficiently mentally developed, cannot understand and therefore cannot respond to training.

Young dogs, when they reach the age of puberty, at around twelve months, will undergo a period of disobedience. This is the animal counterpart of the rebellious teenager, and arises from the same causes. It is as if the dog is testing the owner to see how far it can go, and what it can get away with. Do not be too harsh at these manifestations. Treat them with the same tolerance and understanding that would be given to adolescent human beings. The phase will pass with time, and the dog will settle down again.

Teething

At about four months the first or 'milk' teeth will fall out and be replaced by the permanent ones. The puppy at this time must have plenty of calcium to ensure strong and sound permanent teeth. Keep careful watch on the whole of this teething process. Particularly, ensure that a new tooth is not pushed out of line by the failure of the milk teeth to come out at the appropriate time. Your veterinary surgeon will advise on this.

The erupting of the new permanent teeth frequently causes sore mouths, and may be the reason for the puppy going off its food. If this should occur, take veterinary advice. Sometimes the new tooth emerges alongside the milk tooth, and this again calls for veterinary attention.

On occasions, the milk tooth which is overdue to come out can, if loose, quite easily be pushed out since it has no roots. This operation must be carried out with great care, and on no account must force be used on a tooth that is not sufficiently loose.

Do not be worried if, when the permanent teeth first arrive, the mouth appears to be overshot. This almost always corrects itself with time. Mouths that at first appear dead level may well become undershot later.

When handling the mouths of young dogs, and particularly when removing a loose tooth, be extremely careful and very gentle, otherwise the puppy may develop a dislike of having its mouth handled and put up a spirited fight against it for the rest of its life. This is a serious drawback in a show dog.

Coat

The subject of grooming will be dealt with in Chapter 8, but it must not be assumed that Afghan Hounds need not be groomed unless they are to be put into the show-ring. Regular grooming is an essential part of kennel management, as it keeps the coat vigorous and healthy. It should start at three to four months, long before the length of coat might suggest it to be necessary, and continue throughout the life of the dog. If this is not faithfully carried out, coats will become matted, and look unsightly, and more important still, cause discomfort and unhappiness to the dog. A matted and tangled coat, particularly in tender parts of the body, can be very painful. Grooming is also useful in removing falling hair during a period of coat shedding. The Afghan Hound, unlike some breeds, does not undergo a regular or seasonal change of coat. Bitches tend to have a coat shed after seasons, usually about the time that lactation would be taking place but not always so. Dogs can also have a period of coat change, but it does not follow a definite pattern: some dogs may have heavy coats all their lives, while others may shed them at two to three years of age and be 'out of coat' for as much as twelve months. Some, again, have a very poor coat until about four years of age, when it becomes heavy and luxuriant. The Afghan Hound coat does not come out on one's clothes as do the coats of Alsatians or similar breeds. The change from puppy to adult coat is not a simple matter of the puppy coat growing longer. It is accompanied by a partial shedding of the puppy coat. When a coat is shedding, or about to shed, it loses its lustre, becomes dead, and has a greater tendency than usual to felt or mat. During the puppy change of coat (between ten to eighteen months) a frequent, at least daily, grooming is essential to avoid matting.

If an Afghan Hound is so neglected that its coat becomes a mass of felt and mats it may be impossible to groom it back to normal, and it is then better to cut the whole coat short and allow it to grow again from the beginning. It is the practice of some kennels to cut the coats short on old dogs or dogs that are not exhibited in the ring, and this is preferable to leaving them ungroomed and matted. I would not, however, take this decision lightly as the coat of these beautiful dogs is characteristic and, an essential part of them.

General Points

Some Afghan Hounds have a distressing habit of chewing, and even eating, their own coats. This habit, if it is severe and chronic, can render it useless for showing, as well as making the dog a pathetic sight. I have such a dog in my kennels, and have tried every remedy suggested to me, without the slightest success.

The habit has been compared with nailbiting in human beings, and is probably of psychological origin. The dog does not lose condition and is in every way happy and healthy. I regret not being able to offer any helpful advice on this problem.

In adults the long ear-hair can drop into the plate and be inadvertently chewed with the food. This can best be combated by the use of an old stocking with the foot cut off. The resultant sleeve can be pulled over the head and ears, leaving the foreface protruding and the dog free to eat, while the ears are out of danger.

Car sickness is a problem with some dogs; as with young children, this trouble will normally clear up unaided as the puppy grows up. It is advisable that puppies intended for a show career should be accustomed to car travel from an early age. They can be taken for short car rides from about three to four months, and so generally become accustomed to this form of travel. There are medical remedies for this type of sickness which is probably of nervous origin, and the veterinary surgeon will prescribe if necessary. It has been suggested that the moving view from the window may be a contributory cause of this trouble, and that dogs kept on the floor of the vehicle, where they cannot see out of the windows, are less likely to be affected in this way. It is unusual, but not impossible, for the trouble to continue long into adult life.

Worms can be a problem in adult dogs, on occasion. The symptoms and treatment are the same as described for puppies in Chapter 7, on puppy rearing. If the dog loses weight and condition, has offensive breath and lack-lustre coat, the cause may be infestation with tapeworm. Fortunately, this is easy to clear up with modern remedies, and your veterinary surgeon will prescribe a suitable one. Once again, I must stress the inadvisability of using patent remedies purchased across the counter.

There may be occasions when it becomes necessary to send your dogs to spend some time in a boarding kennel, or to be looked after by friends. I would strongly recommend that this is not done unless absolutely unavoidable. The Afghan Hound does not take too well to strange people and living quarters, and will frequently pine and, possibly, refuse food. It is a good idea when sending a dog away to strange quarters to send an old garment of the owners on which the dog can sleep, which gives it comfort. R. C. G. Hancock in his book *Dogs: Care and Management* tells of a dog he was boarding who refused food for so long that there were fears for its life. The owner, who was abroad, on hearing this sent an unlaundered vest which was given to the dog, who immediately began to eat, and gave no further trouble. It must be realised that separations of this sort, although sometimes quite unavoidable, do cause intense suffering to dogs who cannot know the temporary nature of their banishment, and consider themselves utterly forsaken. If the kennels to which your dog is to be sent has had no previous experience of Afghan Hounds, it is imperative they are told of the escaping potentialities, the disobedience, and the other difficulties they are likely to encounter, with particular emphasis on the difficulty of recapturing them if they are let out.

Another difficulty encountered by many Afghan Hound owners is the unfortunate habit some dogs have of howling. It has caused more trouble to breeders and pet owners alike than any other single factor. There is little that I can offer in the way of advice as to how to overcome this. In my early days with this breed I was obliged to move from the village in which I lived because of the complaints, and since then I have lived in an area without neighbours and have therefore been free from this particular problem.

It has been suggested by R. C. G. Hancock in his book that a microphone, with loudspeakers in the kennels, can be installed so that the owner can control the dogs by voice, and I know Afghan Hound owners who have proved this to be efficient. It does not, however, solve the question of controlling the noise when the owner is away. It is further suggested by Mr. Hancock, as a result of his own experience, that kennels painted primrose inside can have a quietening effect on the inmates. This would seem to suggest that the claim that dogs are colour blind is open to doubt. I have read of the success of colour schemes in factories as a means of improving production, but this application of the principle to dogs is particularly interesting.

The relationship of children with animals is one that calls for careful thought and supervision. The popular practice of well-intentioned parents buying young dogs or animals as presents for their children is, in my opinion, to be discouraged. It may well be that little Johnny has seen a puppy illustrated in a picture book and has asked for one for Christmas, or the fond and doting parents may consider it 'good for him' to own a living creature, and so it may be. It is, however, seldom 'good' for the wretched and helpless little animal that is selected to help form the character of little Johnny. Normal young children are narcissistic and have little understanding, consideration or sympathy for the feelings of other living creatures. It is, therefore, highly immoral to place a young dog or any other animal at the mercy of a child, without rigid and constant supervision. Many years ago I sold a bitch puppy to what appeared to be an excellent home. After only a few hours I was informed that the dog had bitten the child of the house. I immediately collected her, and she lived with us for the remaining thirteen years of her life; a sweeter tempered, more gentle bitch I have never known. I learned afterwards that during her short sojourn as a puppy in the new home, the small son had spent the time hitting her on the head with an electric train! I never knew what further steps the parents took to form the character of the young child, but I sincerely trust that they did not include the purchase of any more puppies.

I consider that the whole concept of dogs as 'presents', as seen in advertisements at Christmas, is highly questionable. Dogs, who are mammals, belonging to the same broad group as human beings, are subject to the same forms of suffering both mental and physical. It must follow that they cannot be considered as inanimate 'things', and be handed around like a box of cigars or a bottle of whisky. A dog should be acquired only after very careful thought and because it is genuinely desired. The act of acquiring a dog carries with it the acceptance of the obligation to tend and care for the animal for the next ten to fifteen years. All too frequently the enthusiasm for the new dog wanes after the charms of puppyhood have passed, and on some occasions it dies even sooner, when the first puddle appears on the floor. The appalling statistics, recently published in the press, revealing that dogs, once the charms of puppyhood have passed, or when holidays draw near, are turned loose on the motorways, or thrown into rivers with their legs tied, should cause grave concern to all breeders. One North London pet shop brazenly displayed an advertisement in its window offering puppies for sale and guaranteeing a free replacement if they died before the age of six months, a clear temptation to unfeeling people to neglect the proper care of the puppy and not to bother with veterinary fees, since a replacement can be had so easily.

If the breeder has a responsibility to his dogs and for the rearing of the puppies, and he certainly has, then he has as great, or possibly a greater, responsibility for the sort of people and homes that his puppies eventually go to. The quick sale and the high price are not, or should not, be the sole aim. He should make absolutely certain, as far as this is possible, that prospective purchasers fully understand the Afghan Hound temperament and all its drawbacks, and the needs of the dog, in the way of exercise and grooming, with the consequent demands on the owner's time. Finally, give an honest estimate of the cost of feeding, and find out if the purchasers have premises suitable to the ownership of a dog of this type. If there are any doubts about the answers to any of these questions, the sale should be turned down.

I shall always remember the occasion when my wife and I went to buy our first Afghan Hound puppy: something I had promised myself as soon as I was released from the Army. To our surprise, when we arrived at the breeder's house, we were not immediately shown the puppies, but were invited in with great courtesy and given a careful description of the breed. It also became apparent that at the same time we were being assessed for our suitability as Afghan Hound owners. We must have proved satisfactory, as we were soon on our way home with a bitch puppy.

If this book should fall into the hands of the gentleman concerned I would like him to know how much we respected him for the care he took over the sale of his puppy, a respect that increased as we learned more of the temperament of the breed and realised their vulnerability in the hands of unsuitable people.

7

Breeding and Puppy Rearing

'The breeder will best solve his problem who does not lose sight of the fact that his is a task rather of preservation than of improvement.'

JACKSON SANFORD

AFTER the acquisition of a reasonably good dog, and possibly some success in the show-ring, the novice owner will probably be fired with a desire to breed. It is the next logical step forward for the enthusiast, and is in accordance with the very laudable human trait of striving for perfection.

It is true that some people begin breeding for quick financial gain, particularly in breeds that are in great public demand, and where rapid and lucrative puppy sales are consequently assured. The current leap in popularity of the Afghan Hound is causing some breeders to place them in the money-making category. I do not, however, think them to be right. It is my considered opinion that breeding Afghan Hounds, if carried out conscientiously, with due care for and careful feeding of the bitch and her subsequent litter, cannot be a profit-making venture. The financial aspect will be discussed more fully later.

Before deciding to breed it is essential to pause and consider carefully some very important factors before embarking on a course of action that may well be regretted later. In the first instance, the Afghan Hound is a fairly large dog that produces large litters. Ten is quite normal, and I have had bitches who produced as many as fifteen. It must therefore follow that unless adequate space is available, both in the form of kennelling and outdoor runs, breeding these hounds should not be undertaken. Any attempt to breed a litter of Afghan Hounds in the kitchen of a small, upstairs flat, is just not fair on the other members of the family; neither is it fair on the bitch or her puppies, which will, in addition to suffering from the cramped and inadequate

I

conditions, almost certainly have to be disposed of too young by their frantic owner.

On the important question of cost, the novice will hear tempting stories, told by breeders, of the high prices obtained for puppies, but dog breeding, like all undertakings, incurs a balance sheet. There is always a profit and loss account, and due thought must be given to the outgoings before anticipating and assessing a possible profit.

In the first place, stud fees are high, particularly if a well-known winning dog is used, and, although this is not essential, puppies sired by a popular champion will sell more easily, and for higher prices than those sired by a less well-known, but possibly equally good, dog. Next, the cost of the whelping box, and possibly some alteration to existing kennels and runs, will all mount up, and the care and feeding of the in-whelp bitch cannot be undertaken efficiently and, at the same time, cheaply, while the puppies, once they are weaned, develop voracious appetites that send the food bills soaring. This can be particularly onerous if sales are not brisk, and the breeder is left with several puppies who, rapidly increasing in size and intake, literally and metaphorically 'eat up' any possible profit there might have been, in addition to damaging carpets, furniture, and so on, if they are indoors. Finally, due allowance must be made for medical fees. These should not be high, if all goes well and only an occasional check up for bitch and puppies is required, but if there are difficulties, and this must always be allowed for, veterinary help and attention may be necessary on a larger scale and can become a considerable item.

I have asked several breeders who are active in the breed today, for an estimated cost of having and rearing a litter of Afghan Hounds, and they all advise the setting aside of approximately a hundred pounds for the venture. Naturally they stress that this could vary either way according to the course of events.

The impatient would-be breeder may have come to the conclusion that I am intent on dissuading him from breeding Afghan Hounds. This is not so, but I do stress the importance of very careful thought before embarking on a course of action that may bring disappointment and regrets.

Three main systems can be followed when planning a breeding

programme. They are, line breeding, in-breeding, and out-breeding (or out-crossing).

Line breeding consists of breeding together animals who are all within a related family, but not necessarily closely related.

In-breeding might be described as a more concentrated form of line breeding, being the mating of closely related dogs: father to daughter, brother to sister, etc. This programme has many pitfalls, and should be carried out with caution, careful thought, and only by experienced breeders. There is nothing basically wrong in mating close relations, provided they are both perfectly sound. It must be realised, however, that the method cannot introduce anything new to the line. It can only reproduce factors that are already present in the parents, but it can, and will, fix not only good points, but faults as well. It is also useful in that it can bring to light factors that, although not so far suspected, have none the less been present, and in this way will enable these factors, if they are faults, to be eliminated by careful culling. It is essential in in-breeding that both parents are very good specimens and as free as possible from serious faults, particularly faults that are common to both.

Out-breeding can best be summed up as the opposite to in-breeding and line breeding, in that the parents are, as far as possible, unrelated. This is inclined to be a hit-and-miss method, but undoubtedly some very good dogs have been produced in this way. Here, as indeed in the other methods, a thorough knowledge of the forebears of both dog and bitch, and what they have produced, will be of tremendous help to the breeder and greatly increase the chances of success.

In general, line breeding and in-breeding are the methods to produce gradual but overall improvements of stock, and to establish an individual kennel type, while out-crossing, although offering the same chances of an outstanding specimen as the first two methods, will not necessarily produce animals that will pass their points on to their offspring with the same degree of certainty.

It should be the aim of every breeder to produce something better in each successive litter. It is essential, therefore, to have a definite ideal in mind as a yardstick when choosing and rejecting puppies.

Too many inexperienced enthusiasts rush into breeding before they have acquired sufficient knowledge to enable them to pick out the best from their litters. Consequently they are left, after all the hard work and expense, with the least good, rather than the best of their puppies. It may be years before a puppy can be selected from a litter with any degree of certainty (*see* Chapter 5) but in fairness to themselves novices will be well advised to restrain their impatience and enthusiasm for breeding until sufficient knowledge of the requirements of the standard has been acquired to make the undertaking worth while.

In my opinion it is of immense value to the breeder to acquire a knowledge of genetics; not because it will provide a short cut to success but because an understanding of the subject will provide added interest and will also explain many points that may otherwise seem inexplicable. It is not within the scope of this work to deal at length with the subject but *The Dog Breeder's Introduction to Genetics,* by Eleanor Frankling, will provide an excellent groundwork.

Many intending breeders are undecided whether to start by buying an adult bitch or whether to buy a bitch puppy and after exhibiting her for twelve months or more withdraw her from the ring to be mated. The purchase of an adult bitch will enable the breeding programme to begin immediately, but acquiring a puppy will give the owner time and opportunity, while exhibiting, to gain a knowledge of the breed, and so enhance the chances of choosing the right puppy when the litter arrives.

The Stud Dog

A stud dog should be in first-rate general condition, well muscled and exercised, and free of excess fat. He should be fed on a well-balanced diet of protein, carbohydrates, and vitamins, and, above all, be free from hereditary defects. It is the responsibility of the owner of the stud dog to ensure that the dog is free from infection, and the owner of the bitch should expect to see a certificate of clearance from hip dysplasia, or under certain circumstances a borderline case can be used (*see* Chapter 11). A good sire may not be a champion, but one who sires good stock. In choosing a suitable stud dog, the bitch owner must not only have a know-

· ledge of the standard, but must be honest enough to admit where the bitch fails so that steps can be taken to eradicate her faults. If the bitch is weak in any particular point or points, then make sure that the dog is as near perfect in these points as possible. For example, if the bitch is heavy in head, then choose a stud dog with a head as near perfect as possible.

Do not fall into the trap of assuming that an overfine headed dog will offset the heavy head of the bitch. It will in all probability produce a litter of some heavy and some fine heads, with possibly no correct ones, whereas the dog with a perfect head will produce some heavy heads, but is also likely to throw some perfect ones. It is a fallacy to imagine that a mixture of extremes will produce a mean. It is also essential to study the pedigrees of the intended parents, and see as many specimens of the lines as you can.

Great care must be taken to keep stud dogs apart from bitches in season. If a dog gets the scent of an in-season bitch, his mating instincts will be aroused, and the consequent frustration will cause fretting and loss of appetite, with resultant falling off of condition as well as real misery. If a stud dog and a bitch are normally kennelled together, attempts must be made to foresee the impending season, as some bitches give off scent prior to the actual start of the season, and once the dog has become aware of this it is too late, and hurried separation is merely closing the stable door after the horse has bolted.

Bitches in season exude scent through the urine as well as from the vagina, so dogs must not be allowed to run on ground after it has been used by them. A dog that shows sexual interest in a bitch should never in any circumstances be reproved or punished. The mating instinct is a fundamental and natural one, and if it is frustrated, or associated in the dog's mind with punishment, it may well render him useless as a stud dog. There is only one remedy for this problem, and that is timely and rigid segregation, to the extent that the paths of the dog and bitch literally never cross. We not only house our in-season bitches separately, but also take them in and out by different gates and use different paths from the dogs.

Opinions vary as to the advisability of using pet dogs at stud.

Some pet owners think that it will be beneficial to their dog to allow him to mate a bitch once or on rare occasions. I very much doubt the wisdom of this dictum, as it is arguable that a single mating may arouse instincts that will only create problems for the owners, in so far as the dog may, if bitches are not provided for him, wander off in search of them. But pet owners will have to make their own decisions in this matter as I would not like to be dogmatic on the subject.

A dog intended for stud work, ideally, should have his first mating fairly young, followed by subsequent matings reasonably spaced out. The first engagement for a young dog should, if possible, be to an experienced bitch that has been mated before and has not shown any signs of being difficult. A maiden bitch that may snap and be generally uncooperative may cause serious loss of confidence in a young dog, and possibly impede his activities at stud.

After serving a bitch it is inadvisable to return a dog immediately to his kennel companions. Afghan Hound dogs are, generally speaking, amenable, and most kennels allow stud dogs to run together, but if a dog is returned at once to his kennel mates with the scent of the bitch on him, a fight may result due to the unwelcome attentions of the other dogs. It is a good practice to wash the genitals of the stud dog in a mild solution of disinfectant before ultimately returning him to his kennel.

The Brood Bitch

Choosing the brood bitch cannot be taken too seriously. I do not agree with those people who say that it is of little importance whether the brood bitch is a good specimen of the breed or not so long as she is healthy, and the stud dog is good. In dog breeding, as in most activities, one tends to get out what is put in. It therefore follows that a bitch that conforms as nearly as possible to the standard, mated to the right dog, will be more likely to produce good puppies than one with several faults. This must not be interpreted as meaning that it is not worth mating a bitch unless she is a champion, or constant winner, but it is advisable for her to be as free from faults as possible, even if she does not possess the personality and glamour that mean so much in the show world. A heavily coated bitch is not essential, but one with a very poor coat will probably throw some poor-coated puppies. The three main requirements of the brood bitch can be generalised as type, soundness, and femininity. By type, I mean a head, expression, and outline that are truly representative of the standard, even though certain individual points may not be as good as could be desired. By soundness, I mean good construction and bone, and faultless movement viewed from any angle: also a good width of loin. Femininity I think, speaks for itself. The bitch should also be certified free from hip dysplasia, or under certain circumstances a borderline case

When the choice of the brood bitch has been made, ensure that she is in first class condition. An over-fat bitch may not conceive, or may experience difficulty in whelping. Hard muscular condition is as essential for her as for the stud dog. Do not breed from a bitch over six years years old or, if a maiden, over four or five years old; in both cases take veterinary advice.

The Bitch in Season

Afghan Hound bitches usually have their first season, or oestrus, between the ages of nine and sixteen months, but it can occur earlier or later. After the first season it will recur at regular intervals of six to nine months throughout her life.

The season is divided roughly into three stages, each of approximately a week in duration. In the initial stage there is a slight and almost colourless vaginal discharge, which gradually increases and becomes bloodstained. During this stage the vulva becomes enlarged and hardens. These symptoms indicate the preparation of the uterus by a reproductive hormone to receive the fertilised eggs. The next stage brings an increase in the discharge, which has the increasing appearance of blood, and after reaching a climax, begins to lessen and becomes paler in colour towards the end of the stage, accompanied by a softening and loosening of the vulva. At this stage and during most of the third week the ovary will be shedding its eggs, and the correct time for mating will have arrived. At the end of this time the genital organs will start to subside and the season will be over on or about the twenty-first day. Fastidious bitches will keep themselves very clean during this time.

The approach of the season may be heralded by a slight mucous discharge, over-frequent urination, and constant licking of the vulva, which will be seen to be enlarged.

There is no truth in the statement that there is an overall 'right' day for mating. The right time in the season is governed by the shedding of the eggs from the ovary, and will vary with different bitches, and from season to season. Careful watch must be kept on the bitch, who will indicate clearly when this time arrives. When in the company of other dogs, male or female, she will stand rigid with her tail turned to one side, and may encourage them to mount her. If she has no kennel companions, stroking her back and hind legs will in all probability produce the same indication of her readiness. There is no truth in the widely held view that mating must wait until the coloured discharge ceases. Many bitches discharge all through the final week of their season, so no hard and fast rule can be made in this matter. It will have to be left to experience plus common sense to tell the breeder when the moment has arrived.

A bitch in season must be accommodated, not only apart from dogs, but in kennels and runs that are escape proof. While most beginners and laymen are fully aware of the persistence and ingenuity displayed by dogs in their efforts to reach a bitch in season, they are seldom prepared for the equal determination shown by bitches in season in attempting to break out to find a dog.

During this period, bitches must never be out unless on a secure lead, and, if possible, either carried away from the home or driven in a car before being allowed to touch the ground. In this way the trail of scent is broken, and the unwelcome attentions of all the dogs in the neighbourhood can be avoided. This is particularly important where the breeder lives in a populated area. Unfortunately, in Afghan Hound bitches, even meticulous segregation and care in avoiding the dogs or their runs does not always prevent them from becoming aware of their attractions. The bitches give a particular call or wail which is instantly recognised by the dogs and very soon taken up by the whole kennel. I can offer no helpful advice on the way to combat or overcome this problem, since to kennel a bitch out of earshot of the remainder of the dogs is virtually impossible for most breeders. Bear in mind that a very short period of freedom is sufficient for a bitch to be mated by any available local dog (and there will be many available at this time). If this catastrophe should occur, contact your veterinary surgeon at once (certainly within twenty-four hours) and he will give an injection to bring the bitch into full season again, and so, in all probability, avoid a litter. This remedy must not be used too often as it will most likely cause womb trouble in later life. This fact must be stressed, as some bitch owners, knowing of the treatment, tend to be careless with their bitches.

The theory of telegony (meaning that a bitch, once mated to a mongrel, will have her future litters tainted with his blood) is now definitely disproved. If an accident of this kind occurs, no fears need be entertained for any future litters. Dual conception, however, is a definite possibility. It is therefore essential to keep a bitch away from other dogs after she has been mated. If there is a further mating in the same season with another dog, there is no way of telling which dog is the sire of any of the puppies. The Kennel Club have a definite rule for these cases; it is that the names of both the dogs that have mated the bitch must appear on the pedigree.

There are many preparations on the market claiming to deter the dog from the in-season bitch. Eucalyptus and citronella are well known, but in my experience not particularly effective unless the dog is not very keen in the first place. Chlorophyll products taken internally or used for swabbing the hind portions of the bitch are better, but I would not place too much confidence in them. The latest innovation is the 'Pill' obtainable from the veterinary surgeon. It is claimed to prevent conception if the bitch should be mated. The best remedy, however, is prevention. In other words, careful and prompt segregation when the bitch shows signs of imminent season, and constant vigilance to prevent escape and access to dogs.

Some breeders will advise a double mating during the season to make more sure of conception, but normally one service is considered sufficient, unless there is any doubt about the first one.

Mating

Many books on animals begin the section devoted to mating with some rather obvious statements to the effect that mating is a perfectly natural function, arising from equally natural instincts, and should therefore require little or no human interference. While I quite agree with this, there is a danger of the novice breeder placing a little too much faith in nature, and consequently not being prepared to lend a helping hand when required.

Many matings will take place easily, and require little or no human assistance. Occasions will inevitably arise, however, when events do not go as nature intended. Bitches may be frigid and resent the advances of the dog, or, on the other hand, the dog may show no interest in the bitch, even when she has shown clearly that the time is right.

It is very important for the breeder to understand and accept the fact that dogs, like all other animals, not being machines, need a period of courtship prior to mating, and that they also show definite likes and dislikes in the choice of their sexual partners. These facts are not always appreciated, and although the local mongrel may be able to dispense with courtship and have no fastidious preferences, it will soon be clear to the novice breeder that this is by no means the general pattern of sexual behaviour.

The practice of sending bitches alone on long journeys to be served is not one to be recommended. I always accompany any bitch to the stud dog. The little extra confidence it gives her at this time is well worth while, and may even make the difference between success and failure. If it is not possible to accompany the bitch, then the utmost care must be taken to ensure a safe and comfortable journey for her. If the trip is to be by rail, a spacious and well-ventilated travelling box must be provided; one that will enable her to stand and turn round in comfort. If the journey is long, arrangements will have to be made for watering, but give the most stringent instructions to prevent her being allowed to escape, and finally ensure that she is promptly met and the neces-

sary arrangements have been made for her return. It is a good
plan to allow the bitch to sleep in the travelling box for some time
prior to the journey, so that she will become accustomed to it
before the day arrives. I must, however, stress again my objections
to sending bitches in this way as I have heard too many stories
of boxed animals being shunted into railway sidings and left
unattended for days; apart from the distress the bitch may feel,
there is also the added danger of a misguided individual who,
with the best of motives, may let the bitch out of the box, and
be unable to catch her again.

It is now becoming quite usual for stud dogs to visit the bitch,
which is in many ways a good idea, but a matter for mutual
arrangement.

When the bitch arrives at the home of the stud dog, she should
be allowed to relieve herself, after which the two dogs can be
introduced, preferably in a small run or other enclosed space.
Initially, both dogs should be kept leashed, until it has been
established that they are well disposed to each other. After they
are freed, it will be as well to leave a collar on the bitch so that
she may be the more easily controlled. If the time is right, they
should soon settle down, and the stud dog will show distinct
inclinations to mount the bitch. It is desirable at this juncture to
stand in front of the bitch and steady her by the collar. This will
prevent her from moving too soon, either during or after the
mating, and possibly injuring the dog, or if the bitch is nervous
or a maiden, will enable her to be reassured and encouraged. It is
preferable for the bitch to be held by her owner rather than by a
stranger, for obvious reasons, but unfortunately this procedure,
while giving confidence to the bitch, may be a deterrent to the
stud dog if he is at all wary of strangers.

Some difficulty may be experienced with pet bitches who are
not used to other dogs, and will thus be nervous and consequently
fractious, and uncooperative. While the bitch's owner holds her
by the head, she can be supported under the body by the dog's
owner, to prevent her sitting down, a very tiresome tactic adopted
by some bitches. If the dog owner takes up this position the stud
dog can be encouraged if he shows any signs of hesitancy in
mounting the bitch. Encouragement can be given in various

ways, either by voice or manually. A good method is to scratch the lower back, down the vertebrae. If the stud dog will not mount while the bitch is held, he may do so if they are both set free, but the bitch should be held again the moment penetration has taken place.

If the bitch persists in snapping, it may be necessary to tape her muzzle, lest she may seriously affect the future activities of the young stud dog. Taping is best done with a soft, two-inch bandage, bound round the jaws, and fastened behind the neck. If the bitch, although ready, does not move her tail to one side, this must be done for her so that the dog may penetrate. Whether a non-cooperative bitch is merely nervous and being obstinate, or is past or before her acceptance period, can be decided only by an experienced person, and the stud dog owner may be able to help here.

Under normal circumstances the dog will penetrate without undue difficulty—a smear of Vaseline will help if the bitch is maiden—and she should then become submissive, but it is important to continue holding her by the collar to prevent her moving during the mating, which might be injurious to either, or both. Difficulty in penetrating by the dog can be caused by many factors. Wide divergence in height might well be the cause: if so, this can be overcome by standing either the bitch or the dog on a slightly raised level. If there should be evidence of an organic cause, such as vaginal structure, then veterinary help should be sought. It is not good policy to persevere too long if success does not seem to be in sight. It is better to rest both dogs separately, and retire for a cup of tea, returning in about half an hour to resume the endeavour. Success is often achieved in this way.

Afghan Hound bitches have a disconcerting habit of emitting a scream at the moment of mating, which can be rather alarming if it is not expected, but it is only momentary, and they soon settle for the remainder of the union.

The period that follows penetration, when the union is taking place, and both dogs are quiescent, is known as the tie and can last for ten minutes to half an hour or even more. During this period the two are locked together and must not in any circumstances be parted, otherwise serious injury may result. Great care must be taken to keep the bitch steady, and to prevent her attempting to sit down or pull away, particularly during a long tie. Quite early in the union the dog will take his forefeet off the bitch and place them on one side of her, and then lift one hind leg over her back, thus bringing them back to back, where they will remain until the union is completed, at which time they will come apart easily and naturally. Some assistance can be given to the dog by lifting his leg into position, but this is best carried out by an experienced person, as it must be done only when the dog is ready. In this respect, if both owners are inexperienced in breeding it will be wise to ask a more experienced friend to attend the mating, whose advice and assistance will be found invaluable during the whole proceedings.

The absence of a tie, or a very short one, does not mean that conception cannot have taken place. If possible, however, if no tie has taken place, it will be advisable to repeat the mating, to the same dog, of course. Never assume that conception has not taken place and mate again to a different stud dog, as there will be no way of knowing who is the real sire of the resultant litter.

Forced matings are sometimes resorted to, due possibly to lack of time, or lack of understanding of the psychology of the dogs. This is not recommended, certainly not for the novice. Dogs will show quite natural choice, as explained earlier in this chapter, and will mate readily with some bitches while steadfastly refusing others. Any mating, however, achieved by any degree of force applied to the bitch is rape, with all its psychological and physiological effects.

Before going on to consider the problems and care of the in-whelp bitch, a word of advice on the business and financial arrangements connected with matings. The normal procedure is for a stud fee to be paid to the owner of the stud dog. This discharges all responsibilities of the bitch owner, who is then in complete ownership of the ensuing litter. I strongly advocate this method, as it is simple, direct, clear, and foolproof against misunderstandings. The other method is for the stud-dog owner to have a puppy, or possibly two puppies from the resultant litter in lieu of the stud fee. The objection to this is that the owner of the dog usually wants the first choice of the litter, and being probably more experienced, will almost always choose the best, thereby robbing the bitch owner of the cream of the litter. I cannot think of any situation more disappointing and depressing than enduring all the anxieties and tribulations of mating, whelp-ing, and rearing the litter, only to see the best puppy whisked away by someone who has contributed little or nothing in the way of time and effort. This arrangement does have the advantage of avoiding the initial outlay of cash for the stud fee, which in a well-known winning dog can be considerable. It is also helpful to the novice breeder if the breed is not selling well, as it ensures homes for one or two puppies that might otherwise be difficult to sell. It is, however, quite a pointless method if the object is to breed a good puppy to win in the show-ring oneself. There is sometimes an arrangement, a mixture of the two, in which a reduced fee is charged in addition to a single puppy, probably not the pick of the litter.

Another form of business agreement much used in dog breed-ing is known as 'breeding terms'. This refers to a situation where a bitch is either loaned or given for mating purposes, on condition the original owner has first call on one or more puppies of the litter or litters. There are many variations of this arrangement, but whatever they are, they must always be in writing. No gentle-man's agreement under any circumstances! The Kennel Club provides a form for this purpose and such details as who pays the stud fee, who pays the veterinary surgeons bills, who chooses the stud dog, what is to be done if the bitch has a singleton (one puppy only), and any others must be clearly laid down and agreed, otherwise misunderstandings and, inevitably, friction will result. The form is signed by both parties and registered at the Kennel Club.

The fee paid to the stud-dog owner is for service only, not for results. A bitch may 'miss' but if the stud dog is proven, this is not considered to be his fault. In most instances of 'missing', the stud-dog owner will offer another stud service free of charge at a future season. This, however, is a concession *not* a right. If a bitch is sent to a stud dog by transport and left overnight and fed, all expenses incurred are in addition to the stud fee and must be paid at the time of service. Owners of unproven stud dogs sometimes offer a service free of charge in order to prove the dog, or may offer to return the fee if no puppies result.

In-whelp Bitch

It is not advisable to breed from a bitch until her second season, unless her first season is very late, i.e. well over a year, in which instance mating her is unlikely to be harmful, but still not advisable. When the decision has been taken to mate a bitch, it is a good practice to worm her before the season starts, and if there is any doubt of her being free after the mating is over and conception has taken place, then a further worming is recommended about a week after the mating. It is essential that she be completely free of these parasites to avoid their transmission to the forthcoming puppies.

After mating it will be difficult to say for sure if the bitch is in whelp for some weeks. The signs are an enlarging and puckering of the teats, and the vulva remains enlarged.

Little change in the shape of the expectant mother will take place in the first few weeks of pregnancy, but gradually a thickening of the body will be noticed, with an increase in weight. In the early days she should be allowed to live a normal life with her kennel companions. The gestation period is sixty-three days, but as with humans and other mammals, it may vary slightly. If the bitch is as much as three days overdue, veterinary advice must be taken.

During the entire period of pregnancy the bitch must have regular exercise to keep her muscles in good condition, which will promote regular bowel movements, and prepare her for the effort she will need to make when the time arrives for her to deliver the puppies. As the period of gestation progresses the bitch must be protected against rough play with other dogs, to avoid injury to the pups or herself, and her whole life and exercise must be strictly supervised. She is not, however, an invalid and must not be treated like one. She must not be overtired, nor, as the pregnancy advances, should she be allowed to jump. A daily walk is essential; but allow her to make her own pace. During the final weeks the movement of the unborn puppies will be easily discernible. Do not fuss unduly, but allow nature to take its course. Keep constant supervision, and in the event of any signs of distress, loss of appetite, rise in temperature or the appearance of a dark discharge, consult your veterinary surgeon at once.

Feeding the in-whelp bitch needs constant thought and care. Normal feeding should be continued for the first month, but from then on the needs of possibly up to fifteen small bodies must be catered for, in addition to the needs of the bitch herself. Protein with its body-building qualities is of great importance during this period, and some starchy foods can be replaced by extra protein foods such as meat, fish, eggs, and cheese, but in any event do not increase the normal intake of carbohydrates. Occasional small quantities of liver are also beneficial at this time. The body needs additional minerals so that the bitch will not go short herself. Lime and phosphorous are necessary but they must be in the correct proportions. Uncontrolled quantities of each given in a haphazard fashion is not the best way. These two important items also need vitamin D to assist in their assimilation; advice from a veterinary surgeon or experienced breeder will be useful. My own opinion is that a proprietary product with the items already present and balanced is the easiest way to administer them. These extra minerals with the vitamin D should be given throughout gestation and lactation if good sound bone is to be assured in the puppies.

Bitches in whelp frequently and understandably develop large appetites. It is difficult to overfeed a bitch during this period, particularly if the food is of the right kind. Obviously her feed must be increased, but some limit must be put on her intake if she is exceptionally greedy, for she must never be allowed to become fat. Towards the end of the pregnancy the daily food must be split into two or three meals in order to avoid distending the stomach, with the resultant discomfort.

Whelping Box and Quarters

The quarters selected for the whelping should be light, clean, and disinfected. They should also be roomy enough for a human to stand and move around in, and to house the whelping box and provide quarters for the puppies to run around in as they grow. My own whelping kennel is approximately eight feet square and

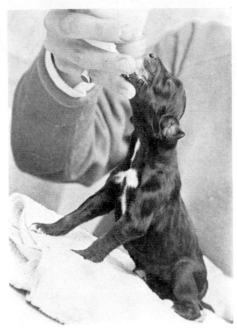

(Evening Post, Hemel Hempstead)

Bondor Busybody—15 hours old. The newly born Afghan Hound
bears little resemblance to the heavily coated adult

(Thomas Fall)

Chs. Cleopatra, Portrait, and Moonbeam of Khorrassan

Jalalabad Barwala of Carloway—dog at 10 months

Ch. Rasta of Jagai—bitch at 11 months

(*Kentish Express*)

eight feet high, with a stable-type door in two parts so that observation can be maintained by opening the top half of the door only, thus preventing the inmates from pouring out every time the door is opened. These quarters must be adequately lighted and heated, particularly for winter litters. It is essential that both the heating system and the lights are out of reach of the bitch or the puppies. The ideal temperature for a newly born family of Afghan Hounds should be about 75° Fahrenheit. An infra-red lamp, suspended about three feet above the whelping box is excellent for this purpose, and the puppies will be relaxed and contented under a direct warmth of this type. It will also allow them to benefit to the full from their food, which will not be used up in combating the cold. Puppies reared in a warm temperature will invariably do better than those brought up in the cold. It is a mistake to assume that to allow new-born pups to live in the cold and dampness is a way of hardening them. Careful and controlled hardening off can be undertaken as soon as the puppies begin to run around, but at the time of birth and for the first few days of life, warmth is of the utmost importance, even more important than food. For winter litters, hardening off must wait longer and be undertaken with great care.

The whelping box should be about three feet six inches square, with sides about eighteen inches high, enough to keep the young puppies in and the draught out, and at the same time allow the dam to step in and out with ease. Inside the box, a rail should be fitted on three sides, five or six inches from the floor and from the side. This will keep the bitch from crushing any of her family against the sides. Bitches are, on the whole, very adroit at avoiding treading on or otherwise harming their offspring, but the precaution is nevertheless very necessary. The front of the box should be in sections so that one or both sections can be removed to allow the puppies to walk in and out, or, alternatively, fixed so that they are kept in.

Some means must be provided for the dam to escape temporarily from her family if she so desires. The concentrated attention of a dozen or so small Afghan Hounds tends to be rather wearing, even to the most devoted of mothers. A small bench, just high enough to be out of reach of the puppies will be adequate for this

K

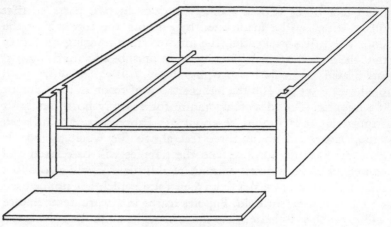

FIG 15 Whelping box
Guard rails (on back and both sides) and one of the two movable front
sections are in position

or, equally good, a flat top to the whelping box will provide the
same means of escape.

The best bedding consists of old woollen pullovers and other
old garments, and pieces of blanket. The bitch will insist on
arranging the bedding to her own pattern and liking, and on no
account must she be interfered with in this, however strange and
uncomfortable the resultant muddle may appear to human eyes.
When the soiled bedding is removed, it can be burnt. The bitch
should be encouraged to sleep in the whelping box for some time
before the whelping, so that she may become accustomed to her
surroundings, and be quite relaxed by the time the litter arrives.

Have the following articles ready for the time of birth:

Tissues
Boiled lint
Sharp, blunt-ended scissors
Brandy
Dry, clean, rough towelling
Disinfectant (T.C.P.)
Surgical thread

All the above must be scrupulously clean and disinfected.

A small box with some towelling or blankets will be useful, which, with a hot-water bottle under the blankets, can be used to place a puppy in temporarily, as explained below.

Whelping

Much well-intended, but ill-informed advice will be offered to the novice on the subject of breeding and whelping by people who claim knowledge of some sort, and the breeder will be advised to treat all this with caution. The most usual are the well-worn platitudes about 'The whole thing being perfectly natural' and 'How do you think the wild animals manage?' There is undoubtedly some truth in all this, but nature left to herself is profligate and does not count waste, being content to scrap many for the survival of a few. The conscientious breeder, however, will be anxious to rear as many sound puppies as he can, in addition to safeguarding the health and future of the dam. Nature is all very well when all goes well, but if anything goes wrong, then human help is needed and, probably, promptly. For this reason I strongly advocate the practice of staying with the bitch during whelping. I have found that bitches are sometimes very frightened at the beginning of whelping, and are much in need of reassurance. I had one who tried hard to jump on to my lap to have her puppies, presumably feeling more secure there. It would certainly be cruel and foolish to leave them unattended at this time.

I have found it convenient when a litter seems likely to arrive during the night, to put up a camp bed in the kennel and spend the night there. In this way you are on hand immediately the puppies start arriving, and it is so much easier than constantly running out to the kennel from a warm bed throughout the night. This is another good reason to have comfortable, warm breeding quarters with all modern conveniences. There can be a drawback to this arrangement if the breeder is a heavy sleeper. I normally sleep fairly lightly, but once, on returning from a 400-mile drive, I found one of my bitches showing distinct signs of an impending whelping. My camp bed was duly erected in the kennel, and I settled down to await events. As the bitch was for the moment peaceful, I lay on the bed for a moment's relaxation and, inevitably, fell asleep. I awoke in the small hours to find the bitch snuggled down by my side and three newly born puppies on my chest. The bitch, fortunately, accepted the move to the whelping box without objection and I was on duty to help deliver the next seven puppies at intervals throughout the night, before escaping for a much needed clean up.

There is, as always, the other extreme, and over-fussing and unnecessary interference with a bitch who is managing perfectly well for herself can only impede, and possibly be harmful. Do not, therefore, take a hand unless reasonably certain that help is needed.

The first indication of approaching whelping will most likely be the bitch making nests of her bedding. This may start several days or even a week before the actual arrival of the puppies. There will be a hardening and swelling of the vulva, accompanied by a discharge that increases as whelping draws near. An infallible indication of imminent parturition is the lowering of the temperature by some 3° to 4° below normal (101.5°F.). During this period there is a gradual softening and dilating of the birth passages, restlessness, and obvious signs of discomfort, with a softening of the vulva. There will also be bouts of panting interspersed with more relaxed periods. This stage can last for anything from one to twenty-four hours. The bitch will have a rather glazed look in the eyes and will almost certainly refuse food when parturition is near, although occasionally bitches will take food up to the last minute.

The second stage is when the birth passages are softened and a puppy enters the pelvis. The bitch will then have bouts of straining downwards with intermittent periods of panting, and even trembling. These periods of straining, which at first will be slight but which will increase in intensity and become more frequent up to the time of parturition, are the beginning of labour, and the time should be noted. Some bitches may have a very short labour and deliver a puppy after a few bouts of straining, others may be much longer, but if labour continues for an hour and a half or so, with no sign of the birth of a puppy, then veterinary help must be obtained.

Puppies are normally born within a membraneous sac, which also contains fluid and have the afterbirth or placenta attached to the umbilical cord; but on occasion puppies can be born without this sac. The first signs of imminent birth will be the appearance of this bag of membranes at the vulva. This will in all probability protrude during a period of straining and be slightly withdrawn in between these periods, but it will eventually be expelled during a downward strain and the puppy will be delivered, normally head first. The head being the largest part of the puppy at this time, the remainder of the body will emerge easily. If the head appears to be stuck it can be gently eased out by gripping very carefully and gently behind the head, this must be done during a straining period (contraction). At this stage puppies are very slippery and hard to grasp with the fingers, so it is advisable to use a piece of boiled lint to assist the grip. Never pull hard, and always in rhythm with the bitch's periods of straining. When the puppy emerges in its membraneous container, it will still be attached to the dam by the umbilical cord. It may sometimes happen that the sac is broken during the puppy's emergence, and the fluid will be released. If this does not occur, the bitch will break it (until she does the whelp cannot breathe), eat the afterbirth, and cut the umbilical cord near the navel with her teeth. It is perfectly natural and correct for the bitch to eat the afterbirth and she must not be restrained from doing this. After the puppy is freed from the dam she will start to lick and clean it with her tongue, turning it over and over as she does so in what may appear to be a very rough and callous manner, until it is opened out, and kicking and crying. She must not be prevented from this as it is her instinctive way to stimulate breathing and promote circulation. It is the origin of the well-known expression 'to lick into shape'.

Although the head-first arrival is the normal one, puppies may sometimes emerge in other positions, the most usual variant being the rump first, or breech birth, but this need be no cause for alarm. If assistance is given, never pull the whelp by the legs, but grip gently round its middle and ease out as already explained, in rhythm with the contractions of the bitch. If the sac should be broken during emergence, especially in a breech birth, the birth must not be delayed, otherwise there is a real danger the puppy will die of asphyxia or drowning.

It sometimes happens that a bitch will show complete indifference to her maternal duties at the birth and take no interest in the newly born litter. This is where the vigilant breeder will have to go promptly into action. If the bitch does not break the sac it must be done for her immediately, lest the puppy suffocates. It is best done by breaking it gently with the fingers in the area of the mouth to permit the immediate start of breathing. Next wait about thirty seconds to allow as much blood as possible to enter the pup from the cord, which should then be gently squeezed flat with the fingers, pressing the blood towards the pup, and then cut with sterilised scissors about half an inch from the navel, taking care to avoid cutting too close, or handling roughly, to avoid the possibility of rupture. This should obviate the necessity of tying the cord, which can be done with sterilised thread if considered necessary. Finally, rub the new-born whelp gently with a dry warm towel to stimulate breathing before returning it to the dam, who will in all probability accept it without further fuss.

If a puppy appears to be limp and lifeless at birth do not be too ready to assume that it is stillborn. Hold it in one hand and rub its back firmly up and down to stimulate life; if this is not effective, administer a few drops of brandy. In many such cases the puppy will soon show distinct signs of life, and is then best put aside in a box with a warm (not hot) water bottle under some bedding, until it is deemed safe to return it to the dam and its brothers and sisters.

Occasionally, a puppy is born without the afterbirth. I remember being very worried when I first experienced this, but it need be no cause for alarm, as the bitch will normally expel the placenta later without trouble. The straining she indulges in to bring this about can very easily be mistaken for the arrival of another puppy, but if the placenta is not expelled, the veterinary surgeon should be consulted.

Some breeders adopt the practice of taking the pups away from the bitch while she is actually engaged in the whelping, and placing them in a separate and suitably warmed box. This is because the bitch, while giving birth, may injure the earlier arrivals during her straining, and there is certainly some substance to this viewpoint. The main argument against the procedure, however, is that the dam may be unduly distressed at these removals, particularly when she hears the puppies crying, and she will then not concentrate on her job, and be more than necessarily perturbed. I find it better to place each puppy on a teat as soon as it is clear, if it has not already found one for itself. This usually tends to quieten and relax the dam during intervals between deliveries. It is essential if this is done to be in constant attendance and, during an actual birth, to place the earlier arrivals to one side out of harm's way. The temperament of the bitch is a very important factor in deciding between these two methods.

There is no fixed or regular interval between the birth of puppies in a litter. Some may be separated by only a few minutes, while others may be an hour apart. Do not be alarmed at a fairly long interval provided the bitch is restful and not in any distress. An occasional drink of warm milk with glucose can be given, and even a teaspoonful of brandy if there are signs of exhaustion. If there is an unduly long period without a birth even though the bitch is straining regularly (say an hour or so), then the veterinary surgeon should be called as there may be a misplaced puppy.

Sometimes, when there is very little time between the births, the bitch may not have completed the separation and release of one puppy before the arrival of the next. This could mean that one of them is left too long before being released from the sac, and so suffocate; also, if the cord is not severed and the puppy is dragged around, an umbilical hernia may result. Umbilical hernias are not uncommon in dogs. The causes can be many, the bitch biting the cord too close to the navel, or dragging the puppy by the cord, as explained above, are examples. If the swelling is small, it can be ignored, but larger swellings are best treated surgically by the veterinary surgeon.

It is often difficult to decide with certainty when the last of a litter has arrived, but when the breeder considers the operation to be complete, the bitch can be taken out for a short spell to relieve herself. Meanwhile the soiled bedding can be removed and replaced with fresh, so that the nest will be clean and ready for her return, which will not be long delayed if she has her way. Indeed, some bitches show a strong reluctance to leave the nest during the first few days after whelping, and must be taken out on a lead, at regular intervals, to relieve themselves.

The teats in the area of the groin usually yield more milk than those on the brisket. The strong and the gluttonous puppies will usually fight their way to the most productive teats, while the weaker will be left with the remainder. Try to obviate this, but it is often difficult, as a litter cannot be supervised all the time.

Some bitches are excessively maternal and will become frenzied if their puppies are removed for even a moment or so, while others seem devoid of normal maternal feelings and are comparatively indifferent to their families. There are those who look with obvious distaste at their offspring and will refuse to feed them. This may be due to the fact that the bitch has no milk, which also calls for veterinary help. In the event of a bitch not feeding her litter, immediate steps must be taken to provide for the hungry mouths. The obvious and most desirable remedy is a foster mother, if one can be obtained. The veterinary surgeon may be able to help, or local kennels can be contacted and other friends and acquaintances may be able to help. The canine press on occasions carry advertisements offering foster mothers.

The bitch to be used as a foster parent need not, of course, be of the same breed as the puppies, and need not be a thoroughbred, as long as her milk is good. She must, however, be healthy, free from infection and parasites, and come from a clean and reputable home or kennel. On one occasion, when an Afghan bitch of mine could not manage all her litter, I put three of the pups to a miniature poodle bitch who had whelped at approximately the same time. She took the little Afghan Hounds along with her own family and did them all very well; there was certainly no difference between them and their brothers and sisters who had been reared by the mother.

In a kennel where there are other bitches, some may start to give milk when they become aware of the newly arrived litter, even though they may not have been mated themselves. There is no reason why they cannot be co-opted to take on some puppies if necessary.

If it does not prove possible to find some form of foster parent for puppies whose mother will not, or cannot, feed them, then there is no alternative but for the breeder to rear the litter by hand, feeding initially by means of a fountain-pen filler or some other form of dropper, and later progressing to a bottle and teat. Or starting straight away with a small teat. This is a stupendous undertaking, and great strength of mind is needed to cull the litter down to a manageable size. The advice of an experienced friend or veterinary surgeon will be essential in this case, as also the help, if possible, of a friend to share the two hourly feeds day and night. I have only reared one litter this way, and I sincerely hope there will not be another. The breeder is literally confined to the kennels for days unless there are several people to share the work. There is, as always, a reward for all this labour in the contemplation of a healthy litter of puppies that would otherwise have been lost.

The best substitute for bitch's milk is goat's milk, which, with its high fat and mineral content, and comparative freedom from T.B. is far superior for puppies to cow's milk in its natural state. Cow's milk can be enriched by the addition of a full-cream dried milk; your veterinary surgeon will advise in this matter. Whichever milk is given, it must be slightly warm (i.e. the bitch's body temperature).

TABLE OF MILK ANALYSIS IN PERCENTAGES

	Fats	Casein	Albumen	Sugar	Ash	Total Solids	Water
Bitch	10	6	5	3.1	0.7	24.8	75.2
Cow	3.7	3	0.5	5	0.7	12.9	87.1
Goat	5	3.2	1	4.5	0.7	14.4	85.6

When the whelping is completed, the inevitable question arises as to how many are to be kept. If the litter is small there will be no problem, but a large litter is too much for one bitch to rear unaided. Bitches will vary in their capacity to rear litters, but I usually consider eight puppies to be enough, if they are all to have the best chance. Remember that a small litter, well nourished, with every pup in top condition, is far better than a larger litter undersized and ill-nourished. To keep every one of a large litter, to avoid destroying what might possibly have been a good puppy can therefore be a fallacy. Some countries impose a compulsory reduction in litters, but in Britain it is left to the breeder. Some breeders are opposed to destroying a healthy puppy however many the dam may produce, and I respect, although I do not agree, with this point of view. If, however, the full litter is kept, it will almost always necessitate help from the breeder as previously described. The decision as to how many puppies to run on will have to be taken on the spot by the breeder, who alone knows all the factors.

Before any final course is decided on, the litter must be examined for malformations, and if any are found they must be put aside for the veterinary surgeon to put down. It is not wise to make a definite decision as to culling for two days or so, as some of the whelps may die or become casualties in spite of constant care, thus reducing the litter without calling on the breeder to make a decision.

To reduce the chance of casualties in the new-born pups, it is wise to cut the bitch's coat short before whelping. If this precaution is not taken, the hair mats and becomes tangled, which in addition to being insanitary tends to form loops in which the pups can be caught by the head and neck, so that when the dam stands up they are quite literally hanged. I have seen this depressing sight too often to risk trying to save the bitch's coat, which she will in all likelihood lose anyway.

After the delivery of her family, the dam may suffer from diarrhoea for a few days, which will probably be black in colour, due to the blood she has consumed when eating the placenta, but it should soon clear up, and the motions become normal. There will also be a vaginal discharge for about a week, which is quite normal. If this discharge should become yellow in colour due to the presence of pus, then veterinary help is required at once. It is also a sensible precaution to keep a check on the bitch's temperature which, after a slight rise following the whelping, will return to normal (101.5°F.) within four days. Keep a watch on the bitch in case she shows signs of restlessness or distress, which will indicate that all is not well.

For the first few days the nursing bitch must be fed on milk and milky foods, but then she must be returned to a full diet of protein foods as soon as she will take it as previously described, with the possible addition of Lactagol or some similar preparation to promote milk production. It is best to give the bitch her food in two or three meals a day.

Sometimes a new-born puppy will persist in crying, and nothing seems able to stop it. This distressing condition usually indicates some internal trouble, possibly injury during birth, and there is normally little that can be done, although medical opinion should be sought. In these cases the bitch often seems to realise this, and will throw the puppy out of the nest however many times it is returned to her. To the human mind this seems cruel, but her instinct tells her that there is no hope of rearing the unfortunate pup.

If the puppies seem unable to relax, appearing fretful and going from teat to teat uttering plaintive and incessant cries, it is a sign that the bitch is not supplying enough milk. Have her checked by the veterinary surgeon and be prepared to supplement the feed three or four times a day with a fountain-pen filler or bottle and teat, as already described.

There is a condition known as fading, in new-born puppies, where they cease to make progress and gradually fade and die if not given prompt medical attention. If this is suspected, send for the veterinary surgeon at once.

Finally, if it is decided to put puppies down, never attempt to destroy them yourself. This can cause quite unnecessary suffering. Send for the veterinary surgeon, who is better equipped both in knowledge and equipment to carry out this sad little task as painlessly and efficiently as possible.

Weaning

Weaning is a gradual process, and as it proceeds the bitch's food will have to be equally gradually returned to normal.

As early as three weeks old, the pups should start their lapping lessons. This is not weaning proper, but it is essential because although some puppies will lap automatically without tuition, others need much time and great patience in order to teach them this simple function. For the first week or so of their lives, puppies' eyes are closed, and they do not hear, but these senses gradually manifest themselves. Initially they will simply crawl about the whelping box, but in about three weeks they will get to their feet and begin to stagger around. The bitch should be able to feed a reasonably sized litter unaided for these first three weeks, but after that time the breeder must be prepared to assist, and this is the time for the first lapping lessons. Put some warm goat's milk or suitably enriched cow's milk into a saucer, hold the pup on the knees, and dip its nose into the saucer. Some will lap at once, others will put up a spirited resistance, but they will all come to it sooner or later, in spite of much spluttering and bubble blowing. This procedure, starting twice a day, can be gradually increased with the addition of a cereal food such as Farex. At this stage, the puppies will become quite active, and the bitch will take to leaving them alone for considerable periods.

At approximately four weeks old, they may be introduced to meat. This should be offered, finely scraped and raw, preferably beef, but not knacker meat. Given in very small quantities at first, it can be gradually increased. Most pups will take to it instantly, but if they seem reluctant, put a small pellet of scraped meat in their mouths and they will soon get the right idea and all too rapidly become meat addicts. The meat feeds must be given in addition to the milk feeds. The dam must still be allowed to feed them when she wishes during the day, and she will be sleeping with them, too, at night. The puppies will now be allowed the run of the kennel from the whelping box, and the bitch, tiring of their attentions, will be sitting on her bench or the lid of the box for increasing periods. The first sharp little teeth will be appearing, probably making feeding something of an ordeal for her. By the time they are five weeks old they should be on a fairly varied diet as the dam's milk supply will be on the wane. At this point an extra milky meal can be introduced, and also some biscuit meal, possibly in lieu of the Farex, and they can also be introduced to some calcium vitamin supplement, as outlined earlier. The whole process of weaning must be carried out gradually because too violent alterations to diet will cause upset stomachs and diarrhoea.

At six weeks the pups will be having about five meals a day, one or two meat meals, and four meal or milk meals. Also, at about this time the dam will start to regurgitate her part-digested food for her offspring. This is a perfectly natural function, and I was surprised to read in a well-known book on dogs that the author considered it should be stopped on the grounds that it was 'disgusting'. No natural function, if it is understood, can possibly be disgusting, but there are grounds for attempting to control this practice since the bitch will be depriving herself of much-needed nourishment in favour of her puppies, who will already be adequately fed. It is also a sign that the youngsters are ready for a more varied diet. If she does seem to be overindulging in this practice, it can sometimes be prevented by holding her head up while she is feeding her family, but many experienced breeders do not believe in interfering with something that is perfectly natural. While the dam is indulging in regurgitation, it is a sound precaution to cut her food into very small pieces, so that if it is brought up and swallowed by the pups they will not choke. For the same reason she must not be given food that might be harmful to the puppies.

Also at six weeks, the dam will show even less enthusiasm for the company of her offspring, and should be apart from them during the day, except when she obviously wishes to feed or play with them. She will still, however, be sleeping with them at night.

At eight weeks the puppies should be completely weaned, and free from their mother. In many breeds this would be a reasonable time to sell to a new home, but I consider that Afghan Hounds, who develop much more slowly than most dogs, should not leave their brothers and sisters until they are at least ten weeks old.

Care of Puppies

The newly born Afghan Hound will normally weigh approximately a pound, and will increase rapidly in both size and weight. At eleven or twelve months it will usually have reached its full height, but not its final weight and proportions. These factors will continue to develop and alter for a considerable time after puppyhood. And it is quite usual for this breed not to reach full maturity for two or three years. Large litters will tend to consist of smaller puppies at birth than smaller litters.

For the first ten weeks of their life the dam will take complete control of the litter, which will need virtually no extra care from the breeder, apart from constant vigilance, to ensure that they all receive fair shares of food and keep in good health. Bitches will almost always permit their owners to handle and attend the puppies at any time, but many will strongly resent any interference from strangers or other dogs. Some will become quite vicious if an unknown person even approaches the vicinity of their family.

Puppies should be played with by humans as soon as possible. Young dogs need affection as much as young children, and lack of it has much the same consequences in both.

The removal of dew-claws is optional in the standard, but I advocate their removal. This must be done by a veterinary surgeon in the first three or four days of their life.

Until such time as the puppies run about on a hard surface and wear their nails down, they will have to be trimmed at regular intervals from the age of about one week. These sharp, hooked little talons can, if unchecked, cause injuries to the bitch and the other puppies, sometimes being responsible for the bitch refusing to feed her litter. Clipping the nails is a simple job and can be carried out with an ordinary pair of nail scissors, but great caution must be exercised to avoid cutting into the quick. Only the points must be cut.

The eyes of newly born puppies, as stated earlier, are closed and will remain so for about ten days: when they first open they must not be subjected to strong light.

The living quarters should have an adequate, outside enclosed run attached to them, with, preferably, a hard surface, concrete being in my opinion the best because it keeps the nails worn down and is easy to wash and keep clean. While the pups have been living with their mother, she will have done all the clearing up of faeces etc., but when they are on their own this task falls to the owner, and the output from a litter of ten or more can be quite astonishing. Most Afghan Hounds are naturally fastidious and will soon show a marked reluctance to foul their beds and kennels. This trait can be encouraged as the first steps in house or kennel training.

It is very rare for a litter to be free from worms and worming can be undertaken at about six weeks and again in about another ten days if necessary. If infestation is heavy and obvious, the worming can be done even earlier than six weeks. The signs of worms will soon be learnt by the new breeder. They are: loss of condition, i.e. poor coat, and diarrhoea, a tendency to distended or 'pot' bellies after food (that is, beyond the ordinary pleasing rotundity of the well fed), and a general lack of normal progress and inability to increase in weight. Most obvious and reliable sign of all is the passing of worms in the motions. The most usual infestation in puppies is by round worms, which resemble small light coloured earthworms with a tendency to form themselves into coils. Never worm a litter, or indeed an adult dog with proprietary remedies sold over the counter. Always discuss your worming problems and subsequent programme with your veterinary surgeon, who will prescribe a suitable remedy. The modern worming methods, which are such an advance on the old-fashioned ways, no longer rely on violent purgatives, nor do they require the period of fasting prior to dosing that characterised the older methods. Most remedies will be in tablet or capsule form, and it is imperative that each pup has its proper dose. The mouth must be opened—a gentle pressure of the finger and thumb each side of the jaw will accomplish this—and the tablet or capsule placed on the tongue, well to the back, after which the mouth must be held closed until the medicine has been swallowed. Puppies and dogs generally are very clever at hiding tablets in their mouths and expelling them later when they think they are unobserved. So make absolutely sure, by observation, that the dose has really gone down. It is also a wise precaution to stay with the pups for a while in case any of them vomit and lose their dose. If this is not seen it will be impossible to tell which has been wormed and which has not. The results of the treatment will probably appear during the next twenty-four hours in the form of dead worms passed by the pups. Finally, never sell a puppy that has not been wormed.

In conclusion, before the final decision to breed is taken, be absolutely sure that the reasons are sound and the aims clear cut.

Never breed because you think it might be amusing for the children to have some puppies to play with.

. Never breed because you think it might be good for the bitch, or possibly prevent future false pregnancies—it won't!

Never breed to make money. I am convinced that if the dam and litter are properly fed and cared for with correct medical supervision and attention, this is an improbability.

Never breed primarily for coat, either in quantity or colour. It is conformation that matters, first and all the time. The coat is merely a garnishing for the structure underneath and must never be an end in itself. The pursuit of colour, if it is allowed to take precedence over conformation, can be disastrous.

Finally, never breed from nervous stock, however good the specimens may be physically. The old wives' tale that a nervous bitch will improve after a litter, or that a nervous dog will be less so after serving a bitch is complete nonsense. All that will happen is that more nervous puppies will be born to live wretched lives, and possibly pass the affliction on to yet another generation.

No breeder of any form of livestock should ever breed from stock known to be unsound mentally or physically, or which is known to carry hereditary abnormalities. They should, in fact, be prepared to make sacrifices, financial or otherwise, rather than do this.

A constant criticism of show-dog breeders is the fact that they pursue physical perfection without considering mental attributes, and this is certainly true. Perfection in either is extremely hard to achieve, while perfection in both is so rare as to be, for all practical purposes, impossible. However, when making breeding plans consider the psychological as well as the purely physical, so that our breed will never degenerate into glamorous neurotic hairdresser's dummies.

As with humans, early environment and care play an important part in the mental and physical development of young animals. Puppies that have been correctly fed, housed, and reared, and have established the right relationships with human beings and other dogs, will have a better chance of a happy and healthy life when they grow up.

American, German, Belgium, Dutch Ch. Ophaal v.d. Orange Manege of Crowncrest (*right at 9 years old*). This unique pair of photographs reveals the true balance and conformation beneath the glamorous coat of a top-class Afghan Hound.

American Ch. Shirkhan of Grandeur

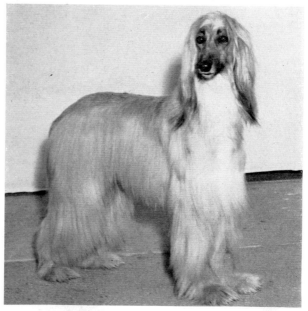

American Ch. Barberryhill Dolly

8

Shows and Showing

AFGHAN owners enter the show world in one of two ways. On the one hand, they may be one of those fortunate people who acquire a puppy with no thought beyond the pleasure of owning a glamorous and fascinating dog, but who subsequently find out that they have unwittingly become possessed of a specimen good enough to show. On the other hand, they may have set out with the deliberate intention of buying a dog for the purpose of entering the show-ring. The first category depends entirely on luck, and it is to be hoped that they will appreciate their good fortune and while enjoying their successes realise that they have still much to learn, and take care that their easy early successes do not spoil them for the inevitable setbacks that will surely come when they breed or acquire new stock.

The second category, however, can take conscious steps to increase their chances of acquiring a good dog, although even here the element of luck is not entirely absent. The prospective owner of the show dog should take every opportunity of visiting dog shows and learning all he can by talking to exhibitors and breeders of experience. He should also observe the dogs that are given awards by responsible judges. While it will soon be obvious that different judges, however experienced, will have widely divergent preferences, no competent judge should ever give a high award to a bad dog. It must be stressed that however hard and diligently the would-be exhibitor follows this advice, if he does not possess a reasonable eye for a dog, no amount of instruction can put it there, although it can, in a limited way, be developed. This does not mean that by serious study and application a knowledge of the various points required by the standard cannot be acquired; the purchase of the first show dog can with this background be approached, if not with the certainty born of experience, at least with some hope of success. I make no excuse

L

here for repeating the platitude that there is no short cut to experience. It is clearly not possible to learn everything in a few months, and only after years of experience is it possible to pick a good puppy with any degree of certainty (*see* Chapter 5). If, however, the new exhibitor can make his debut in the ring with, if not a flyer, at least a good sound typical hound, he will have little cause for complaint.

A word of caution at this point: prospective buyers of dogs should be wary when taking advice from breeders with stock for sale. Advice received from these sources may well be biased in favour of their own dogs. It is generally speaking better to take advice from more disinterested people, although it must be added that some breeders are scrupulously fair in this way.

Having acquired the dog, the first step towards showing is to make sure that it is registered at the Kennel Club. In all probability this will have been done by the breeder before sale, in which case a transfer is required to record the change of ownership. Forms for both registration and transfer can be obtained from the Kennel Club for a small charge. It is possible that the Registration Certificate and transfer form will be handed over with the pedigree by the breeder at the time of purchase. A Class I registration at the Kennel Club is possible only when both parents are registered. It is most important to understand that while the transfer is the official recognition by the Kennel Club of a change of ownership, it is not recognised in civil law as proof of ownership. Failure to comprehend this simple fact has caused much waste of time, money, and emotion in doggy circles.

If it is desired to enter a dog at a show while awaiting the completed registration or transfer forms, it is permissible to do so by affixing the letters N.A.F. (name applied for) or T.A.F. (transfer applied for) after the name of the entry.

Training for Show

No dog may be shown under Kennel Club regulations under the age of six months. This does not mean that training for the show ring cannot begin much earlier. It is essential for the novice exhibitor to understand that no judge, however competent, can assess the merits of a dog if it is so boisterous and uncontrolled that the handler is virtually flying it like a kite at the end of the lead; or if it is so slovenly that it will neither stand nor move without being dragged or supported by its handler. This is a state of affairs seen far too frequently in the puppy classes at all types of dog shows, clearly indicating that no steps have been taken at all to prepare the young entrant for its first appearance in competition in public. There is no excuse for this, as dogs are essentially creatures of habit, and with reasonable trouble and understanding it is incredible how quickly they come to realise what is expected of them in the show-ring.

The first step with a very young puppy is to train it to walk on a lead. At first, the raw youngster will fight back, and even roll on the ground in a frantic endeavour to free itself from the new and unpleasant restriction to its freedom. While doing this it will probably emit blood-curdling screams that will convince everyone within earshot that you are inflicting unspeakable tortures on it. This is only one of the many crosses that will have to be borne in the process of becoming a seasoned Afghan exhibitor. It is important in the early stages to associate the lead with something pleasurable. We always carry our very young puppies from the kennel to the grass exercise runs, a daily trip that they all enjoy. At about three and a half to four months we start to walk them up on a lead. They quickly realise that the lead is connected with the trip to the runs, which to them is sheer pleasure, so the desire to arrive at the destination overcomes a tendency to fight the new restriction. Of course, it is not the same thing when the time arrives for the return journey, unless this happens to coincide with feeding time, but the ice will have been broken, and with patience and determination they soon accept the lead without undue fuss. Do not indulge in tugs of war which may harm the pup or set it back rather than improve it; coax all the time rather than use force.

The next stage can be carried out concurrently with the lead training: this is teaching the prospective show dog to stand. It is quite contrary to the normal instincts and desires of any young creature to be still. Some dogs, however, will stand perfectly still and steady at a very tender age, while others will be fidgets most of their lives. This is purely a matter of temperament, but training in the form of endless patience, understanding and guile on the part of the owner will stand the puppy in good stead when he enters the ring. I find that going through the routine of grooming, i.e. standing the pup on a table and holding it still with one hand (with or without a lead) while gently brushing it with the other, is something it enjoys, and without apparently realising it stands still. If this routine is repeated daily for short periods, the sight of the grooming brush will be automatically connected in the puppy's mind with standing still, possibly because it relishes the attention it is being given. I have had Afghan Hounds that, on sight of my approach holding a brush, automatically jumped on to the nearest table and stood waiting. This is only one example of how a little thought and guile can assist in training. New owners will undoubtedly work out methods and ruses of their own.

The next major requisite of a show dog is that it must become accustomed to noise and crowds and to being handled by human beings. This part of the preparation for showing may be difficult for busy owners who live in isolated areas, but it is essential if the dog is to stand and move in a ring surrounded by crowds, and to stand relaxed while being handled by the judge. It is a good idea to utilise one's friends and other visitors to the kennel by asking them to run their hands over the new youngster whenever possible, so that it becomes accustomed to handling by strangers, with the result that the judge at the first show will be no surprise to it. Country dogs should be acclimatised to populated areas. Efforts must be made associate human contacts with pleasure in the puppy's mind. Dogs who only experience strange humans when visiting the veterinary surgeon can hardly be blamed for assuming that all human beings conceal hypodermic needles up their sleeves.

It is essential to understand that puppies, like children, are highly volatile, and cannot maintain interest for long periods. Lessons, therefore, must be short and often, lest the pupil become stale, and more harm than good ensue. As with the training of all young things, patience is the one all-important attribute needed by the teacher. The use of titbits can be usefully employed with some dogs as an aid to training, and as an inducement to move and stand in an alert manner. A rabbit's foot, or something similar, is used by some exhibitors to good account. The owner who knows and understands his dog will quickly work out ways and means of bringing out the best results. The good handler establishes a sympathetic relationship with his dog in the same way that a good horseman becomes one with his horse, developing a bond that is something special to them alone.

Finally, it must be understood and accepted that dogs, like humans, vary considerably in temperament and character. Some will—almost without training—stand perfectly, move gaily when required, and generally conduct themselves exactly as the handler wishes. These, the extroverts, we call 'born showers', and lucky is the exhibitor who possesses one. Conversely, there are those that obviously loathe every moment in the show, that crawl up and down on the move, refuse to stand still for the judge's appraisal, and present a picture of dejection and misery that completely belies their normal gay and happy behaviour at home. The owner will have to decide at some stage whether it is worth persevering with dogs of this type. If no progress is made after endless time and patience, it is better to abandon showing it, as it can only produce frustration, exasperation, and useless financial loss.

There is also hereditary nervousness. When the sufferer is a dog of beautiful conformation and type, the owner is prompted to persevere hopelessly in the show-ring long after the time when common sense and experience dictate the acceptance of defeat. It is, after all, better for the breed that such dogs should not win or be used for breeding, quite apart from consideration for the mental agony that these unfortunate animals undergo when being forced to endure experiences that, to them, are sheer terror. I have heard breeders, who profess concern for, and interest in, their breed, say: 'This bitch is too nervous to do any good in the show-ring, I shall retire her, and breed from her'. Such reasoning appals me.

It must be mentioned here that not all nervousness is hereditary. Sometimes the trouble can be traced to some unfortunate happening, or bad early environment. In these cases time, gentleness and patience can work a complete cure.

Finally, in training a puppy never, never lose your temper.

Remember that dogs, like children, are essentially logical; everything they do (or do not do) has for them a very sound reason. It is for the owner to so understand and penetrate the mind of the dog that these reasons become discernable. In short, it is necessary to be a dog psychologist.

Bathing

Before the day of the show it is usually advisable to bath your dog, particularly if it is light in colour. This is best carried out by standing the dog in the bath and using a hand shower attachment fitted to the taps. Great care must be taken to ensure that the flow of water is adjusted to the right temperature before applying it to the dog, otherwise scalding is likely, which will certainly put it off bathing forever. Having thoroughly soaked the coat, apply a good veterinary shampoo and work up a lather with the hands. When this has been done, rinse thoroughly until all trace of the shampoo has disappeared. Repeat this process a second time. Afterwards, excess water can be removed by towelling, and the final drying can be helped with a hand hair-dryer, or by allowing the dog to run in the sun and fresh air. It is advisable to complete the drying process by brushing while there is still some dampness in the coat. It is not good to bath an Afghan too often, and care must be taken in choosing a good veterinary shampoo. Detergents must not be used.

Grooming

Grooming is by no means limited to dogs who are about to be exhibited at a show. To keep an Afghan's coat in good condition it is essential first to keep the dog in good health. All the grooming in the world will not transform a scrappy, unhealthy coat into a glamorous healthy one. Opinions vary as to how often an Afghan Hound should be groomed. I have found that a thorough grooming approximately once a week is far better than short bouts of ineffectual dabbing at the surface of the coat daily. After much experimenting I have also found the best equipment to be a Mason Pearson brush—preferably nylon and bristle—and a simple metal canine comb, with the addition of a pair of blunt-ended scissors to be used rarely in cases of emergency. It is best to begin brushing with the coat slightly damp. This can be done after a bath, before the coat is completely dry, or by spraying with water or a suitable coat dressing. Brushing a bone-dry coat is likely to cause the hair to break, and consequently damage the coat. Individuals will work out their own sequence of working over the dog. Some owners like to work with the dog lying on its side, others—and I am one—prefer to stand the dog on a table of suitable height and to work round it in this way. The coat should be brushed gently but firmly in layers, carefully unravelling and teasing out mats and tangles (taking care not to cause discomfort by tugging and pulling at matted hair). It will sometimes be found advisable to abandon the brush and comb and use the fingers to unravel tangles that are very obstinate, and in the last resort, if the matting and felting has gone too far, to use the scissors and cut the mat completely away. If possible, cut the mat with the grain of the coat and tease apart. This operation must be carried out with great care as it is easy to cut the skin if the mat is very close to the body, particularly if the dog is struggling or fidgeting, in which event it is helpful to have an assistant to hold the dog steady while the scissors are in use.

Mats can occur anywhere on the Afghan Hound, but are particularly prone to the chest, between the forelegs, in the groin, and on the feet. I have found that it pays to wash the feet of my hounds nightly during wet and muddy weather—this can easily be done by dipping them into a bucket of water—otherwise the mud and hair form into a solid mass that can be removed only by cutting the hair away.

The comb should be used with caution and sparingly, but is useful to put finishing touches to a coat that has already been well treated with the brush.

Finally, never, ever brush a muddy dog. Always remove the mud by washing first.

The regular grooming period provides an excellent opportunity to examine the skin and coat for signs of pests such as lice and fleas. They can be quickly spotted in this way, and if promptly dealt with by using one of the many efficient remedies on the market, the danger of a serious infestation can be avoided. Lice and fleas are both sources of disease, and must be eliminated.

Ears can also be examined for cleanliness and freedom from mites. Always treat ears with great care and do not probe inside.

There is no stigma connected to the possession of these visitors; dogs from the most meticulous homes can easily pick them up at shows and elsewhere.

Grooming for a show is no different essentially from the normal process described above, except, of course, that a greater degree of glamour is desired, and consequently more time must be spent on the operation. If the regular grooming programme has been faithfully adhered to it should not be too arduous a task to bring the coat up to show standard. Be sure to do all this before the show, so that if you are late in arriving, or restricted in space at the venue, you will have only the final touches to apply before entering the ring.

The Show

As soon as the new puppy has passed six months and the decision to exhibit has been taken, it will be necessary to find a suitable show for its debut. In this, the advice of more experienced friends in dogs can be most helpful, and the canine press gives full details of forthcoming shows. It is a rule of the Kennel Club that a puppy must not be entered under a judge from whom it has been purchased until a period of twelve months from the date of sale has elapsed. There are four types of shows held under Kennel Club authority. They are:

Sanction Shows

This is the smallest show at which entrants are required to be registered at the Kennel Club, and are restricted to members of the organising society or club. These shows are open to entries from dogs that are eligible for classes up to post-graduate, i.e. which have not won five or more prizes of £1 or more in postgraduate or higher classes. This type of show, of course, excludes all challenge certificate winners. Both the entries and prize money are lower than other types of shows. The sanction show is an ideal training ground for new entrants but, unfortunately, few societies run them these days.

Limited Shows

This is one up the scale from the sanction show, but is also limited to members of a club and to dogs that have not won a challenge certificate. The prize money and entrance fees are more than those of a sanction show, but less than those of an open or championship show.

Open Shows

These shows are, as their name implies, open to all people and all dogs whatever they have won. This type of show will usually provide several classes for your breed, and the larger ones will be benched. That is, the exhibit will be confined to a bench that bears its number when not in the ring or being exercised. The prize money will be at least £1 for a first prize, and the win of a first prize at an open show counts one point towards a junior warrant (referred to under Titles and Awards).

Championship Shows

This is the largest and most comprehensive type of show. More classes will usually be scheduled for your breed than at any other kind of show, but most important, the Kennel Club challenge certificate for best dog and best bitch is offered only at this type of show: three such certificates, under three different judges entitles a dog to be called a champion (see Titles and Awards). Prize money is higher than for other types of show (£2 for a first), as also are entry fees.

Another type of show that is not restricted to dogs registered at the Kennel Club is the exemption show. This is open to all, including mongrels, and wins are not taken into account when entering shows under Kennel Club rules. They are usually held in conjunction with fêtes etc., and are not really intended for the serious show competitor, although they can be useful practice for a new young puppy. Some exhibitors do enter this type of show with a winning dog on a purely pot-hunting basis, and I have even seen show champions entered, but it is very bad form and not to be encouraged.

Kennel Club Titles and Awards

Champion. Three challenge certificates for best of sex in breed, won under three separate judges, gives the recipient the title of champion. Champion dogs can still be entered at championship and open shows, but are confined to the open class. There is no limit to the number of challenge certificates that may be won by an individual dog, neither is it against the rules to win more than one certificate from the same judge, although this is not a usual practice.

On the challenge certificate the judge signs a statement to the effect that the exhibit is, in his opinion, of such outstanding merit as to be worthy of the title of champion. If, in his opinion there is no exhibit that fulfils this requirement, he may, and indeed should, withhold the award.

Junior Warrant. This is an award introduced by the Kennel Club just prior to the Second World War to give some recognition to young winning dogs up to eighteen months. It is awarded on a points system, 25 points are needed to qualify—awarded as follows: 1 point for a first prize at an open show, 3 points for a first at a championship show. This award is sometimes criticised on the grounds that it may cause young dogs to be overshown in a frantic endeavour to obtain the requisite number of points before time runs out; unlike the seeker after challenge certificates which has its whole lifetime to qualify.

There is not much foundation for this criticism, as a young fit dog who enjoys shows cannot take harm from a fairly concentrated bout of showing of, say, one or two shows a week for a limited period. The only real harm may be that he becomes stale, and the owner should be quick to discern this and ease up accordingly.

Having selected a suitable show from the above varieties, write to the secretary for a schedule, which will contain full details of place, time, classes, and prize money but, most important, accompanying it will be an entry form which calls for certain information about the exhibit such as name, breed, date of birth, parents, and the numbers of the classes it is desired to enter. The normal classes for a puppy are: Special Puppy (for ages six to nine months) and Puppy (ages six to twelve months). It is permissible to enter a puppy in Junior (ages under eighteen months) or indeed any other adult class, but for the beginner I would not recommend this. Fill in the entry form clearly and accurately, noting carefully the date of closure for entries, and send it off with the entry fees to the secretary of the association organising the show. Don't forget to sign and date the form. Failure to complete entry forms correctly causes endless extra work and delays for the already over-burdened show secretary.

It is helpful if the prospective exhibitor can visit some shows prior to entering, in order to gain some knowledge of the procedures adopted by judges. They are briefly as follows:

1. To move all dogs in the class round the ring two or three times with the judge in the centre. This is valuable in loosening up the dogs and enables the judge to make an overall preliminary assessment.
2. To examine and handle all the exhibits individually including the 'bite', which the judge will probably ask the handler to show by parting the dog's lips.
3. To move the exhibits individually away from and towards the judge, to assess fore and hind action.
4. To move the exhibits individually past the judge to give a side view, from which length of stride and propulsive power of quarters and general balance can be judged.
5. To make final choice from the exhibits posed at the standstill position.

There is no fixed procedure laid down for judges, but most will follow some variation of the above.

To handle a dog successfully in the show-ring it is essential to have a clear mental picture of the ideal, with an equally clear knowledge of where one's own exhibit fails. Pose the dog as advantageously as possible; fig. 14d (page 87) gives an indication of the correct position. It is useful to practice in front of a mirror.

In handling your dog in the show-ring, be as unobtrusive as possible, while remaining in complete control, and never stand between the judge and your dog. Handlers should avoid flapping coats or other garments likely to obstruct the judge's view of the dog. When asked to move, keep at a steady controlled pace (every dog has a pace that suits it best, and you will have decided on this when training and practising). Move in a straight line away from and towards the judge. It is difficult to judge fore and hind action if the exhibit moves diagonally across the ring. Avoid flashy or 'gimmicky' handling techniques, such as holding the tail up at the standing position (unnatural and ugly) and stringing the dog up by the neck, as in terriers. Keep the dog on a slack lead if possible, and allow it to assume a natural movement and stance. Concentrate on the job in hand all the time and watch the judge and stewards so that their requests can be instantly complied with.

A few points for the day of the show. Provide yourself with a roomy bag or holdall to contain a rug for the bench, grooming equipment (brushes, etc.), a towel in case of a wet walk from the car park, water bowl, some titbits as an aid to showing, if used, a collar and bench chain, and a suitable show lead. Usually a lead of the slip variety is preferred, but this is an individual choice, as long as the show lead used is as unobtrusive as possible and does not spoil the outline of the neck. Never use a collar in the ring. Some exhibitors take a midday meal for their dogs, but I do not do this as my dogs always eat better in their own home, and a long wait for a meal does no harm to a well-nourished dog. Give your dog as much opportunity as possible to relieve itself before leaving for the show. There is usually an area set aside at shows for this purpose, but some dogs will not avail themselves of it. Bitches will frequently go the entire day rather than use these strange facilities, but do not be alarmed by this. I have never known a bitch be harmed in this way.

Showing—Points to Remember

First, always arrive at the show venue in good time. A flustered and bad-tempered handler with a hastily groomed dog is not the best passport to success.

Don't forget to check the contents of the show bag before leaving home, a missing brush with no shop handy can be a calamity.

Always have a pin or brooch to hold your ring number card.

On uneven ground, as sometimes encountered at outdoor

shows, take care to stand your dog facing uphill, the converse will over-accentuate the rump and spoil the outline.

Never address remarks to the judge; answer only any questions that may be put to you. Volunteered information concerning past successes under other judges will not endear you to him.

Always keep your dog between yourself and the judge. This is not as easy as it sounds, and may sometimes call for minor feats of acrobatics. Do not keep your dog posed for long periods while the judge is examining other exhibits. Allow as much relaxation as possible, but take care and be ready to alert your dog should the judge wish to glance at you for comparison with a dog that is being examined. Never engage in longwinded conversations with other exhibitors or ringside acquaintances, otherwise you may pay for your lack of concentration with a lost opportunity.

Although there is no rule against taking a bitch in season to a show, it is very much frowned on by other competitors, and it must be admitted that it is an unsporting thing to do. The chances of a male dog who is benched next to a bitch in full season, or worse still has to stand next to one in the ring, of behaving well and possibly winning, are slender indeed.

The newcomer will find regular showgoers very friendly and ready to answer any questions and help in a variety of ways. Do not, however, ply them with questions while they are preparing their dogs for their classes. Approach them after the judging has finished and they will give you their undivided attention.

Do not make unkind remarks about a judge because he does not share the high opinion that you have of your dog. He is probably more experienced than you are, and in any case he may have a point. Take your placings philosophically and do not give displays of emotion. Accept your winnings with reasonable modesty and your losses with dignity and sportsmanship. The over-gloating winner, looking like a cat that has got at the cream, is almost harder to take than the loser who storms out of the ring with a face like thunder, emitting a stream of invective and casting thinly veiled doubts as to the judge's legitimacy.

Finally, remember that there are all types of people in dogs: the generous and the ungenerous, the kind and the unkind. Do not, therefore, be too sensitive to unwarranted criticism of your dog.

In all probability this may mean that your dog is feared as a rival in the ring and is, therefore, in a roundabout way, a compliment. You will find that few people will waste time in pulling to pieces a dog who is obviously a poor specimen.

Remember always that the showing of dogs is, for the majority at least, a sport, and try to treat it as such. Strive to keep the whole picture in proportion and perspective. Do not become a neurotic on the subject, one of those for whom a win is a necessity to be obtained at any price, giving temporary satisfaction only until the next show, just as a drug addict gains a boost from a shot. One look at the faces of such people will quickly reveal that they derive little real pleasure from their dogs.

9
Judging

JUDGING is the most controversial and certainly the most important aspect of the entire gamut of the dog exhibitors' activities.

For amateur or small breeders and one-dog owners who exhibit in the show-ring, the dog show is the *raison d'etre* of all their efforts and expense, and success at the shows is their ultimate goal.

For larger, possibly professional, breeders, wins in the show-ring, particularly championship titles, are of paramount importance as advertisements for stock and to attract lucrative stud work for their winning dogs, whose fees increase in line with their wins. Overseas sales are also influenced by success in the show-ring, particularly in a breed whose popularity is rapidly expanding.

All this depends ultimately on the judge, who, if he cannot actually make or break a dog, can certainly boost or damage its reputation. It therefore follows that in agreeing to officiate in this capacity, a tremendous responsibility is incurred; one that should not be undertaken lightly.

A further aspect of this responsibility is the fact that the type of dog that finds favour in the show-ring determines what is produced by breeders, and not the reverse, as many would persuade themselves. Few breeders have the single-minded strength of purpose to continue breeding a type of dog that does not win at shows, however much they may consider themselves to be right.

W. L. McCandlish writing on the 'Judge at Shows' in Brian Vesey-Fitzgerald's *Book of the Dog,* starts the chapter with the following statement: 'Shows are opportunities for going one better than your neighbour, and for substantiating personal pride. To decide which has gone better than t'other, someone's opinion is required. The person chosen to give it is called the judge.' This certainly describes one aspect of dog showing: the very human and laudable striving after perfection, and the equally natural desire to compete with, and if possible go one better than, your neighbour. It does not, however, mention at all the important effect of the show-ring on puppy sales and stud work. The summing up of the duties of the judge, however, could not be put more succinctly: 'To decide which has gone better than t'other.' Later in the chapter, Mr. McCandlish continues his views on the judge's duties thus, 'To decide the order of merit of a number of individual dogs, which requires a well ordered mind and a high mental concentration,' and later, 'judging largely consists in the ability to weigh comparative merits and defects'.

If I were asked to add a final comment I would say that the judge must have two attributes: first, a knowledge of the breed to be judged, and secondly the courage to apply this knowledge without fear or favour, whatever the consequences.

When I agreed to include a chapter on judging in this book I decided that this difficult and in many ways touchy subject must be presented honestly in all its aspects, or not tackled at all.

I have little patience with the professional 'glad boys' of doggy journalism who are at pains to present the whole world of dog showing in terms of rosy platitudes, seeking to assure us that all judges are both competent and honest, and that the system by which they are appointed is ideal, the obvious implication being that anyone who disagrees or questions the whole set up is in some way *de trop*.

The newcomer to the show-ring will soon realise that this is not so, and apart from being an insult to the intelligence, this sort of humbug deceives nobody and achieves nothing. The truth of the matter is that the system for appointing judges is virtually non-existent, and many judges, being mortal, fall far short of the ideals of knowledge, concentration, and moral courage outlined above.

It is my intention to discuss the ways that judges are appointed, and the problems that have to be faced, as objectively as possible, so that the new judge will know something of the background to the whole situation. In addition, I hope to be able to give some advice that may be useful when the first judging engagement is undertaken.

There may be those who are expecting this chapter to contain some simple instructions on how to become a judge: if this is so, I regret that they will look in vain.

I do not consider that anybody can be 'taught' to judge dogs or any other livestock. The practical knowledge necessary can only be acquired by constant association and contact over a long period with the breed concerned, as owner, breeder, exhibitor, and general enthusiast. This can be assisted by study of the standard and discussion with knowledgeable judges and breeders, and further helped by books and lectures, but these can never take the place of the long practical apprenticeship.

The mental and psychological requirements certainly cannot be taught. An individual either possesses them or does not.

Beauty, as we are constantly told, is in the eye of the beholder, and therefore what constitutes the ideal Afghan Hound will vary from person to person. This must not blind us to the fact that there are some who are basically incapable of appreciating proportion, balance, and beauty of outline. This is no disgrace, but it is as futile to expect such people to appreciate a beautifully proportioned dog as it would be to expect a tone deaf man to appreciate a Beethoven symphony or one who is colour blind to enjoy an Impressionist painting. It is, in my opinion, the lack of this faculty that causes some people to judge a dog by sections, rather than as an entirety.

The question will inevitably be asked, how is it possible to decide if and when an exhibitor has reached the required standard to warrant a judging engagement. I would say that this can only be decided by the answer to one question: has the person shown, over a fairly long period, dogs of a constantly high standard (not necessarily champions)? If they have, then this must be accepted as proof that they are able to recognise and pick out a good specimen. If the answer is no to either part of the question, it is difficult to see how they could possibly be entitled to pass judgment on the dogs of others. Sheer length of time in which a long and consistently poor sequence of dogs has been produced can

M

only be evidence of an inability to pick or appreciate a good one. At the other extreme, the newcomer who has made a lucky purchase cannot be credited with the knowledge until the initial successes have been confirmed by the production of further high quality dogs over a period of time.

There are two distinct categories of judges in the dog-showing world: one is the 'all-rounder', who possesses a wide knowledge of many breeds and judges variety classes (classes scheduled for more than one breed), groups, and competitions for Best in Show. This type of judge will also officiate for single-breed classes.

The other type of judge is the specialist who judges, and indeed only claims expert knowledge of, one breed, or possibly two. It is from the ranks of the breeders and exhibitors that this type of judge is recruited, and this is the category we are most concerned with here.

It will be instantly realised that while this system produces judges who are knowledgeable on the breed, it will also produce judges who are clearly not in the best position to give disinterested and unbiased judgments, being emotionally involved in the competition and politics of dog showing. The system, in fact, absolutely ensures that a completely objective and detached approach is a virtual impossibility. Herein lies the fundamental weakness of all dog showing.

Consider for one moment some of the more obvious stresses and strains to which the specialist judge is subjected. In the first place he will be expected to judge between dogs owned by friends and those owned by people with whom he is not on good terms. He is equally likely to be faced in the ring by exhibitors who, as judges, have given him high awards and to whom he will feel a natural gratitude, alongside others who have, in all honesty, left his own dogs unplaced. If the judge is a breeder, he will sooner or later be faced with dogs who bear his own prefix, and towards which he will feel a perfectly understandable psychological bias. The most difficult situation of all for the novice judge is the well-known winning exhibitor with the equally well-known winning champion dog. The psychological pressure of being confronted by a champion dog which has been highly placed by many experienced judges is formidable, and to resist this pressure, to look upon the dog dispassionately and consider it on equal terms with the other exhibits, and even place an unknown but better dog above it, calls for a high degree of integrity and moral courage.

Having established the role of the judge, and listed some of the problems that will have to be faced, let us now consider how judges for dog shows are chosen and appointed.

The Kennel Club, governing body of the entire pedigree dog-breeding and showing world, takes no part in the choice and appointment of judges for sanction, limited, and open shows. As these three types of show will be of most interest to the novice judge, they will be discussed first.

Dog shows are normally organised and run by canine societies; that is to say the committee on behalf of the members decides on the type of show, the venue, and a date on which it is to be held. After the Kennel Club has given its sanction to the date, and the venue has been booked, the next and all important task of the organiser is the appointment of judges for the individual breeds, the variety classes (and obedience classes if they are scheduled) and, finally, for the groups and the competition for Best in Show.

It is from the secretary of one of these canine societies or clubs, that the first invitation to judge will be received. How then does the secretary decide on an individual to invite to officiate at his association's show? At the outset, it must be made clear that there is no official way for an association, or its secretary, to choose a judge for their show. It is also a fact that there is no official qualification of specified length of experience or necessary degree of showing success required to qualify anyone to judge at a sanction, limited, or open show. Incredible as it may seem to the uninitiated, the hard fact is that a person who has never seen an Afghan Hound could easily be appointed to judge the breed at an important open show. To quote W. L. McCandlish once more, referring to the judge and the breed standard, he says, 'Yet a judge is not compelled to swear that he knows it, or to abide by it.'

Faced with this situation, the organising society, through its secretary, either invites someone known to be an accepted judge of the breed, or the secretary may ask one of his committee or a personal friend for the name of a suitable person, whom he will of necessity accept on trust. It is hardly necessary in this imperfect world to point out the obvious weaknesses in this last procedure.

Another method is for the organising association to ask one of the breed clubs for its approved list of judges, and to select a name from this list. The official breed club lists of judges are usually compiled by the members, and added to or reduced at general meetings. Some breed clubs have two lists, one for championship shows, and one for more junior shows.

When breed clubs run their own shows, the judge is normally elected by ballot from their own official list. Unfortunately, as the breed club secretaries will confirm, very few requests are received from canine associations and clubs for their approved judges lists, which means that most appointments are made by the show secretaries as a result of their own experience, or by personal recommendation. And it is in this way that the new judges will be most likely to receive the first invitation to officiate.

The names of prospective championship show judges are selected in the same manner as for the other types of show. In this instance, however, the Kennel Club does take a hand, and the proposed name must be submitted to it for approval. This will entail the completion of a questionaire giving particulars of past judging experience, the number of dogs entered in the stud book, and other pertinent details needed to enable them to assess the suitability of the proposed judge. Until the Kennel Club officially gives its approval, no judge can award challenge certificates.

I have referred above to dogs entered in the Kennel Club stud book, and this may require further explanation. A dog is automatically entered in the stud book when it is awarded a first, second, or third prize in the open or limit class at a show where challenge certificates are awarded for the breed. This provides a rather rough and ready method of assessing whether an exhibitor has shown dogs of merit. Clearly, anyone who has a reasonable number of dogs that have achieved these placings at championship shows can claim to have fairly consistently shown dogs of a certain standard.

The time will eventually arrive when an enthusiast will have exhibited for a sufficiently long period and have achieved enough success, to warrant an invitation to judge at a show where the breed is scheduled.

When I first started to show dogs, it was the custom for new judges to make their debut at sanction or limited shows, where the entries were possibly four to six per class, and where champions were not permitted. Today, these two types of show are seldom held, and new judges are forced to undergo their initiation at open shows, where the number of entries may well exceed twenty in each class and may also include well-known champions. This can be a formidable undertaking for even the most experienced judge.

It is therefore more necessary than ever before that prior to accepting an engagement, would-be judges should ask themselves honestly if they are capable of undertaking this task. To be more precise, have they been active in the breed long enough, and have they won enough to merit the respect of their fellow exhibitors and morally entitle them to pass judgment on other people's dogs? Also, and equally important, are they temperamentally suited to the task? Can they apply their knowledge impartially, knowing as they do so that many friends and exhibitors will inevitably be bitterly disappointed and some antagonised!

The first invitation to judge is usually received with a mixture of pleasure and trepidation, and this is the time to be brutally honest and decide whether it is the normal apprehension of any modest and conscientious person faced with a responsible task, or an indication that a little more experience is required before taking this vital step.

I have known very experienced, knowledgeable and kindly people in the world of dogs who will not accept a judging appointment because they cannot endure the thought of disappointing and possibly upsetting friends and exhibitors; and let there be no nonsense about this, because it is an inevitable result of a judging engagement.

How much more admirable are these conscientious people, who honestly assess themselves and face facts, than those judges who, although obviously scared and unable to cope, none the less accept the appointment because of the kudos involved. This type of judge invariably gives himself away in the ring by attempting to give awards to everybody he considers to be important, irrespective of the merits of the dogs they are showing, and usually ends in a hopeless muddle, as well as upsetting most of those they so assiduously sought to please.

When the decision to accept the invitation to judge has been taken, notify the secretary at once, in writing, and make a careful note of the date, place, and time at which you are required to be present.

On the day of the show, be punctual at the venue, and on arrival report your presence immediately to the show secretary, who will give you some idea when your breed is to be judged, and in which ring. He may also introduce you to your steward, and in all probability tell you what arrangements have been made for your lunch.

When your breed is called, be promptly in the ring and start as soon as possible. Unnecessary delays are irritating to keyed up exhibitors, who may have been waiting around for hours. Make sure that you understand how to fill in your judge's book. This is quite simple, and consists of marking in your placings against the ring numbers of the competitors. Any friend who has judged will show you how to do this. As you will also be asked to furnish a critique of winners for the canine press, you will require a notebook, or tape-recording equipment.

There is no fixed or official procedure laid down for judging dogs. Some of the usual procedures have been outlined in Chapter 8, but a judge may adopt any reasonable method in order to assess the merits of the exhibits he is judging. I once saw a well-known all-rounder judge take a dog and its handler out of the ring into an adjacent meadow in order to assess the movement in an unrestricted area. I do not know what the official Kennel Club reaction to this would be, but I respected him for it.

Remember that, as the judge, you are in complete control, and your decisions are final and binding. The ring stewards are there to assist in ring organisation, and control of the exhibitors, but definitely not to assist in the actual judging. However indecisive and lost you may feel, never seek help from your stewards. This, although human and understandable, is wrong and would inevitably be spotted by the exhibitors. Remember that it is your opinion they come for, and yours alone.

Before starting, the judge should inform the steward what procedure is going to be adopted and any other points considered necessary. At this juncture it may be of some assistance if I outline the procedure I adopt, and give the reasons for it. This will provide a basis on which novice judges can work out their own procedures: but before this I would stress one aspect that I consider of paramount importance. Whatever methods are adopted always remember that movement is vital in assessing structure and balance in a dog. To judge this fully, it must be viewed not only from front and rear, but also from the side. Some judges omit this side view of movement, but it is difficult to understand how length of stride and drive can be assessed without it.

At the start of judging, when the steward has reported that all is ready, I move all exhibits round the ring in a wide circle (sometimes difficult if the entry is large). This has two main purposes. First, it gives the exhibits a chance to loosen up and settle down. It also allows me to have an overall view of the exhibits on the move, and it is frequently possible to pick out several possible winners at this stage.

After this initial run round, I call each dog out, in turn, for a detailed examination at the standstill. When the handler has set the dog up (do not hurry this), I stand well back and inspect the picture presented by the dog in entirety, noting particularly outline, topline, head carriage, balance and rhythm of line. I then examine the dog manually, feeling the body for shoulder placement, depth of brisket, spring of rib, length and firmness of loin, hip bones, and general muscular condition. If the dog is sparsely coated many of these points can be assessed visibly.

In the case of male dogs I ensure that they are entire (both testicles present in the scrotum). I next examine the hindquarters for angulation, height, and position of hocks, tail and tail set, slope-away, and muscular condition.

I then check the forelegs for weight of bone, parallelism, straightness and the feet for size and alignment (pointing straight to the front).

I then examine the head for size, width of skull, refinement, balance, and shape of muzzle, also chiselling. The eye for shape and placing, and the mouth and teeth for correct bite, and the neck for length, shape, and muscle. Some judges advocate the practice of starting at the head and working down to the tail, and while this method certainly minimises the risk of overlooking anything, I do not consider it suitable for Afghan Hounds. The breed in my experience is averse to a direct frontal approach from strangers, and I have noticed that when a judge advances with hands outstretched to examine the head, the reaction of the dog is frequently to back away or display some symptoms that might be mistaken for nerves, but is in fact a manifestation of the natural breed suspicion of strangers. If, on the other hand, the examination is started with the body or quarters, by the time the head is reached, the judge will have been accepted and the dog will be acquiescent.

Finally, I move each exhibit independently, away from, and towards me, to assess front and hind action, and again for a side view to assess length of stride, propulsion from hindquarters, freedom from inhibition, and general balance. After this I make my final selection from all exhibits at the standstill.

A word of warning here. Good showmanship is not the same as good movement. A bad specimen with bad action, can show well, while a beautifully conformed dog can move well but display indifferent showmanship. This can be a dangerous trap for the inexperienced judge.

Do not hesitate to move an exhibit many times if you consider it necessary. It is my firm belief that much more can be seen of a dog in movement than at the standstill, where a clever handler can stack it up in such a way as to conceal many faults that would be obvious on the move.

On the subject of handlers, it is the legitimate task of the good handler to make the very most of his exhibit, which means that he will use all his skill to hide any faults (of which he should be well aware) and emphasise the good points in order to create the best picture possible. The better the handler, the more successful he will be. His attitude is much the same as the barrister who, knowing the weaknesses of his client's case, none the less does his best to minimise them and make the most of the good points in order to create the best possible impression.

If it is the handler's job to minimise the faults, it is the duty of the judge to see through the clever handling to the true dog beneath. In this he is really engaging in a perfectly legitimate battle of wits with the handler. Do not deduce from this that all good handling of necessity conceals a multitude of faults. A good dog well handled will appear a very good dog, while the same dog indifferently handled may well look only average.

At this point it will be useful to consider some of the more usual tactics employed by handlers to conceal faults, and against which the alert judge should be on guard. First, the surreptitious hand under the body holding up a very dippy back, also the equally crafty knee propping up the nervous cringing exhibit. Hind legs that are pulled too far back are usually there because if the dog were allowed to stand naturally it would be high on the hindquarters. Be suspicious of the brushed forward topknot, it may well conceal a thick skull or indifferent eye. Careful stripping can also minimise faults if expertly done, and the way the coat is brushed can do the same.

Be very suspicious indeed of the exhibit moved on such a short, taut lead that the forequarters are virtually off the ground, and the resultant movement is controlled by the handler as if the dog was a puppet. Insist that all exhibits are allowed to move freely and naturally and are not interfered with in any way by the handler. In this way only can a true assessment be made.

Do not be influenced by flashy handling techniques, or by over-forceful exhibitors. Your stewards should control the exhibitors in the ring, but stewards are not always experienced or efficient, so be on guard against one exhibitor deliberately masking another, or allowing a dog to interfere with that of another competitor. When the successful competitors are called out to take their place in the final line up, make absolutely certain they take up the places you intended. It is hard to believe, but I have actually witnessed a case where a forceful individual placed herself at the top of the line, contrary to the judge's instruction, and was not corrected by the stewards, who may not have been aware of the situation. The judge, however, displaying a disgraceful lack of moral courage, allowed the placings to stand—presumably fearing a 'scene'—and the wrong competitor received the red card. This type of judge has no right to be officiating.

After the judging is over, some exhibitors will approach the judge and ask questions concerning their dogs. This kind of interrogation will come mostly from the less successful. The winners, content in the knowledge that their own high opinion of their dogs has been confirmed, will not require further enlightenment. I believe in being truthful in answering these questions, but if possible, not hurtful. If a dog is not a show specimen, it is surely kinder to tell the owner so, rather than allow further waste of time and money in exhibiting all over the country without any hope of success. If possible, explain simply and truthfully where the dog fails. This is not always easy today when entries are high and failure to win an award by no means proves a dog to be a poor specimen.

Never fall into the habit of judging dogs in sections. Body, neck, shoulders, quarters, head are all parts of the whole dog and it is the whole animal that is to be judged. To do this it is imperative to stand well back and to take an overall view. Individual sections of the dog are important, but only as parts of the whole, and it is the final balance and rhythm that is created by the joining together of these parts that matters. To put this in a slightly more practical way, a dog may have a straight tail or be slightly plain in head, but still be well proportioned and sound and should always be placed higher than an indifferent and unsound specimen with a ringed tail or superb head. Too many judges tend to judge on head alone, and while this is an important part of the dog (embodying as it does expression) it is still only a part.

A dog must first of all be absolutely sound before consideration is given to individual points. When judging dogs, never lose sight of the basic purpose for which the breed was designed, even though it may no longer be fulfilling this role.

There is no scale of points for each part of the dog to assist the judge in this country, so each one will have an individual scale of his own, and this will differ between judges.

One of the complaints against specialist judges, compared to all rounders, is that they tend to be 'faddists', and it must be admitted that there is some substance in this accusation. Guard against it at all times. The worst type of faddists are the 'black

mask' and 'beautiful coat' fetishists. Coat is only an embellishment
of the basic dog underneath and sheer length and quantity of coat
is not necessarily a good point and can spoil the outline. Grooming is of still less importance. Although a well-groomed dog looks
well and is a compliment to the judge, a good dog with some
mats in its coat is still a good dog and must go over a well-
groomed 'also ran'.

The black mask, undeniably an attractive feature, can be a snare
for the inexperienced judge. Most people on first becoming
acquainted with this breed are captivated by the black-masked
dogs, and I was no exception to this. As time progresses one
grows more accustomed to them, and they consequently cease to
have the same impact: in fact, one slowly becomes aware that in
many instances the black mask conceals a coarse or indifferent
head. I have now reached a stage when this particular feature
does not influence my judging at all, and I know this to be true
of most of my contemporaries.

I genuinely believe that the well-proportioned, beautifully
chiselled self-coloured head, owing nothing to camouflage, is the
most attractive of all.

One aspect of the judge's legitimate powers, which causes
controversy, and on occasions ill feeling, is the withholding of
awards. Any judge officiating at a dog show under Kennel Club
regulations is empowered to withhold an award if he so desires.
This power is seldom exercised and, in the opinion of some,
should never be exercised at all.

To discuss this question further it is necessary to take it in two
parts. First, the withholding of challenge certificates, and second,
the withholding of awards other than challenge certificates.

When a judge awards a challenge certificate to a dog, he is
required to sign a statement to the effect that he considers the
exhibit to be of such outstanding merit as to be worthy of the
title of champion. This clearly indicates to me that if there is no
exhibit the judge considers to be worth the title of champion, then
he cannot honourably sign such a statement. In other words, the
challenge certificate must be withheld, and a conscientious judge
should have the courage to do this. If a challenge certificate is
awarded to a dog because it is the best exhibit present, although

clearly an indifferent specimen and not in the opinion of the judge suitable for the title of champion, it is not only dishonest but lowers the value of all such certificates and makes a mockery of the entire system.

In awards other than challenge certificates, in other words the normal prizes awarded in the various classes in any type of show, the situation is entirely different. In this instance the judge is not required to sign any certificate of merit or standard of excellence, but merely to place the exhibits in the order he considers they should be, the best first, the next best second, and so on. If the exhibits are of very poor quality, his task is exactly the same. The best of the bad lot must be the first, however poor a specimen it may be.

It has been suggested to me that where a class has only one entrant and that a very bad specimen, it might injure the reputation of the judge to award it a first prize. I would still insist that he should award the exhibit the red card (1st prize), as it is undeniably the best Afghan Hound there and he would have to take a risk with his reputation.

The only instance that I can visualise where this type of award should be withheld is in the unlikely event of a single entry that is so poor a specimen that the judge has sincere doubts as to whether it is an Afghan Hound at all.

I would stress that the views I have expressed are my own interpretation of the judge's obligations. There will undoubtedly be some disagreement with them, and it must be emphasised that the judge at a dog show is entitled to withhold any award if he wishes.

One of the most persistent fears that haunts the judge of dogs particularly, although not necessarily the novice judge, is the possibility of reversing a decision. This can happen in two very different ways. The deliberate and intended reversal of placing, or the accidental.

Any judge in the show-ring is entitled to reverse a decision, and indeed there are occasions when this definitely should be done. If a good dog misbehaves and refuses to move or be handled, it cannot obviously be placed, yet the same dog may be entered in a later class and possibly under a different handler, move and show perfectly. In this case the judge is perfectly correct in placing the dog where its merits entitle it to be: over other competitors that had previously beaten it.

The accidental reversal is very different, and let us be honest about this, it could, but should not, happen to anyone. This type of error is more likely to occur in large entries where some exhibits are repeated in various classes. It is, however, most likely to happen if the judge is placing exhibitors rather than dogs. The stewards should also be alert to assist the judge in these instances so that errors of this kind can be avoided.

Taking this theme a step further, it is not generally known that a judge is permitted to alter his placings up to forty-two days after the show. This right is, fortunately, rarely exercised, as it causes trouble and embarrassment all round. As to its merits and demerits it must be admitted that it enables a courageous and conscientious judge, who honestly considers he has made a mistake, to remedy the matter, but it must also be admitted that it enables other people to contact, and possibly influence the judge at, and after, the show.

When judging, consider the exhibitors at all times. Remember that many have travelled long distances and all have paid you the compliment of placing their dogs under you for your opinion, and good manners at least dictate that they receive if not a prize, at least consideration. Remember the time when you timidly entered the show-ring for the first time, and be patient with nervous and inexperienced exhibitors.

Make sure that every competitor receives equal attention, even the least good is entitled to a thorough examination, and no exhibitors must feel that they are ignored or do not count.

Try to look cheerful and as if your task is a pleasure. The type of judge who looks disagreeable or bored, or glowers at the competitors as if they were the most obnoxious collection he had ever seen, is depressing to watch and irritating to exhibit under.

Lady judges should avoid long jangling necklaces, bracelets, and bizarre hats which can be disquieting to a highly strung dog when being handled.

Resist the temptation to prejudge a show. This will be difficult if the engagement is in your area, where previous knowledge of the likely exhibits and their usual placings are almost inevitable. Put the whole matter from your mind until you step into the ring, advice that is easier to give than to take, but none the less sound.

Do not hesistate to reward a dog you consider deserves it, even though you know that other judges have left it unplaced. Likewise, a well-known winner that you genuinely consider inferior, must be penalised.

Never give a thought to your reputation or to what others may think. It is as dishonest to withhold an award from a friend whose dog deserves it, for the sake of appearances, as it would be to give one to a friend whose dog does not.

Never play to the gallery, or seek popularity by penalising top quality winning dogs. It is sometimes more courageous to confirm the placings of other judges than to contradict them.

Mrs. Winnie Barber, writing on the subject of judging recalls the advice given to her as a young judge by her father: 'Keep your eyes on the dogs and don't look at the exhibitors.'

To those reading this chapter it will be apparent that I am far from content with the judging position in the world of dog shows. I would go further, and claim that the situation surrounding the appointment and qualifications of judges could hardly satisfy anyone who has a genuine interest in thoroughbred dogs.

It is no part of the task of this book to suggest or discuss ways and means of improving this situation. It is gratifying, however, to know that some efforts are afoot to tighten up control, both of the method of appointment and the standard of experience and knowledge required before a candidate can be appointed to judge in the show-ring.

I have recently served on a sub-committee set up by the Afghan Hound Association to examine and report on this subject, and to make suggestions as to how the situation could be improved. It is therefore possible that by the time this book is published, some steps, however tentative, may have been taken to this end.

On the brighter side, I would say without any hesitation that I enjoy judging more than any other aspect of my association with Afghan Hounds.

The prospect of a ring full of these delightful dogs is a sight that never ceases to thrill me, and the challenge presented by the task of placing them in order of merit is both immense and satisfying.

In conclusion I would claim that there are few greater satisfactions than the knowledge that one has been among the first to recognise and reward a dog that subsequently becomes a famous champion. I would place this pleasure above—perhaps only just above—the thrill of receiving a challenge certificate with one's own dog.

My final words to the novice judge fulfilling his first engagement are, make up your mind to enjoy every minute of it and do exactly what you want to do; it is your day and you cannot be gainsaid. A great newspaper man once made the now famous remark 'Publish and be damned', I would say to the new judge 'Judge honestly and be damned', and if you do, you probably will be.

The Afghan Hound Overseas

IT HAS been described in previous chapters how the Afghan Hound first came to Europe and gained a foothold as an established breed in this country in the early days of the century. As would be expected, it was not long before these captivating dogs attracted supporters in other countries on both sides of the Atlantic. Today the breed is strongly entrenched in the U.S.A., and in many continental countries, particularly in Scandinavia. In addition, Australia and Canada have a vigorous body of breeders and enthusiasts.

As many of the pioneer British kennels supplied foundation stock to these other countries, it will be of particular interest to discuss briefly how the breed has fared in these distant lands, and trace some of the links with our own strains.

U.S.A.

The Afghan Hound in America is founded on much the same basic stock as our own. Joan McDonald Brierly in her book *This is the Afghan Hound* estimates that 15 to 25 per cent of American breeding is founded on the Bell Murray strain, and 20 to 30 per cent on the Ghazni strain.

The first three Afghan Hounds to be registered with the American Kennel Club in 1926 were of Miss Manson's breeding. In 1928 the first American-bred litter was registered. An excerpt from a breed column in the canine press by Mrs. Amps in 1929 reads:

'There is a growing demand for Afghans from America. Mrs. Cooper, of the Flandre Kennels, Hornsea, tells me she could sell all her puppies in the States if they only had the three generations pedigree. We all regret the lack of this, but the unchanging east has never kept dogs' pedigrees, and never

(Ludwig)

American and Canadian Ch. Crown Crest Mr. Universe

Australian Ch. Laukera Shah

Int and Scandinavian Ch. Tajmahal Abd-ul Djari

Int Ch. Bohem Python

will. The breeder will tell you his hounds' histories, who the sires and dams were bred by, the strain and district they came from, and there he stops. Fortunately this is a difficulty quite a short time will overcome.'

In 1930, Zeppo Marx, of the famous Marx Brothers, imported a pair of Afghan Hounds from England. They were Westmill Omar and Azra of Ghazni. These two were eventually sold to Q. A. Shaw McKean who owned the Prides Hill Kennels. Azra, at the time of her death, at fourteen years, had produced some seventy puppies, thus making a considerable contribution towards establishing the breed in the U.S.A.

Mr. Shaw McKean imported the famous English brindle dog Badshah of Ainsdart, and his litter brother Tuftan of Ainsdart. Badshah was the first Afghan Hound to win a Best in Show award in the U.S.A.

It is noteworthy that a puppy of Westmill Omar out of Azra of Ghazni, Barberry Hill Illusive, was the mother of the beautiful Barberry Hill Dolly. The same pair also produced Kundah of Prides Hill, the maternal grandsire of Ch. Rudiki of Prides Hill and Zahera of Prides Hill.

Mr. Shaw McKean was a great pioneer worker for the breed in America, as were many of the early breeders, including Mrs. Sherman Hoyt, Mrs. Marion Foster Florsheim, Mrs. Jack Oakie, Mr. and Mrs. Wernsman, Mr. and Mrs. Robert Boyer, and Mrs. Leah McConaha. As a result of the efforts of these early enthusiasts, many new kennels appeared, among which were two names destined to reach world fame in the breed: the Crown Crest prefix of Mrs. Katherine Finch and the Grandeur affix of Mrs. Sunny Shay, about which more will be said later.

The first Afghan Hound champion to gain the title in the U.S.A. was Ch. Kabul of Prides Hill, in October 1934 (a further result of Omar mated to Azra). The first bitch champion was Barberry Hill Dolly, gaining her title in 1935.

In the middle 1930s, a foreign correspondent, Laurence Peters, after much searching and some difficulties, imported a pair of Afghan Hounds from Afghanistan. A dog, Tazi of Beg Tute, and a bitch, Saki of Paghman. The names indicated the

N

villages from which they had been obtained. Saki was grey in colour and was the forebear of the famous Felts Thief of Baghdad, and influential in the pedigrees of other 'blues'. Another import from India was Fatima, which arrived in 1936 and was mated to Tuftan of Ainsdart, and produced several champions.

There were also imports from England during this era, including Ch. Garrymhor Kishtwar, Garrymhor Khasa, and Jalalabad Kara.

In 1937, a litter brother to Barberry Hill Dolly, Barberry Hill Charlie, came to the fore, winning a Hound Group and going on to be first Best in Show Afghan Hound in California. Also in the same year, Barberry Hill Dolly left the kennels of Charles Ruggles and came into the possession of Mrs. Jack Oakie, of the Oakvardon Kennels, under whose love and care she blossomed to be the famous winner of many great awards, including the first Best in Show bitch in California, and the second in the U.S.A.

The Oakvardon Kennels imported a dog from India (Umberto) which became a champion in 1938, and a dog from Ireland, Hanuman of Enriallic, also two from England, Ch. Westmill Natanz, and Westmill Razuran.

The first speciality show for the breed, held in 1938, was organised by the Mid West Afghan Hound Club, in conjunction with the Detroit Specialities Group, and the Best in Breed was the British bitch import Garrymhor Pearie.

A great Afghan Hound of the 1930s was Amanullah of Kandahar, which is delightfully described by Constance O. Miller and Edward Gilbert as one 'who picked off Groups and Best in Shows like bones from a plate'. He was by Ch. Badshah of Ainsdart out of Zahera of Prides Hill.

In 1939, a heavily coated cream bitch from England, Lakshmi of Geufron Catawba, made a great impact in the U.S.A. where the heavy coats that were winning in England had not yet become commonplace. Lakshmi became the first Best in Show bitch in the U.S.A.

Another import was Garrymhor Zahardart of Arken which, in addition to winning in the ring, was a great stud force for this kennel and was the sire of Ch. Rajah of Arken.

The autumn of 1938 was memorable for the first appearance of the young Rudiki of Prides Hill, probably the best-known American Afghan Hound among English enthusiasts. International Ch. Rudiki of Prides Hill, bought by Mrs. Marion Florsheim of the Five Mile Kennels, was a Best in Show winner fifteen times, forty times Best Hound, and seventy-seven times Best in Breed. A great-grandson of Ch. Sirdar of Ghazni, he sired over 200 puppies and was a leading sire during the war years.

Another famous dog, mentioned before in this book, was exported from Britain during the immediate pre-war period. He was Rana of Chaman of Royal Irish, exported by Mrs. Molly Sharpe to Mrs. Florsheim, where he joined Rudiki and daughter Rudika as the foundation of the Five Mile Kennel. As a ferry pilot during the war, Marion Florsheim was able to campaign Rana and Rudiki over a wide area.

Also escaping from Britain at war were the two dogs from Dr. Betsy Porter's kennel, brother and sister, Sardar Khan el Kabul and Rani el Kabul, two brindle grandchildren of the great Westmill Tamasar. They arrived on the liner *Somaria*, which was sunk on its return journey. Received into the Elcoza Kennel of Mrs. Laver Froelich, Sardar Khan became a champion, and the bitch Rani produced five champion offspring. Ch. Sardar mated to Flo Flo of Ghazni produced nine champions.

Rudiki's daughter Rudika was a top winning bitch during and immediately after the war.

Contrary to the ideas held by most British people, dog breeding and showing were seriously curtailed in the U.S.A. during the Second World War, for much the same reasons as they were here. Likewise, when hostilities ceased, there was an upsurge of breed activities and registrations, accompanied by many new breeders and exhibitors.

During the war the great champion Aly Khyber came to prominence. He was a son of Rudiki out of Pommel Rock Kashan, which was a great-grand-daughter on the mother's side of Ardmore Anthony and Ch. Garrymhor Souria. Aly Khyber was also a great-great-grandson of Taj Mahip of Kaf which was the first dog to win a challenge certificate in England.

He sired thirty-five champions in the U.S.A., notable Ch. Karach of Khanhasset, whose phenomenal show career was abruptly halted with his sudden death from leptospirosis when barely two years old, and after siring only one litter, out of Far Away Loo. Karach, however, had a litter sister said to resemble him, which also had a great show career.

A repeat mating of Rudiki to Kashan, produced Ch. Khanhassets Kanda, owned by Charles Costabile, which was the first Afghan Hound to win the Quaker Oats award for top winning dog all breeds in the Southern States.

In 1948, after much discussion and deliberation, the new American Standard was produced and adopted. About this time a young silver blue dog began to make his presence felt in the show-ring. He was Felts Thief of Baghdad, owned by Mrs. Kay Finch. Concurrently another future champion and stud force made his debut, he was to be Ch. Five Miles Punjab Ben Ghazi owned by Ruth Tongren.

Other great winners of the 1940s were Ch. Majara Mahabat, the imported Ch. Turkuman Nissims Laurel and Ch. Majara Mirza, the only Afghan Hound bitch to win the afore-mentioned Quaker Oats award. Also of the Majara prefix was Ch. Majara Mihrab, a great stud force.

The now world famous Crown Crest Kennel of Mrs. Kay Finch had come to the fore with the previously mentioned Ch. Felts Thief of Baghdad. This dog, a silver anniversary gift from her husband, Braden Finch, was known as 'Thumper', and was the first of many great winners from this kennel. His pedigree contained many important and interesting blood lines, including influences from the old imports Tazi of Beg Tute, and Saki of Paghman. Indeed, Mrs. Finch writing in *The Hound's Tale*, under pedigree profiles, says she attributes Thief's singular colour (silver grey) to Saki of Paghman. Mated to Felts Fatima, he produced Ch. Felts Allah Baba.

In 1951 Mr. and Mrs. Finch, as the result of a photograph sent to them by Mrs. Leo Conroy, visted Decatur, Illinois, and purchased a young dog called Taejon (after the Korean battle on the day of his birth). This dog, later to become the famous Ch. Taejon of Crown Crest, was a great favourite with his owner and a famous show-winner, dominating the show-rings of the West for some years and breaking all records. He sired thirty champions, including a daughter, Ch. Crown Crest Taejoan.

In 1954, Mrs. Finch imported the great German, Belgian, and Dutch Champion Ophaal from the V.D.O.M. Kennels of Mrs. Eta Pauptit. He was four years old and kept at private stud at Crown Crest, unavailable to the public. He none the less produced twenty-seven champions from five litters, including such names as Zardonx, Rubi and Topaz. Mated to Ch. Hope, he sired a litter of nine bitches and one dog. The single dog was the great Crown Crest Mr. Universe, the most outstanding Afghan Hound of the 1960s, winning twenty-eight All Breed Best in Show, ninety-six Group competitions, and siring many champions.

On the East Coast, the other great producer of winning hounds was Mrs. Sunny Shay's Grandeur Kennel. Outstanding among the top quality winning hounds of this breeder was Ch. Shirkhan of Grandeur, born in 1954 and owned by Mrs. Shay and Dorothy Shenades, he was described as pewter grey, and had a brilliant career, winning the supreme award at the Westminster Show in Madison Square Garden in 1957, the first Afghan Hound to do so. He was also the third Afghan Hound to win the Quaker Oats award. It will be remembered that Mrs. Shay has been mentioned earlier as the co-owner with Sol Malkin of Turkuman Nissims Laurel, imported from Miss Juliette de Bairacli Levi, which brought further fame to this kennel and was much used as a sire.

Ch. Blue Boy of Grandeur, the sire of Ch. Shirkhan, was unfortunately killed in a road accident. Mrs. Joan McDonald Brierly, of the Shadi Kennels, used Shirkhan on a daughter of the great Ophaal, Ch. Crown Crest Khalifah, to produce champion offspring.

Mrs. Lois Boardman also used this great sire to obtain Akaba's Top Brass, the famous winning brindle. An outstanding daughter of Shirkhan, another brindle, the champion bitch Pandora of Stormhill, bred by Virginia Withington, also had a distinguished show career.

Mrs. Betty Richards's Ch. Javelin of Camri was yet another winning brindle. His son, Garlands Talisman of Camri has been imported to Britain by Miss Stephanie Hunt-Crowley of the Chandhara prefix.

Today the breed is thriving in the U.S.A. It would be invidious, and I think improper, to mention dogs that are actually competing in the ring at the present time. I have tried to give a very brief picture of the rise of the breed in America for the benefit of British enthusiasts, a virtually impossible task in such limited space. If this book should fall into the hands of any American Afghan Hound people, I hope they will appreciate my difficulties and be tolerant of any omissions and shortcomings.

In the chapter on the Standard and Conformation (Chapter 4), I mentioned that the American Breed Standard was different from the British and Continental one. It should be interesting and useful to English breeders, so it is included as Appendix D.

Canada

In Canada the well-known El Myia Kennels owned by Mrs. Mary Matchett have produced many champions. This kennel was founded on Chaman stock exported from England. The Kophi Kennels of Mr. and Mrs. Myles Phillips are also top winners at shows.

Scandinavia

Afghan Hound breeding in Scandinavia is a very international affair. In addition to the stock regularly imported from Great Britain, Holland, and to a lesser extent, the U.S.A., there is a regular exchange of puppies and stud services between all the Scandinavian countries. As there is normally no quarantine regulations, breeders are able to exhibit their dogs freely in neighbouring countries. In consequence of this it is now hardly realistic to speak of Swedish or Finnish or Danish Afghan Hounds as separate groups, and I will therefore deal with the Scandinavian countries as a single entity.

The first dogs imported were in the 1930s, but these are seldom found even far back in the pedigrees. It was in the late 1940s that Sweden really launched the breed with some very successful imports, while the Norwegian prefixes of Khasru and Knurrebo, as well as the Danish Tscharikar, became more and more rarely seen. The first really successful import came from Belgium in the shape of International Ch. Baghdad R'Akela, by Ch. Achmed

Sjach van de Oranje Manege out of Ch. Bagheera de Ruwen-dael, owned by one of the breeds greatest enthusiasts in Scandinavia, Mme. Ingrid af Trolle.

Akela was followed in a few years by four other dogs from Belgium, a sire and dam with two puppies. The sire was International Ch. Amanulla Khan of Acklam, and the dam was International Ch. Suki of Chaman, both bred in England. These two had come via Belgium, where they had been successfully shown and bred from. With Akela, and their Belgian bred offspring, they formed the foundation of Mme. af Trolle's kennel, and over the years produced a number of El Khandahar champions.

Another dog, imported at the same time, was Suki's litter brother, International Ch. Taj Arad of Chaman. He was rather sparsely used at stud, but his few litters in the av Indra Kennels produced a large number of champions, particularly Ch. Shah Amanullah av Indra.

In 1953, a new dog arrived from Holland. It was destined to exert a tremendous influence on the whole breed, and appears constantly in the pedigree of the top winners, not only in Scandinavia, but also on the continent and in the U.S.A. He was International Ch. Xenos van de Oranje Manege. Born in 1949, he was by Barukhzy's Dhrstadyumna out of Rashna du Chateau des Roches, and was much sought after as a stud. Two of his offspring—International Ch. Tanjores Domino and International Ch. Tajmahal Kenya—went to the U.S.A., and there helped to produce one of the greatest winners in Ch. Sandhihi Joh-Cyn Taija Baba (whose dam was by Domino out of Kenya), while the greatest sire in Scandinavia during the 1960s, International Ch. Tajmahal Abd-ul Djari, has Xenos as his double grandsire.

Xenos's winning offspring dominated the show-ring in the middle 1950s. At the close of the decade some new blood lines were introduced. From England came Reuben of Carloway, by Ch. Bletchingley Hillsman out of Ch. Carloway Sharmain of Virenedale, and from the U.S.A. came Ch. Crown Crest Kaejorg. Unfortunately, Reuben died in a motor accident less than two years after his arrival, which of necessity curtailed his stud

activities. Owned by the Sultan Kennels, he found time to win
Best Sight Hound twice in Gothenburg, and sired some excellent
stock, including International Ch. Saphir, whose dam goes
back to Chaman blood, and the bitch Ch. Ariadne el Khandhar,
whose dam also sprang from Acklam-Chaman lines.

Ch. Crown Crest Kaejorg has a long and successful stud career.
As he was the first American dog available in Scandinavia, he
was in great demand. He was owned by the Tajmahal Kennels,
and his most famous offspring was probably the bitch, International Ch. Tajmahal Nefertiti, who was the top winner in
Best of Breed and Groups for a long time.

England, however, really came to the fore with the importation
of Ch. Bletchingley Houndsman, in 1961. Houndsman was bred
by Mrs. Riley and was by Ch. Bletchingley Hillsman out of
Bletchingley Shirin. Purchased by Mme. af Trolle, Ch. Houndsman was Dog of the Year in 1961, although he was imported
when more than half the year had passed. He continued winning
Groups for many years, and his tragic death, together with
Mme. af Trolle's other hounds in a disastrous fire in 1966, was
a great loss to the breed in Scandinavia.

Houndsman sired almost a dozen champions, several of them
out of a Dutch bitch owned by the Ismail Kennel, and his work
has been carried on by other English dogs in Mme. af Trolle's
kennel, notably Ch. Menthe Rebel, by Ch. Horningsea Khanabad
Suvaraj out of Menthe Khara of Khorrassan.

Houndsman defeated the great Nefertiti at the Stockholm
show in 1962, under Mr. J. H. Braddon. The following summer,
Nefertiti's outstanding daughter International Ch. Tajmahal
Kenya II was ready to take up the battle, and on at least one
occasion did beat Houndsman. Kenya II also broke the records
set by her dam, and is now top winning bitch of all time, as well
as being the dam of the present top winners.

During the first years of the 1960s Swedish exhibitors began to
realise the fact that they were no longer first in Afghan Hounds
in Scandinavia. Finland had very few Afghan Hounds during
the 1950s, but by the turn of the decade they had acquired some
excellent breeding stock from England and Sweden, and they
made use of it to the best advantage. There were the British bred

bitches International Ch. Cleopatra of Scheherezade, by Ch. Bletchingley Ragman of Scheherezade, out of Chandhara Sheba Khanoum, also Zomahli Asu, and, above all, the great domino stud dog International Ch. Tajmahal Abd-ul Djari who went on to produce outstanding champions in all his litters. Soon the Finns began to take every possible award at the Swedish shows, nearly all the winners being sired by Djari. The prefixes most in the limelight were Tuohi-Tikan, Mazar-I-Sharif, and el Miharaja.

Denmark was also coming to the fore. The El Kamas Kennel was founded on the English import Ch. Horningsea Jamussah, by Horningsea Jehan out of Sirella of Davlen, which produced International Ch. El Kamas Wladimir. This kennel also imported other successful dogs including Ch. Horningsea Shakari, and Badakshan Tigran, a daughter of Badakshan Rani by Ch. Horningsea Tigers Eye.

Finland and Denmark have also started an exchange of puppies and stud dogs, which has at times threatened to leave Sweden behind. Norway has far less activity among its few Afghan Hound breeders, and the Norwegian hounds are seldom shown in other countries.

Sweden, during these years of Finnish-Danish improvements, had little to offer in the way of international competition. The best results came from bitches mated to Finnish dogs. Djari sired the brothers International Ch. Bohem Python, and Ch. Bohem Waalph, while an el Miharaja dog sired Ch. Jawahars La Femme, and Ch. Jawahars Tiffany out of Kenya II, all from dogs carrying the old el Khandahar blood to some degree. Python has indeed beaten some of the Finnish and Danish champions on occasions, and done quite well in Group competitions, while the others have not been so extensively campaigned. Ch. Moontha of Carloway, by Ch. Pasha of Carloway out of Crown Crest Zardeeka was also successful at that time, while Ch. Khinjan Baryak, by Khinjan Jespah of Carloway out of Khinjan Bilindar of Carloway gained championship status in 1969, and Ch. Pussy Willow of Jagai is another winning bitch.

The greatest excitement during the last two years has been provided by Finland with the importation of International

Ch. Panameric of Stormhill, by Ch. Holly Hill Black Magic out of Ch. Pandora of Stormhill, owned by the Tuohi-Tikan Kennel, and an influential sire. From his first litter came Ch. Tuohi-Tikan Naskali (Swedish owned), and Ch. Tuohi-Tikan Nalja. Out of Swaadenas Star Kenya II and one of her daughters came Ch. Jawahars Campari, and Ch. Jawahars Dante. All great winners in Group competitions in 1969.

The number of Afghan Hounds in Scandinavia is not large by British standards. Sweden, which has the largest number, never had more than 100 registrations a year until 1968. The comparatively small number of dogs keeps the breed free from many of the difficulties that beset us in England.

Holland

On the continent of Europe the old-established Van de Oranje Manege Kennels of Mrs. Eta Pautit in Holland, were founded on Ghazni stock, and have maintained this original type. The imported silver Chota was true to this. The famous Ophaal was exported to the Crown Crest Kennels in the U.S.A.

Australia

It was not until the beginning of the 1960s that the breed really arrived in Australia. Afghan Hounds had been imported into Australia over the years, but the early imports are no longer to be found in any Australian pedigrees. The present-day Australian Afghan Hound developed from the imports of the 1950s, which were the dog Zarussef Zso Zso, by Yussef of Carloway out of Ch. Bletchingley Zara, and the bitches Radiant of Carloway (Ch. Bletchingley Hillsman out of Ch. Carloway Sharmain of Virendale), and Khorrassan Horningsea Tarbouka by Belshazzar of Khorrassan, all of which became Australian Champions. Also taken to Australia in the 1950s were the Afghans belonging to Mrs. Barbara Skilton (née Catt) who was an exhibitor in England. Her foundation stud was Aust. Ch. Aghai of Hawkfield by Meshki Baz-i-Pushtikuh and her bitches of Bletchingley and Netheroyd lines. For several years the offspring of these hounds and Mrs. Skilton's later import Taj Amigo of Chaman were combined.

The 1960s saw a vast inflow of imports from Britain, U.SA., and Europe all of which have had some influence on the development of the modern Australian Afghan Hound. Amongst prominent kennels and importers of the 1960s (in addition to Mrs. Skilton's El Tazzi Kennels as above) probably the best known to British breeders is David Roche of the Fermoy Kennels, who imported Ch. Walliwog of Carloway, and Ch. Mazari of Carloway into Australia, as well as Crown Crest, Khinjan, and Pooghan bitches. Another visitor to England has been Mrs. Helen Furber of the Furbari Kennels who purchased Aust. Ch. Kasra el Kabul and Aust. Ch. Furbari Kusan Kabul from Dr. Porter. An emigrant from England was Mrs. Herta Buxey who took the black Aust. Ch. Ajman Shunawar and Aust. Ch. Shiba of Abdillya to Australia with her. The first kennel to import new blood in the 1960s was the Emir Kennel of Joyce and Lester Davey, who purchased the Wazir son Tarababa of Carloway, and later a Shirkan grandson, Chandhara's Emir of Gray Dawn in partnership with the Calahorra Kennels of Wendye and Stuart Slatyer. The Slatyer's also imported a dog from the U.S.A. with Swedish and Dutch background.

The second kennel to import was Shaaltarah, owned by Lyn and George Schelling. Their first import was Chandhara Wazir Shah, another Wazir son, which was tragically killed shortly after gaining his Australian title at just one year of age. He was followed by Chandhara Tarkuhn Khan and Horningsea Kishta from England, and Aztrajid of Kazah from New Zealand (although N.Z. born she was by Waliwog out of a Moonswift bitch that had been exported from England in whelp), all of which gained their championship titles, and lastly Chandhara Talukdar from England, a son of Talisman. Following the Shaaltarah lead in the early 1960s, another kennel that imported extensively was Shahzada, owned by Graham Paelchen and Lyle Dally. Their first three imports were from England, Chandhara Hashim Yakoub, Chandhara Shirazada and Chandhara Tardis Arrakesh. Hashim and Arrakesh both gained their championship titles, and the latter will always be remembered as a great Best in Show winner, having taken this award at three of the Royal shows. The last import to this kennel was the blue Akaba's Blue Max, from the U.S.A. 'Blues' are well established in Australia, as other blue imports included one from the Dic-Mar Kennels in the U.S.A., and Aust. Ch. Khanabad Blue Frost from England. As can be seen, these hounds and other imports from Moonswift, Shanshu, Rabiouw Wahad, Bletchingley, Jagai, Oranje Manege, etc., give the Australians the opportunity to work with the best lines in Britain, U.S.A. and Europe. Australia uses the British standard.

The Afghan Hound in Sickness

IT IS not intended in this chapter to deal with all the ills and diseases that beset dogs. This is the province of the veterinary surgeon. Nevertheless, a book on this aspect of dog owning is essential, and I would recommend *First-Aid and Nursing for Your Dog* by F. Andrew Edgson and Olwen Gwynne-Jones, published by Popular Dogs.

When a dog is ill, do not dabble with patent medicines and supposed cures, but obtain veterinary help promptly.

The Afghan Hound, given proper feeding and care, is a healthy, hardy dog, able to withstand extremes of temperature and showing remarkable powers of recuperation, with a strong will to live when sick. As with human beings, even the healthiest can be attacked by disease, and for successful treatment early diagnosis and veterinary attention is essential.

A healthy dog has bright eyes—free from discharge—is lively, has good appetite, sweet breath, and exudes an overall aura of wellbeing. On the other hand, listlessness, loss of appetite, diarrhoea, vomiting, and high temperature, are unmistakable signs that all is not well, and that medical help is needed.

To take a dog's temperature, use a blunt-ended clinical thermometer and insert gently about one inch into the anus in a forward direction, and hold in that position for a minute or two. If the dog resists, obtain help in holding it steady, lest the thermometer be broken. A little Vaseline on the thermometer will sometimes help. The normal temperature for a dog is 101.5° F. Remember that temperatures tend to rise after exercise or as a result of excitement, even in healthy dogs.

Owing to advances in veterinary science, many diseases that were once accepted as killers, can now be largely avoided or minimised by inoculations, particularly the three dangerous scourges, distemper, canine virus hepatitis, and leptospiral jaundice, which can all be dealt with together in one inoculation. It is criminal negligence to deny this protection to our dogs, and no young puppy should be permitted to leave the environs of its home until this has been done. Three months is a good time for this inoculation, with boosters throughout its life under the direction of the veterinary surgeon.

Hereditary Defects in Afghan Hounds

A healthy Afghan Hound should not only be free from disease, it must *not* have inherited serious defects from an unwise choice of parents. Almost all faults are inherited, but it is important for the novice breeder to have in mind a clear order of priority. First, and least important, are the faults of appearance—light eye colour, details of coat, shortness of ear leather, for example. These are all to be avoided in a show dog if possible, but are to be preferred to more serious faults, those that affect temperament or structure. The British Veterinary Association and the Kennel Club have drawn up a list of the most dangerous inherited faults of structure—that is those that are most serious for the health and comfort of the dog—and they have, where possible, organised official joint schemes to help breeders eradicate them. Details of these can be got from the Secretary, the Kennel Club, 1–4 Clarges Street, London, W.1. The Animal Health Trust will supply a leaflet giving short descriptions of these conditions, and lists of breeds affected. Their address is 24 Portland Place, London, WIN 4AU.

Only two major hereditary defects are known to be troublesome in the Afghan Hound. One is juvenile cataract, a disorder of the eye, which brings total blindness at an early age. So far, breeders in the U.S.A. and some European countries have reported this defect, but it does not seem to be known in England. Breeders should, however, be on the watch for it, and, if in doubt, should have their dogs checked by an eye specialist before breeding from them. There is an official scheme covering this condition, but at present it is only open to a few breeds in which it is known to be common in this country, and Afghan Hounds are not among them.

The second major hereditary defect that affects Afghan

Hounds is hip dysplasia. This means malformation of the ball and socket joint which joins the top of the leg to the pelvis. It is a difficult condition to deal with because it varies in seriousness in different dogs, from a slight malformation that shows only on X-ray and causes few or no symptoms, to one so bad that the dog is lame and possibly in great pain. There is no treatment or cure. The mode of inheritance is also a complicated one, involving several genes; and as a joint is something that is used all the time and that grows with the dog, environment can also play a part. As far as this factor is concerned, the best and most practicable advice is to give the best possible rearing, with the puppy neither too fat nor too thin. It should not be over exercised, or overstrained in any way, but allowed plenty of space in which to play and develop steadily. Strong, thick muscle, which is itself, in part at least, inherited, is also desirable as it helps to keep the joint in the right position; but one must not, of course, expect to see a young puppy in hard muscular condition.

Until January 1969 it was not known that hip dysplasia affected Afghan Hounds. A number of X-rays taken from a wide selection of most known bloodlines, however, showed that it is common in the breed. As in other breeds it was found to vary greatly in severity. Afghans Hounds with only slightly abnormal hips showed nothing to the eye when they moved. Others, with bad X-ray plates had a 'bad' hind action—that is they rolled, shuffled, or failed to flex the leg joints fully. In two bad cases quite severe lameness was reported. This was noticed at about twelve to eighteen months. In other breeds it is not uncommon for dogs with severe hip dysplasia to suffer so much pain that they have to be destroyed. At present this seems rare in Afghan Hounds although cases have been reported from Australia and from Europe. Every breeder has an obligation to see to it that they do not become more common.

The way to do this is to be conscientious in the choice of breeding stock. Because of the complicated mode of inheritance the eradication of hip dysplasia will always be slow and difficult, but it can be controlled if dogs suffering from it are not bred from. The novice should remember that unless he starts with sound stock he is handicapping himself and injuring the breed.

Foundation stock should always be X-rayed, and if possible should come from parents that have also been X-rayed and certified free. It is not sensible to pay high prices for dogs that may, or may not, pass this test, when it is so easy to make sure. X-rays should not be taken until the dog is at least twelve months old. Before this age, as the bones are still developing, the result would not be reliable. The official scheme of the British Veterinary Association and the Kennel Club offers the best protection to the owner. It gives him access to a panel of experts in the field, and it also supplies an officially recorded form of certificate that is of great value in stud or export transactions. This scheme divides cases into three grades: passes, fails, and borderline cases. These last should not be bred from if it is a matter of urgency to exclude any possibility of passing on hip dysplasia but if there is danger of too close in-breeding through shortage of fully certified stock, or if some important characteristic, like good temperament (but *not* a minor point of appearance!) is to be preserved they could be used. Slight cases can produce offspring that are worse affected, and therefore need to be used with care.

All this represents something new to dog-breeders, and it is not surprising that many of them have felt a sense of shock and even outrage on hearing that inherited defects are widespread in their breed. Some have even refused to admit the fact and prefer to stick to the costly method of trial and error instead of welcoming a chance to test their dogs to find out whether they have a tendency to produce unsound offspring before they breed from them. What has really happened is that advances in veterinary knowledge and new and improved methods of diagnosis make this preliminary assessment of a dog possible, without the expense, and possibly heartbreak, of rearing a large number of puppies from it. Such testing is, of course, restricted to a few conditions, but they are serious ones, which every breeder would wish to avoid. Breeders have got used to carrying out a plan of immunisation for young puppies to prevent the common virus diseases that used to kill so many of their best dogs; they must now get used to another kind of planning, put into effect before the puppies are born, or even conceived, to prevent the development of conditions that would cripple their dogs in later life. Although progress will probably be slow, the result in the long run will be healthier dogs and better satisfied owners.

Advanced old age

Afghan Hounds can, and frequently do, live long lives. Whatever the length of life, the time must come with all living creatures when the body begins to fail. I do not specifically refer to definite disease, or violent pain, but rather to the condition where there is a gradual loss of the ability to enjoy a doggy life. Lassitude, weariness, and a general feeling of illness, possibly combined with the failure of normal bodily functions, can all occur without actual pain, for pain is not the only criterion of distress. It is at this stage that the most difficult decision of the dog owner has to be faced.

It is clearly our duty to spare our dogs this final misery, but while the decision is comparatively simple in violent pain or disease, the slowly deteriorating dog presents a far more difficult problem. The temptation to allow an old friend a few more days of life, coupled with a natural reluctance to terminate a life, can lead to unnecessary suffering. Looking back I have the feeling that I may have been guilty of this form of self indulgence, and I now try to be brutally honest and assess the situation purely from the point of view of the dog.

Unlike human invalids, who, when the body fails, can seek pleasures of the mind, the dog lives a very physical life, and when this is no longer possible he must be unhappy. The question is basically a straightforward one: is the old dog's life a pleasure or a burden? If it is still a pleasure, then any amount of nursing and personal trouble are worth while to allow it to continue (I have nothing but contempt for those people who instantly put a dog down as soon as it falls ill or becomes a trouble). If, on the other hand, its life is obviously a burden, then the course of action is clear.

Modern veterinary science has provided humane methods of destruction that are completely painless, and cause no distress if properly administered.

One final word on this sad but inevitable subject. Do not take

o

or send your dog to the veterinary surgeon, but ask him to call, so that the dog may be allowed to die in the familiar surroundings of its own home, and if the owner stays with it to the end there need be no mental stress at all. This is a simple final service that we can give, and I can vouch for the fact that there is nothing unpleasant or frightening about the process.

APPENDIX A

BREED REGISTRATIONS

1946 —	274	1954 —	205	1962 —	450
1947 —	278	1955 —	280	1963 —	388
1948 —	262	1956 —	247	1964 —	537
1949 —	273	1957 —	237	1965 —	576
1950 —	278	1958 —	257	1966 —	774
1951 —	323	1959 —	250	1967 —	1096
1952 —	217	1960 —	273	1968 —	1486
1953 —	220	1961 —	335	1969 —	2914

BREED CLUBS

Afghan Hound Association
Secretary D. Paton, Southlands Cottage, Broadham Green, Nr. Oxted,
Surrey. Oxted 3411.

Southern Afghan Club
Secretary A. D. A. Munro, 8 Appledore Close, Edgware, Middlesex.
Edgware 3667.

Northern Afghan Hound Society
Secretary Mrs. J. Van Schaick, Alicia Cottage Kennels, Rochdale.
Rochdale 47606.

Midland Afghan Hound Club
Secretary Mr. and Mrs. Heath, Bumblebee Hall, Sandby, Nr. Retford,
Notts.

Western Afghan Hound Club
Secretary Mrs. L. Cook, The Crooked Shoad, Cowbridge Road,
Llantwit Major, Glamorgan.

Afghan Hound Society of Scotland
Secretary Miss E. M. Holmes, Whitebog, Rosewell, Midlothian,
Scotland. Lasswade 2311.

Afghan Hound Society of Nothern Ireland
Secretary R. Margrain, 64, Charlott Street, Ballymoney, Co. Antrim.
Ballymoney 3656.

CHAMPION AFGHAN HOUNDS 1927–70

Year	Name	Sex	Birth	Sire	Dam	Breeder	Owner
1927	Buckmal	D	21-3-23	Ooty	Pushum	Major Bell Murray	Miss Manson
1927	Sirdar of Ghazni	D	?-6-23	unknown	unknown	an Afghan Shikari	Mrs Amps
1927	Ranee	B	?-3-19	Rajah	Begum	Major Bell Murray	Miss Manson
1928	Taj Mahip of Kaf	D	17-4-24	Khym	Daghai	Major Bell Murray	Mrs Barton
1929	Asri Havid of Ghazni	D	4-3-27	Ch. Sirdar of Ghazni	Roshni of Ghazni	Mrs Amps	Mrs Robson
1929	Shadi	B	27-7-24	Baluch	Oolu	Major Bell Murray	Mrs Williams
1930	Alfreda	B	3-9-26	Shahzada	Afroz	Mr Duffy	Miss Simmons
1931	Ashna of Ghazni	D	18-8-29	Ch. Sirdar of Ghazni	Shireen of Ghazni	Mrs Amps	Mr Chamberlain Mr Watt
1931	Marika of Baberbagh	B	23-4-28	Ch. Sirdar of Ghazni	Sada of Ghazni	Mrs Cannan	Mrs Prude
1931	Nush-ki of Ruritania	B	17-9-27	Ch. Sirdar of Ghazni	Tarza	Mrs Cooper	Miss Doxford
1931	Sirfreda	B	26-1-28	Ch. Sirdar of Ghazni	Ch. Alfreda	Miss Simmons	Mrs Squibb
1932	Badshah of Ainsdart	D	28-5-30	Ch. Sirdar of Ghazni	Ku-Mari of Kaf	Mrs Morris-Jones	Mrs Wood
1932	Garrymhor Souriya	B	13-7-31	Ch. Ashna of Ghazni	Ch. Alfreda	Miss Simmons	Mrs Cooper
1933	Yakub Khan of Geufron	D	2-3-30	Omar of Geufron	Zabana of Kaf	Mrs Drinkwater	Miss Doxford

Year	Name	Sex	Birth	Sire	Dam	Breeder	Owner
1933	Manaprajapati of Geufron	B	16-4-31	Omar of Geufron	Zabana of Kaf	Mrs Drinkwater	Mrs Drinkwater
1933	Maharani of Cheltside	B	29-8-32	Ch. Raj	Ch. Marika of Babarbagh	Mrs Prude	Mrs Prude
1934	Agha Lala of Geufron	D	16-4-31	Omar of Geufron	Zabana of Kaf	Mrs Drinkwater	Mrs Drinkwater
1934	Raj	D	28-6-30	Kymn	Ch. Sirfreda	Mrs Squibb	Mrs Coombes
1934	Westmill Ben Havid	D	26-1-31	Ch. Asri Havid of Ghazni	Elsa of Ghazni	Mrs Wood	Mrs Wood
1934	Westmill Tamasar	D	28-1-32	Int. Ch. Badshah of Ainsdart	Ranee of Geufron	Mrs Wood	Mrs Wood
1935	Chankidar	B	17-1-33	Ch. Firdausi of Geufron	Safiya	Mrs Carlton	Mrs Carlton
1935	Westmill Karabagh	B	6-6-33	Kymn	Ranee of Geufron	Mrs Wood	Mrs Rhodes
1935	Zandi of Enriallic	B	26-12-32	Rupee	Souriya of Enriallic	Mr Cronin	Mr Cronin
1936	Chota Sahib	D	17-1-33	Ch. Firdausi of Geufron	Safiya	Mrs Carlton	Mrs Bhanubandh
1936	Firdausi of Geufron	D	16-4-31	Omar of Geufron	Zabana of Kaf	Mrs Drinkwater	Mrs Drinkwater
1936	Westmill Natanz	B	9-7-34	Mukhlis Saramad	Illima of Geufron	Mr Holford	Mrs Wood
1937	Garrymhor Faiz-Bu-Hassid	D	23-3-35	Ardmore Anthony	Ch. Garrymhor Souriya	Mrs Couper	Mrs Sharpe

Year	Name	Sex	Date	Sire	Dam		
1937	Shah Shuja of Geufron	D	16-4-31	Omar of Geufron	Zabana of Kaf	Mrs Drinkwater	Dr Porter
1937	Azura Goldstar	B	1-10-35	Int. Ch. Chota Sahib	Madirekshana of Geufron	Mr & Mrs Bhanubandh	Mrs Peake
1937	Kisagotami of Geufron	B	21-3-33	Lakki Marwat	Sita of Geufron	Mrs Drinkwater	Mrs Drinkwater
1937	Wanawallari of Geufron	B	28-6-34	Omar of Geufron	Sheba of Wyke	Mrs Drinkwater	Mrs Gibson
1938	Taj Akbar of Chaman	D	24-4-36	Kulli Khan of Kuranda	Safiya	Mrs Sharpe	Mrs Sharpe
1938	Westmill Bayezid Ansari	D	24-4-32	Int. Ch. Badshah of Ainsdart	Elsa of Ghazni	Mrs Wood	Miss Ide
1938	Kinsuku of Geufron	B	25-9-34	Omar of Geufron	Ch. Sirfreda	Mrs Drinkwater	Mrs Rhodes
1938	Malati of Geufron	B	11-5-36	Omar of Geufron	Sheba of Wyke	Mrs Drinkwater	Mrs Bhanubandh
1939	Westmill Purdil Khan	D	6-2-35	Westmill Azadulla	Westmill Matta	Mrs Wood	Mrs Wood
1939	Faxhill Bathsheba	B	16-9-37	Faxhill Dost Hammad	Faxhill Kalana	Mr Hall	Mrs Rhodes
1939	Westmill Kariza	B	14-10-33	Ch. Westmill Ben Havid	Westmill Matta	Mrs Wood	Mrs Wood
1947	Ravelly Patrols Ali Bey	D	3-6-43	Turkuman Damar Pine Tree	Patrols Crerne Chenille	Mrs Harrison	Mr Floyd
1947	Ajawaan Chita Mia	B	16-12-45	Nosnikta's Nissim Tango	Silvercaul Sa-De-Miranda	Mrs King	Mrs Rhodes
1948	Rajah Bey of Ravelly	D	3-10-45	Ch. Ravelly Patrols Ali Bey	Buko of Bletchingley	Mrs Clarke	Mr Floyd

Year	Name	Sex	Birth	Sire	Dam	Breeder	Owner
1948	Taj of Chaman	D	27-3-39	Ch. Taj Akbar of Chaman	Thofar	Mrs Sharpe	Mrs Sharpe
1948	Vendas Tash Down	D	6-8-39	Tash Garift of Pushtikuh	Fay Down	Mrs Smith	Mrs O'Toole
1948	Mitzou of Acklam	B	25-5-39	Ch. Westmill Ben Havid	Ch. Wanawallari of Geufron	Mrs Gibson	Mrs Gibson
1948	Netheroyd Turkuman Camelthorne	B	18-9-43	Turkuman Pomegranate	Golden Rance	Mrs Polson	Mrs Abson
1949	Bletchingley Tajomeer	D	21-6-45	Taj Ameer of Chaman	Shiba of Chaman	Mrs Riley	Mrs Riley
1949	Ajawaan Ranee Tamba	B	17-1-47	Azad of Chaman	Silvercaul Sa-De-Miranda	Mrs King	Mrs Rhodes
1949	Bletchingley Zara	B	28-4-47	Ch. Bletchingley Tajomeer	Ravelly Badrea	Mrs Riley	Mrs Riley
1950	Patrols Ali Khan	D	19-7-44	Turkuman Damar Pine Tree	Patrols Creme Chenille	Mr Kent	Mrs Harrison
1950	Netheroyd Alibaba	D	10-11-47	Netheroyd Ansari	Netheroyd Camelthorne	Mr & Mrs Abson	Mr & Mrs Abson
1950	Marika of Three Streams	B	29-7-48	Zhuba of Chaman	Watmor Amber	Mr Parker	Mrs Dods
1951	Bletchingley Tribesman	D	13-9-48	Ch. Bletchingley Tajomeer	Ravelly Badrea	Mrs Riley	Mrs Riley

216

1951	Mohamed Ali of Acklam	D	19-5-46	Turkuman Damar Pine Tree	Ch. Mitzou of Acklam	Mrs Gibson	Mrs Gibson
1951	Moonbeam of Khorrassan	D	1-8-47	Kassim of Khorrassan	Water Lily of Khorrassan	Miss Snelling	Miss Snelling
1951	Netheroyd Red Eagle	D	24-11-48	Ch. Bletchingley Tajomeer	Ch. Netheroyd Turkuman Camelthorne	Mr & Mrs Abson	Mr & Mrs Abson
1951	Taj Abu of Chaman	D	12-8-46	Taj Ameer of Chaman	Flavia of Chaman	Mrs Sharpe	Mrs Sharpe
1951	Cleopatra of Khorrassan	B	9-5-50	Ch. Moonbeam of Khorrassan	Sunrise of Khorrassan	Miss Snelling	Miss Snelling
1951	Kyronisha el Kabul	B	25-8-47	Kuranda Turkuman Opium Poppy	Zara El Kabul	Dr Porter	Dr Porter
1951	Portrait of Khorrassan	B	9-6-47	Chota Nissim of Ringbank	Natara of Westover	Miss Snelling	Miss Snelling
1952	Tanza of Acklam	B	19-5-46	Turkuman Damar Pine Tree	Ch. Mitzou of Acklam	Mrs Gibson	Mrs Gibson
1952	Carloway Sharmain of Virendale	B	30-5-50	Jalalabad Barwala of Carloway	Shireen of Kenavon	Miss Trevitt	Mrs Devitt
1952	Tajavia of Chaman	B	21-6-45	Taj Ameer of Chaman	Flavia of Chaman	Mrs Sharpe	Mrs Sharpe
1953	Bletchingley El Basrah of Ravelly	D	28-4-47	Bletchingley Tajomeer	Ravelly Badrea	Mrs Riley	Mr Floyd
1953	Jabari Tango	D	5-3-50	Ch. Netheroyd Alibaba	Ajawaan Ranee Sabina	Mr Parrat	Mr Parrat

Year	Name	Sex	Birth	Sire	Dam	Breeder	Owner
1953	Taj Amrit of Chaman	D	4–5–48	Int. Ch. Taj of Chaman	Ch. Tajavia of Chaman	Mrs Sharpe	Mrs Sharpe
1953	Circe of Khorrassan	B	3–6–51	Ch. Moonbeam of Khorrassan	Sunrise of Khorrassan	Miss Snelling	Miss Snelling
1954	Bletchingley Hillsman	D	27–6–52	Jalalabad Barwala of Carloway	Ch. Bletchingley Zara	Mrs Riley	Mrs Riley
1954	Taj Aleh of Chaman	D	20–3–51	Ch. Mohamed Ali of Acklam	Taj Alfreda of Chaman	Mrs Sharpe	Mrs Sharpe
1954	Yussef of Carloway	D	28–6–52	Zog of Carloway	Dana Khan of Carloway	Mrs Devitt	Mrs Devitt
1954	Bletchingley Bedra el Kabul	B	15–5–53	Ch. Bletchingley Hillsman	Bletchingley Badrea	Mrs Riley	Dr Porter
1954	Kumari of Three Streams	B	4–3–50	Ben Havid of Three Streams	Zulieka of Khorrassan	Mr Parker	Mrs Leest
1954	Taj Arab of Chaman	D	20–3–51	Ch. Mohamed Ali of Acklam	Taj Alfreda of Chaman	Mrs Sharpe	Mrs Sharpe
1955	Taj Assum of Chaman	D	13–10–52	Ch. Taj Aleh of Chaman	Ch. Tajavia of Chaman	Mrs Sharpe	Mrs Sharpe
1955	Bletchingley Tolo-Na-Kha	B	1–7–50	Ch. Bletchingley Tribesman	Shurakhan of Barukhzi	Mrs Riley	Mrs Francks
1955	Marjanah of Khorrassan	B	21–12–51	Ch. Moonbeam of Khorrassan	Taj Aziz of Chaman	Miss Snelling	Miss Snelling

1956	Achilles of Khorrassan	D	3-6-51	Ch. Moonbeam of Khorrassan	Sunrise of Khorrassan	Miss Snelling	Miss Snelling
1956	Horningsea Majid	D	31-5-54	Horningsea Turridu	Ch. Marika of Three Streams	Mrs Dods	Mrs Dods
1956	Bahia of Khorrassan	B	28-5-52	Sirdar of Khorrassan	Sunrise of Khorrassan	Miss Snelling	Mrs Mitchell
1956	Baluch Ranee Ashraf	B	14-2-54	Bletchingley Barzara of Carloway	Havmora's Wild Rose	Mrs McGregor-Cheers	Mrs McGregor-Cheers
1956	Tijah of Carloway	B	10-10-54	Ch. Yussef of Carloway	Ch. Carloway Sharmain of Virendale	Mrs Devitt	Mrs Devitt
1957	Taj Achmed of Chaman	D	1-5-55	Ch. Mohamed Ali of Acklam	Ch. Taj Arab of Chaman	Mrs Sharpe	Mrs Sharpe
1957	Bletchingley Talookdar	D	13-5-53	Ch. Bletchingley Hillsman	Stonesby Asmara of Khorrassan	Mrs Riley	Mrs Riley
1957	Fantasia of Carloway	B	14-2-54	Bletchingley Barzara of Carloway	Havmora's Wild Rose	Mrs McGregor-Cheers	Miss Barnes
1957	Saleh Bey of Khorrassan	D	7-4-54	Montezuma of Khorrassan	Ajamais Amber of Menthe	Miss Snelling	Miss Snelling
1958	Wild Iris of Khorrassan	B	7-2-55	Montezuma of Khorrassan	Zanella	Miss Snelling	Miss Snelling
1958	Bletchingley Statesman	D	15-11-54	Ch. Bletchingley Talookdar	Ch. Bletchingley Zara	Mrs Riley	Mrs Riley
1958	Mir Kush Farida	B	10-9-54	Montezuma of Khorrassan	Safia of Three Streams	Mrs Wills	Mrs Wills

Year	Name	Sex	Birth	Sire	Dam	Breeder	Owner
1958	Khym of Carloway	D	29-11-55	Ch. Yussef of Carloway	Bletchingley Aurora	Miss Leyder	Mrs Devitt
1958	Enchantress of Tarjih	B	29-11-55	Ch. Yussef of Carloway	Bletchingley Aurora	Miss Leyder	Mrs Gent
1959	Chrishna of Barbourne	D	18-11-52	Zabu of Barbourne	Kishkinda of Kabul	Mrs O'Sullivan	Mrs Masters
1959	Nanda Devi of Khorrassan	B	13-11-54	Ch. Moonbeam of Khorrassan	Ch. Portrait of Khorrassan	Miss Snelling	Miss Snelling
1959	Muphytt of Carloway	B	29-11-55	Bletchingley Barzara of Carloway	Vashti of Carloway	Mrs Devitt	Mrs Devitt
1959	Pasha of Carloway	D	21-9-56	Ch. Yussef of Carloway	Shiba of Carloway	Mrs Devitt	Mrs Devitt
1959	Khanabad Azravi of Vishnu	D	27-3-56	Ch. Horningsea Majid	Khanabad Azrar	Miss Niblock	Mr & Mrs Harrisson
1959	Khanabad Astrajid	B	27-3-56	Ch. Horningsea Majid	Khanabad Azrar	Miss Niblock	Miss Niblock
1959	Yashmak of Khorrassan	B	3-12-57	Ch. Saleh Bey of Khorrassan	Ch. Cleopatra of Khorrassan	Miss Snelling	Miss Snelling
1959	Rifka's Tarquin of Carloway	D	3-10-54	Ch. Yussef of Carloway	Ch. Carloway Sharmain of Virendale	Mrs Devitt	Mrs Race
1960	Horningsea Sheer Khan	D	20-5-58	Ch. Horningsea Majid	Tillum of Carloway	Mrs Dods	Mrs Dods

1960	Taj Althea of Chaman	B	18-2-57	Ch. Taj Amrit of Chaman	Taj Abida of Chaman	Mrs Sharpe	Mrs Sharpe
1960	Jil of Carloway	B	4-5-58	Watsatari of Carloway	Undine of Carloway	Mrs Devitt	Mrs Devitt
1960	Mandodari of Carloway	B	30-3-57	Ch. Yussef of Carloway	Pari Banu Bin Sreebas	Mrs Devitt	Mrs Devitt
1960	Netheroyd Elibaba	D	22-6-58	Ch. Achilles of Khorrassan	Yasmin of Shibakhan	Mrs Stainton	Mrs Morton
1960	Bletchingley Houndsman	D	12-5-57	Ch. Bletchingley Hillsman	Bletchingley Shirin	Mrs Riley	Mrs Riley
1961	Tranwells Yana of Carloway	B	8-9-56	Ch. Horningsea Majid	Tillum of Carloway	Mrs Dods	Mrs Jackson
1961	Horningsea Khanabad Suvaraj	D	16-9-57	Am. Ch. Horningsea Salim Dar	Khanabad Azrar	Miss Niblock	Mrs Dods
1961	Bletchingley Saluna	B	2-1-58	Ch. Bletchingley Talookdar	Bletchingley Yana	Mrs Riley	Mrs Riley
1961	Bletchingley Zelda	B	18-3-60	Ch. Bletchingley Hillsman	Bletchingley Lana	Mrs Riley	Mrs Riley
1962	Shere Khan of Tarjih	D	29-8-57	Tajammul of Tarjih	Bletchingley Tara of Tarjih	Miss Leyder	Miss Willis
1962	Conygar Janze of Carloway	D	15-5-56	Ch. Yussef of Carloway	Conygar Gabel	Miss Venn	Mrs Bowdler
1962	Jinga of Carloway	B	4-5-58	Watsatari of Carloway	Undine of Carloway	Mrs Devitt	Mrs Devitt

Year	Name	Sex	Birth	Sire	Dam	Breeder	Owner
1962	Badakshan Rani	B	3-8-58	Ch. Khanabad Azravi of Vishnu	Rahane of Ladysmyle	Mrs Adams	Mrs Adams
1962	Kubla Khan el Kabul	D	17-1-57	Khanabad Abdul Hamsavi	Ch. Bletchingley Bedra el Kabul	Dr Porter	Dr Porter
1963	Waliwog of Carloway	D	21-3-61	Ch. Horningsea Sheer Khan	Ilexis of Carloway	Mrs Devitt	Mrs Devitt
1963	Zaza of Khorrassan	B	10-3-60	Rajput of Khorrassan	Ruanda of Khorrassan	Miss Snelling	Mr McCarthy
1963	Jali of Vishnu	D	7-4-59	Ch. Khanabad Azravi of Vishnu	Woodland Lassie	Mrs Hughes	Mrs Harrisson
1963	Barbille Houri of Carloway	B	15-10-58	Ch. Conygar Janze of Carloway	Horningsea Samsie	Mrs Devitt & Mrs Dods	Mrs Hall
1964	Empress of Carloway	B	11-4-60	Ch. Pasha of Carloway	Alida of Khyber	Mrs Bowdler	Mrs Gent
1964	Mazari of Carloway	D	15-5-62	Ch. Pasha of Carloway	Crown Crest Zardeeka	Mrs Devitt	Mrs Devitt
1964	Bondor Serenade	B	18-10-62	Ch. Wazir of Desertaire	Yazeena of Carloway	Mr Brooks & Mr Swallow	Mr Brooks & Mr Swallow
1964	Kismati Khan of Tarril	D	10-1-62	Ch. Wazir of Desertaire	Chandi B'Har of Tarril	Mrs Pollock	Mrs Pollock
1964	Kalbikhan Ravi	D	1-10-61	Ch. Kalbikhan Ali Bey of Carloway	Woodland Lassie	Mrs Hughes	Mrs Hughes
1964	Horningsea Mitanni	D	21-10-61	Ch. Horningsea Sheer Khan	Horningsea Marue	Mrs Dods	Mrs Clark

1965	Pina of Carloway	B	8-2-62	Anzari of Takabbor	Narriman of Carloway	Mrs Etheridge	Mr & Miss Ross
1965	Ueda of Carloway	B	1-8-61	Watsatari of Carloway	Horningsea Samsie	Mrs Crosby	Mrs Andrews
1965	Alphonse of Khyber	D	4-6-57	Ch. Yussef of Carloway	Hanyman Takrityah	Mr Walmsley	Mr Walmsley
1965	Patchouli Khanabad Surasu	B	16-9-57	Am. Ch. Horningsea Salim Dar	Khanabad Azrar	Miss Niblock	Mrs Purdue
1965	Shemsuki Deva Raya	D	21-4-62	Ch. Horningsea Sheer Khan	Riffari of Davlen	Mrs Young	Mrs Efford
1965	Aryana Shalym	D	7-8-61	Ch. Horningsea Khanabad Suvaraj	Sharima of Davlen	Mr & Mrs Robbins	Rev. Ford & Miss Barnes
1965	Tara of Pooghan	B	31-12-61	Ch. Pasha of Carloway	Gina of Anzani	Mr McCarthy	Mr McCarthy
1966	Bondor Lezah	B	20-8-61	Ch. Pasha of Carloway	Bletchingley Zuleika	Mr Brooks & Mr Swallow	Mr Brooks & Mr Swallow
1966	Chandi Bibi of Kushra	B	27-8-59	Subadar Karim Khan	Sha Sha of Fu-Tu-Yu	Mrs Morgan	Mrs Morgan & Mr Hedges
1966	Takabbor Tiaga	D	8-3-64	Horningsea Kublai Khan	Ilexis of Carloway	Mrs. Etheridge	Rev. Ford & Miss Barnes
1966	Ch. Conygar Kanika	B	25-4-59	Chitral Kirkuk	Conygar Judana	Miss Venn	Mrs Gilligan
1966	Kalbikhan Ali Bey of Carloway	D	5-6-60	Ch. Yussef of Carloway	Ch. Muphytt of Carloway	Mrs Devitt	Mrs Hughes
1966	Horningsea Mustagh Ata	D	30-11-63	Horningsea Sagittarius	Horningsea Marue	Mrs Dods	Mrs Dods

Year	Name	Sex	Birth	Sire	Dam	Breeder	Owner
1967	Rifka's Tabaq D'Rar	D	28-4-65	Ch. Horningsea Khanabad Suvaraj	Rofka's Rajeena of Carloway	Mrs Race	Mrs Race
1967	Rifka's Musqat D'Rar	B	28-4-65	Ch. Horningsea Khanabad Suvaraj	Rifka's Rajeena of Carloway	Mrs Race	Mrs Race
1967	Takabor Golden Eagle	D	9-4-62	Chandra of Takabor	Ilexis of Carloway	Mrs Devitt	Mrs Etheridge
1967	Rifka's Moti of Carloway	B	15-5-62	Ch. Pasha of Carloway	Crown Crest Zardeeka	Mrs Devitt	Mrs Race
1967	Horningsea Kayacci	B	30-11-64	Horningsea Sagittarius	Khorissa of Carloway	Mrs Dods	Mrs Dods
1968	Horningsea Tigers Eye	D	29-8-62	Ajman Branwen Kandahar	Horningsea Sardi	Mrs Dods	Mrs Dods
1968	Wazir of Desertaire	D	29-7-59	Am. Ch. Crown Crest Mr. Universe	Am. Ch. Zar-Kari of Shamalan	Mr & Mrs Buchanan	Mr Bridges
1968	Safiya of Sacheverell	B	11-6-65	Ch. Horningsea Sheer Khan	Zena of Sacheverell	Miss Booth	Miss Booth
1968	Kalbikhan Kara	B	10-7-65	Ch. Kalbikhan Ali Bey of Carloway	Ch. Pina of Carloway	Mrs Hughes	Mr & Mrs Severn
1969	Moonraker of Moonswift	D	23-11-63	Ch. Horningsea Sheer Khan	Indira of Carloway	Mrs Bowdler	Mrs Bowdler
1969	Myhorlyns Maharanee of Davlen	B	12-6-65	Ch. Aryana Shalym	Myhorlyns Tullah of Davlen	Mrs Brennan	Mrs Montgomery
1969	Ranjitsinhji of Jagai	D	17-3-65	Ch. Waliwog of Carloway	Shari of Amudarya	Mrs Gie	Mrs Holden

1969	Ophira of Davlen	B	12-8-65	Ch. Aryana Shalym	Takabbor Shiraz	Rev. Ford & Miss Barnes	Mrs Wolley
1970	Tzara of Pooghan	B	28-8-66	Ashley of Pooghan	Arafekh of Pooghan	Mr McCarthy	Mr McCarthy
1970	Bondor Azim Khan	D	10-5-66	Int. Ch. Moonraker of Moonswift	Ch. Bondor Serenade	Messrs Brooks & Swallow	Mrs & Miss Sams
1970	Xzari of Carloway	B	5-5-65	Ch. Waliwog of Carloway	Yazmin of Carloway	Mrs Bowdler	Mr Allison
1970	The Calif	D	23-3-64	Hiltonsay Alpine Merlin	Red Sheba	Mr Sutton	Mrs & Mr Severn
1970	Khonistan El-Cid	D	4-9-65	Sabu Barakzai of Fartonia	Khonistan Weinwater Azun	Miss Heaton	Messrs Walker, Wilson & Mrs Adam Faith
1970	Rasta of Jagai	B	17-4-65	Ch. Waliwog of Carloway	Sahri of Amudarya	Mrs Gie	Mrs Gie
1970	Hajubah of Davlen	D	15-1-67	Ch. Takabbor Tiaga	Khandi B'har of Tarril	Rev Ford & Miss Barnes	Rev Ford & Miss Barnes
1970	Miyasht Empress	B	17-12-66	Horningsea Aramis	Ch. Ueda of Carloway	Mrs Andrews	Mrs Doe

AMERICAN BREED STANDARD

General Appearance

The Afghan Hound is an aristocrat, his whole appearance is one of dignity and aloofness with no trace of plainness or coarseness. He has a straight front, proudly carried head, eyes gazing into the distance as if in memory of ages past. The striking characteristics of the breed—exotic, or 'eastern' expression, long silky topknot, peculiar coat pattern, very prominent hip bones, large feet, and the impression of a somewhat exaggerated bend in stifle due to profuse trouserings—stand out clearly, giving the Afghan Hound the appearance of what he is, a king of dogs that has held true to tradition throughout the ages.

Head

The head is of good length showing much refinement, the skull evenly balanced with the foreface. There is a slight prominence of the nasal bone structure causing a slightly Roman appearance, the centre line running up over the foreface with little or no stop, falling away in front of the eyes so there is an absolutely clear outlook with no interference; the underjaw showing great strength, the jaws long and punishing: the mouth level, meaning that the teeth from the upper jaw and lower jaw match evenly, neither overshot nor undershot. This is a difficult mouth to breed. A scissor bite is even more punishing and can be more easily bred into a dog than a level mouth, and a dog having a scissor bite, where the lower teeth slip inside and rest against the teeth of the upper jaw, should not be penalised. The occipital bone is very prominent. The head is surmounted by a topknot of long silky hair.

Ears

The ears are long, set approximately on level with outer corners of the eyes, the leather of the ear reaching nearly to the end of the dog's nose, and covered with long, silky hair.

Eyes

The eyes are almond shape (almost triangular), never full or bulgy, and are dark in colour.

Nose

The nose is of good size, black in colour.

Faults

Coarseness; snipiness, overshot or undershot; eyes round or bulgy or light in colour; exaggerated Roman nose; head not surmounted by a topknot.

Neck

The neck is of good length, strong and arched, running in a curve to the shoulders, which are long and sloping and well laid back.

Faults

Neck too short or too thick; a ewe neck, a goose neck; a neck lacking in substance.

Body

The backline appearing practically level from the shoulders to the loin. Strong and powerful loin and slightly arched, falling away towards the stern, with the hip bones very pronounced; well ribbed and tucked up in flanks. The height at the shoulders equals the distance from the chest to the buttocks; the brisket well let down and of medium width.

Faults

Roach back, sway back, goose rump, slack loin, lack of prominence of hip bones, too much width of brisket causing interference with elbows.

Tail

Tail is set not too high on the body, having a ring or curve on the end; should never be curled over, or rest on the back, or be carried sideways and should never be bushy.

Legs

Forelegs are straight and strong with great length between elbow and pastern; elbows well held in; forefeet large in both length and width; toes well arched; feet covered with long, thick hair; fine in texture; pasterns long and straight; pads of feet unusually large and well down on ground. Shoulders have plenty of angulation so that the legs are set well underneath the dog. Too much straightness of shoulder causes the dog to break down in the pasterns, and this is a serious fault.

All four feet of the Afghan Hound are in line with the body, turning neither in nor out. The hind feet are broad and of good length; the toes arched, and covered with long thick hair; hindquarters powerful and well muscled with great length between hip and hock; hocks well let down; good angulation of both stifle and hock; slightly bowed from hock to crotch.

Faults

Front or back feet thrown outward or inward; pads of feet not thick enough or feet too small; or any other evidence of weakness in feet; weak or broken down pasterns; too straight on stifle; too long in back.

Coat

Hindquarters, flanks, ribs, forequarters and legs well covered with thick, silky hair, very fine in texture; ears and all four feet well feathered. From in front of the shoulders, and also backwards from the shoulders along the saddle, from the flanks and ribs upwards, the hair is short and close, forming a smooth back in mature hounds—this is a traditional characteristic of the Afghan Hound. The Afghan should be shown in its natural state; the coat is not clipped or trimmed; the head is surmounted (in the full sense of the word) with a topknot of long, silky hair—this also is an outstanding characteristic of the Afghan Hound. Showing of short hair on cuffs on either front or back legs is permissible.

Faults

Lack of a short-haired saddle in mature dogs.

Height

Dogs, 27 inches plus or minus 1 inch: bitches 25 inches plus or minus 1 inch.

Weight

Dogs, about 60 pounds: bitches, about 50 pounds.

Colour

All colours are permissible, but colour or colour combinations are pleasing: white markings, especially on the head, are undesirable.

Gait

When running free, the Afghan Hound moves at a gallop, showing great elasticity and spring in his smooth, powerful stride. When on a loose lead, the Afghan can trot at a fast pace; stepping along, he has the appearance of placing the hind feet directly in the footprints of the front feet, both thrown straight ahead. Moving with head and tail high, the whole appearance of the Afghan Hound is one of great style and beauty.

Temperament
Aloof and dignified, yet gay.

Faults
Sharpness or shyness.

BIBLIOGRAPHY

Ash, E. C., *Dogs: Their History and Development*, Benn, 1927.

Barber, Winnie, 'On The Canine Cult', in Vesey-Fitzgerald's *The Book of the Dog*, 1948.

Brierly, Joan McDonald, *Here Is The Afghan Hound*, T.F.H. Publications, 1965.

Broughton, Thomas D., *Letters Written In A Mahratta Camp during the year 1809*, John Murray, 1813.

Bylandt, Count Henri de, *Dogs of All Nations*, Kegan Paul & Co., 1905.

Croxton-Smith, A., *About Our Dogs*, Ward, Lock, 1931.

Drury, W. D., *British Dogs*, L. Upcott Gill, 1903.

Edgson, F. Andrew and Gwynne-Jones, Olwen, *First-Aid and Nursing for Your Dog*, Popular Dogs, 4th edn, 1968.

Elphinstone, Hon. Mountstewart, *An Account of the Kingdom of Caubul and its Dependencies*, Longman & J. Murray, 1815.

Fiennes, Richard and Alice, *The Natural History of the Dog*, Weidenfeld & Nicolson, 1968.

Frankling, Dr. E., *The Dog Breeder's Introduction to Genetics*, Popular Dogs, 1966.

Handcock, R. C. G., *Dogs: Care and Management*, Faber, 1964.

Hubbard, Clifford, *The Afghan Hound Handbook*, Nicholson & Watson, 1951.

Lane, Charles Henry, *All About Dogs*, J. Lane, 1900.

Lorenz, Konrad, *King Solomon's Ring*, Methuen, 1952.

Lorenz, Konrad, *Man Meets Dog*, Methuen, 1954.

McCandlish, W. L., 'On The Judge at Shows', in Vesey-Fitzgerald's *The Book of the Dog*, 1948.

Miller, Constance O. and Gilbert, Edward M. Jnr, *The Complete Afghan Hound*, Howell Book House, 1965.

Mowat, Farley, *Never Cry Wolf*, Dell, 1963.

Richardson, H. D., *Dogs, their Origins and Varieties*, James McGlasham, Dublin, 1847.

Smythe, R. H., *The Anatomy of Dog Breeding*, Popular Dogs, 1962.

Vesey-Fitzgerald, Brian, *The Book of the Dog*, Nicholson & Watson, 1948.

The Complete Dog Book, published by the American Kennel Club.

Hutchinson's Dog Encyclopaedia.

Index

Kennel Club, 32, 33, 41, 43, 49, 50,
58, 61, 62, 65, 69, 71, 137, 162,
168, 169, 170–2, 179, 180, 182,
187, 206, 208
 Afghan Hound Standard, 71–2
Kennel Club shows, 168–9
Kennel kitchen, 109
Kennelling, 107–10
Kelly, W., 59
Khonistan Kennels, 56
Khorassan Kennels, 53
Kophi Kennels, 198

Lance, Brig.-General, 50
Lane, Charles Henry, 30
Langtry, Lily, 45
Lead training, 120
Leemans, Mme N. de, 59
Letters written in a Mahrotta Camp
 . . ., 24
Levi, Miss Juliette de Bairacli, 49,
52, 197
Leyder, Miss Pauline, 57
Lighting and heating in kennels,
108–9
Limited shows, 169
Line breeding, 131
Litters, 153–4
London Scottish Drill Hall, 50
Lorenz, Dr. Konrad, 18, 115, 117,
121

McCandlish, W. L., 175, 176, 179
McCarthy, Denis, 59, 63
McConaha, Mrs. Leah, 193
McKean, Shaw, 193
McKenzie, Major, 22, 32
McKenzie, Miss Marjorie, 55, 56
Maddigan, Mrs. Cynthia, 56
Malkin, Sol, 52
Manson, Miss Jean, 35, 43, 44, 192
Marx, Zeppo, 193
Masters, Mrs. Margaret, 56, 59
Mastiff, 19
Matchett, Mrs. Mary, 198

Mating, 138–43
 financial arrangements, 141–2
 right time for, 136
Matthews, Miss Marjorie, 48, 53, 70
Meat, 95–6
 puppy and, 156
Midland Afghan Hound Club, 63
Milk analysis, 153
Miller, Constance O., 47, 194
Minerals, 98
Moonswift Kennels, 57
Morton, Mrs. Ida, 52, 58, 63
Mountain of Moses, 23
Mountain wolf, 19
Mouth, 71, 75
Mowat, Farley, 120
Munro, A. D. A., 51

Natural History of the Dog, The, 18, 26
Neck, 71, 75
Nervousness, hereditary, 165
Netheroyd Kennels, 52
Never Cry Wolf, 120
Niblock, Miss M., 55
Noah, 27
Northern Afghan Hound Club, 51,
63
Nutrition, 94–100

Oakie, Mrs. Jack, 193, 194
Oakvardon Kennels, 194
Obesity, 103
Old age, 209–10
Olympia, 51
Open show, 169
O'Toole, Mrs., 51
Our Dogs, 36
Out-breeding, 131

Paelchen, Graham, 203
Pariah dog, 19
Patiala, Maharajah of, 36, 38
Patrols Kennels, 53
Pauptit, Mrs. Eta, 197, 202
Pekingese, 19